Colección Támesis

SERIE A: MONOGRAFÍAS, 210

A COMPANION TO LUIS BUÑUEL

Luis Buñuel (1900–1983) was one of the truly great film-makers of the twentieth century. Born in the Spanish village of Calanda and shaped by a repressive Jesuit education and a bourgeois family background, he reacted against both, escaped to Paris, and was soon embraced by André Breton's official surrealist group. His early films are his most aggressive and shocking, the slicing of the eyeball in *Un Chien andalou* (1929) one of the most memorable episodes in the history of cinema. Subsequently, Buñuel worked in Mexico where, in spite of tight budgets, he made films as memorable as *The Forgotten Ones* (1950) and *He* (1952). From 1960, greater financial and technical resources allowed him to make, in Spain and France, the films for which he is best known: *Viridiana* (1961), *Belle de jour* (1966), *Tristana* (1970), *The Discreet Charm of the Bourgeoisie* (1972), and *That Obscure Object of Desire* (1977). Although the French films in particular are less aggressive and more ironic than his early work, they nevertheless reveal Buñuel's continuing preoccupations: sex, bourgeois values, and religion.

In this study, Gwynne Edwards analyses Buñuel's films in the context of his personal obsessions and suggests that, in contrast to many of his fellow artists, he experienced a degree of sexual inhibition surprising in a surrealist.

GWYNNE EDWARDS is Professor of Spanish at the University of Wales, Aberystwyth

GWYNNE EDWARDS

A COMPANION TO LUIS BUÑUEL

TAMESIS

First published 2005
by Tamesis, Woodbridge

Transferred to digital printing

ISBN 978-1-85566-108-0 hardback
ISBN 978-1-85566-205-6 paperback

Tamesis is an imprint of Boydell & Brewer Ltd
PO Box 9, Woodbridge, Suffolk IP12 3DF, UK
and of Boydell & Brewer Inc.
668 Mt Hope Avenue, Rochester, NY 14620, USA
website: www.boydellandbrewer.com

A CiP catalogue record for this book is available
from the British Library

This publication is printed on acid-free paper

CONTENTS

ILLUSTRATIONS

All illustrations are courtesy of the Filmoteca (Madrid). The stills from *Un Chien andalou* and *L'Âge d'Or* are reproduced by courtesy of Contemporary Films Ltd. Every effort has been made to trace the other copyright holders; apologies are offered for any omission in this regard, and the publishers will be pleased to add any necessary acknowledgements in subsequent editions.

PREFACE

The influence of Luis Buñuel on other film-makers has been immense and is a clear indication of his importance and artistic stature in what has come to be known as the seventh art. Following the award of an Oscar in 1972 for *The Discreet Charm of the Bourgeoisie*, Buñuel was invited for lunch by the film-director, George Cukor, and found himself in the company of a number of other famous film-directors: Billy Wilder, George Stevens, John Ford, William Wyler and Alfred Hitchcock. Hitchcock rarely referred to the work of other film-directors, but he admired much of Buñuel's work, and on this occasion mentioned his fascination with Tristana's artificial leg. Quite clearly, the image had impressed itself on Hitchcock's memory in a way that most visual images do not, and it points to the way in which, in Buñuel's films as a whole, there are so many unforgettable images, from the sliced eye-ball in *Un Chien andalou* to the struggle for the piece of meat in *The Forgotten Ones* and Don Lope's decapitated head in *Tristana*.

The explanation for the haunting nature of these images lies, of course, in the fact that they are the very stuff of dreams and nightmares, floating to the surface from the unconscious, which Buñuel and the surrealists in general so admired. Their love of the irrational, and therefore of instinctive behaviour unfettered by reason, was also, needless to say, the source of their hostility towards the empty way of life embodied by the bourgeoisie, in which good manners, good taste, self-control and respectability were, and indeed still are, everything. And it explains too the opposition of the surrealists to the behavioural restrictions imposed by the teachings of the Church. In short, Buñuel's work, far from merely entertaining audiences, grappled with issues that were and are to do with how to live one's life in the face of pressures that, in his view, seek to deny life. His career as a film-maker was one of uncompromising commitment, and this undoubtedly accounts for the lasting vitality of his films.

The author and publishers would like to record their thanks to the
Instituto Cervantes
for assistance with the publication costs of this book

FOR GARETH

INTRODUCTION

The first half of the twentieth century is arguably, from an historical, cultural and artistic point of view, the most interesting period in modern times. In historical terms, no other era has witnessed two wars of such cata- strophic proportions, and no previous age has experienced such a cultural and artistic explosion as that which saw the appearance, over a relatively short space of time, of movements as innovative and dynamic as Cubism, Dadaism, Expressionism, Futurism and Surrealism. The creative artists who came to the fore during the first thirty years of the century have become familiar throughout the world. In painting, Cézanne, Salvador Dalí, Max Ernst and Picasso quickly come to mind. In music, Stravinsky's 'Rite of Spring' created a sensation in Paris in 1913. In the developing world of cinema, silent film, soon to be followed by the arrival of 'talkies', produced actors of the calibre of Charlie Chaplin, Buster Keaton and Harold Lloyd, and film-directors as influential as Eisenstein, Fritz Lang and Renoir. It is, though, Surrealism which, of the artistic movements mentioned above, has probably had the greatest and most lasting impact on future generations. More than a purely artistic movement, Surrealism consisted of a revolutionary attitude to life, a philosophy which, drawing in part on the psychoanalytical experiments of Freud, emphasised the importance of the unconscious, of instinctive desire, as opposed to the exercise of reason and logic, and which, because of its revo- lutionary aspect, also had a political dimension that allied it in some ways with Communism. Consequently, Surrealism, of which the Paris surrealist group of the 1920s and 1930s was perhaps the most important element, contained in its ranks both intellectuals and creative artists. André Breton, leader of the Paris surrealists, formulated its ideas. Among its painters, Dalí, Marcel Duchamp, Max Ernst and René Magritte figured prominently, Paul Éluard was a leading surrealist poet, and Luis Buñuel became by far the movement's most important film-maker. Even though he left the surrealist group in 1932, he remained a true surrealist until his death fifty years later, by which time he had made thirty-two films.

In the Spain of the 1920s and 1930s, there were many emerging stars, among them Picasso, Joan Miró and Manuel de Falla, but three who merit particular attention are Buñuel, Dalí and the great poet-dramatist, Federico García Lorca, for they form a fascinating triangle and were linked in ways which, at least in part, help to explain the nature and direction of their creative work. Firstly, all three came from bourgeois or at least well-to-do backgrounds, which meant that they enjoyed a privileged childhood in a country where there was much backwardness and poverty. Born in the Aragonese village of Calanda which, even though his family moved to the city of Zaragoza when he was only four months old, Buñuel revisited for many years, he was always conscious of the hardships experienced by the majority of its people, as well as those of others like them in the remoter parts of Spain. This, in conjunction with his father's considerable wealth, undoubtedly played a major part, as it did in the case of Lorca, in shaping Buñuel's strongly left-wing views and anti-bourgeois sentiments.

Secondly, like Lorca and Dalí, Buñuel attended a religious school – in his case the Jesuit Colegio del Salvador (School of the Saviour) in Zaragoza – whose effect on his life we will later see to have been profound. This was a time when the religious Orders controlled much of Spain's educational programme and, through their imposition upon their young charges of fierce discipline and narrow-minded views, practised what can only be described as moral and intellectual indoctrination, in addition to which there was also frequent sexual abuse of young and defenceless boys. In Pedro Almodóvar's *Law of Desire*, made in 1986, there is an episode in which it is suggested that Father Constantino's relationship with one of the young choristers, Tino, had not been entirely fatherly, and Almodóvar himself has also suggested that sexual abuse was quite common in the school run by Salesian priests which, as a child, he attended in the town of Cáceres.[1] There is no suggestion that Buñuel suffered in this way, but, as we shall see later, the kind of indoctrination imposed upon their pupils by the Jesuits had a profound emotional and psychological effect upon him, as well as turning him into a vigorous opponent of the Catholic Church and its practices.

In contrast, Buñuel's arrival in 1917 at the Residencia de Estudiantes in Madrid could not have been more liberating, both in terms of his personal and his intellectual life. Founded seven years earlier and modelled on the Oxbridge college system, the Residencia was in effect a university hall of residence which, under the guidance of its enlightened head, Alberto Jiménez Fraud, brought together under its roof talented young men and distinguished visiting speakers. There Buñuel would meet and become firm friends with Dalí and, in particular, Lorca. Contact with them and also with the cultural life of the capital in general undoubtedly deepened his knowledge of contemporary Spanish and European developments in the arts, though at this stage there is no indication that he had any interest in making films.

Life at the Residencia also revealed certain important elements of Buñuel's character. He took great pride in his physical conditioning, devoting

---

[1] See María Antonia García de León and Teresa Maldonado, *Pedro Almodóvar, la otra España cañí* (Ciudad Real: Biblioteca de Autores y Temas Manchegos, 1989), 37.

himself to all kinds of exercise, including running, boxing and wrestling. Together with his friends he drank a great deal of alcohol, which came to play a major part in his adult life. And he delighted in pranks that were often of an aggressive or bizarre character. On one occasion at the Palacio del Hielo he marched up to 'a sober, moustachioed, bespectacled gentleman', who was dancing with La Rubia, one of the dancers who worked there, and abruptly informed him: 'You make her look ridiculous. Do me a favour and go dance with somebody else!'[2] With a group of friends who constituted the self-styled Order of Toledo, he would often visit the city of that name, and on one of their visits there, he knocked down two military cadets who had insulted and grabbed one of the girls in the group (Buñuel, 73). These and other incidents clearly portray Buñuel as a tough, aggressive, intransigent character – qualities that explain the hard-hitting, unsentimental character of his later films.

Although Buñuel's exposure to avant-garde movements in the arts, both in Madrid and afterwards in Paris, was considerable, it is also important to bear in mind his familiarity with, in particular, Spanish literature of the sixteenth and seventeenth centuries. In this context he has expressed his love of the picaresque novel:

> I adore the picaresque novel, especially *Lazarillo de Tormes*, de Quevedo's *La vida del buscón*, and even *Gil Blas*, which, although written by the Frenchman Lesage, was elegantly translated by Father Isla in the eighteenth century and has become a Spanish classic. It paints a stunning picture of Spain, and I think I've read it a dozen times. (Buñuel, 220)

The picture of Spain to which Buñuel refers is one distinguished by its total lack of sentimentality. In *Lazarillo de Tormes* and *La vida del buscón* (*The Life of the Swindler*), published in 1554 and 1626 respectively, a young boy born in poor circumstances is obliged to find his own way in life, using his wits, availing himself of lies and deception in order to survive, and eventually becomes as corrupt as the characters he serves or meets along the way. The protagonist's experiences present a picture of a society in which hypocrisy and cruelty are much to the fore, not least in individuals who are connected with the Church, and where there is humour, it is frequently dark and even sardonic. Given Buñuel's unsentimental character, his love of realism, and his anti-clericalism, it is easy to understand his attraction to the picaresque novel and its influence on a film such as *The Forgotten Ones* (*Los olvidados*), made in 1950, and *Nazarín* eight years later.

While the picaresque novel embodied Buñuel's love of realism, Cervan-

---

2 Luis Buñuel, *My Last Breath*, trans. Abigail Israel (London: Jonathan Cape, 1984), 65–6 [hereafter Buñuel].

tes's *Don Quixote*, its two parts published in 1605 and 1615, personified in its protagonist the idealism that Buñuel considered to be pointless in a harsh and cruel world. Don Quixote, in imitation of the knights of old, sets out in search of adventure and resolved to right wrongs wherever he encounters them. He is, though, not merely a deluded individual in the sense that he sees windmills as giants, sheep as soldiers, and prostitutes as refined ladies; he is also intolerant inasmuch as he attempts to impose his view of the world on other people, and in this respect a parallel can be drawn between Quixote and the well-intentioned but naïve Christian who seeks to convince others that only he or she is correct in their beliefs. As we shall see later, Buñuel created Quixote-like characters in the protagonists of *Nazarín* and *Viridiana*, both of whom set out to improve an imperfect world and, like Quixote, fail. Their failures are, moreover, often presented with an ironic humour that Buñuel would have found in abundance in Cervantes's portrayal of the knight's misguided escapades.

Nazarín, despite its links with *Don Quixote*, has as its direct source the novel of the same name by the nineteenth-century Spanish novelist Benito Pérez Galdós, to whose work Buñuel also turned for *Tristana* in 1970. Galdós, comparable in the range, quantity and quality of his writing to Balzac, Dickens and Tolstoy, was, above all, the great chronicler of Spanish and, in particular, Madrid society. In more than twenty novels, the majority set in the capital, he vividly depicts the broad spectrum of the social classes, among which the bourgeoisie figures prominently. Essentially a moralist, but not a preacher, Galdós explores such themes as hypocrisy, pretentiousness, intolerance and the corrupting influence of money and of social aspiration. In this context it is easy to see his influence in relation to Buñuel's depiction of similar bourgeois vices.

Although, by his own admission, Buñuel had little interest in painting (Buñuel, 82), it would be difficult to deny the influence of Goya on his work. Both men were, after all, from the northern province of Aragón and, like many others from that region, had a down-to-earth, practical, hard-headed approach to life. Buñuel's *The Phantom of Liberty* (*Le Fantôme de la liberté*), made in 1974, begins with an execution by firing-squad that is clearly based on Goya's famous painting *The Executions of the Third of May*, but the Aragonese painter's influence is evident in much more than specific borrowings. In the series of drawings completed between 1795 and 1797 and entitled *Los caprichos*, Goya ruthlessly exposed the deceit and hypocrisy of the society of his day, each drawing accompanied by such captions as 'It is all lies', or 'No one knows himself'. Buñuel undoubtedly shared Goya's vision of social and moral ills. More than twenty years later, deeply affected by political events in Spain and recovering from deep depression, Goya painted on the walls of his house the series of paintings known as *The Black Paintings*, which depict Spain as a kind of hell peopled by madmen, riddled with superstition and given to violence. These nightmarish paintings, as much the product of Goya's unsettled mind as of his view of Spain, clearly had a considerable appeal for those Spanish creative artists, including Buñuel, who were drawn to Surrealism. Given that the dreams and nightmares that appear in Buñuel's films – *The Discreet Charm of the Bourgeoisie* (*Le Charm discret de la bourgeoisie*) is a particularly good example – also have other sources, Goya's influence on his fellow Aragonese cannot easily be dismissed.

Buñuel arrived in Paris in 1925, one year after completing his studies in Madrid and two years after his father's death. At this stage he appears not to have had any particular career in mind, but, from the moment of his arrival in the French capital, he found himself in the company of many Spanish artists who were resident there, such as Juan Gris and Picasso, and his cultural interests inevitably developed apace. Among other things, Buñuel discovered the writings of the Marquis de Sade, whose *One Hundred and Twenty Days of Sodom* – later to influence the ending of *L'Âge d'or* (*The Golden Age*) – he read when he was about twenty-five (Buñuel, 217). This and other works by the French aristocrat created a profound impression on him, not least in relation to de Sade's unconventional ideas on sex and his advocacy of freedom and a cultural revolution in general. But other French writers influenced him too, including the Comte de Lautréamont and the iconoclastic Alfred Jarry.

As far as cinema is concerned, Buñuel has noted that in Paris he went to the cinema far more often than he had done in Madrid (Buñuel, 87–8). Availing himself of a press pass, he frequently saw three films a day. In addition, Buñuel began to write film reviews for the Paris magazine *Cahiers d'Art*, as well as for various Spanish magazines. And it was not long before he enrolled in an acting school run by the famous French film-director Jean Epstein, as a result of which he began to work as a general dogsbody on the film *Mauprat*, which Epstein was shooting in 1925, and which was followed a couple of years later by *The Fall of the House of Usher* (*La Chute de la Maison Usher*), on which Buñuel was employed as Epstein's second assistant. The experience taught him a great deal and he became particularly interested in the camera, operated by Albert Duverger who subsequently became his cameraman on both *Un Chien andalou* (*An Andalusian Dog*) and *L'Âge d'or*. Nevertheless, Buñuel disliked Epstein's often melodramatic and romantic style of film-making. The fast, precise, objective and unsentimental style that became the hallmark of his own films could not be more different.

Although he did not become a member of the official Paris surrealist group headed by Breton until after the première of *Un Chien andalou* in June 1929, it is quite evident that Buñuel was already familiar with surrealist ideas. His contact with avant-garde movements in Madrid, his frequent returns there, his Paris associations, his wide reading and his ever closer friendship with Salvador Dalí in the late 1920s, all guaranteed that this would be the case, so it is not surprising that Buñuel's film should have immediately been acknowledged by Breton as a true surrealist film. In the course of the next four years he would make two more – *L'Âge d'or* in 1930 and *Las Hurdes* in 1933. These three early films point, as we shall see later, to the various stages of Surrealism as defined by Breton in his *Manifesto of Surrealism* of 1924 and his *Second Surrealist Manifesto* of 1929. Furthermore, acceptance into the Paris surrealist group exposed Buñuel's existing left-wing attitudes to the allure of Communism, with which the surrealists had firm links. He would retain strong communist sympathies for another thirty years or so.

The Paris screening of *L'Âge d'or* led in 1930 to Buñuel's first visit to the United States and to Hollywood, where, it was suggested, he should study the techniques of American film-makers. There he observed the activities of cinema bosses such as Louis B. Mayer, the directing techniques of Josef von Sternberg, and there too he encountered such film celebrities as Charlie Chaplin, Greta Garbo and Mack Swain. But he was not impressed by the standardised pattern of Hollywood film-making, and in less than a year he was back in Paris.

Initially, he was employed by Paramount to dub films at their Paris base, but in 1934, the year of his marriage to Jeanne Rucar after some eight years of courtship, he moved to Madrid, where he worked for Warner Brothers as supervisor of their dubbing operations. Ten months later he was invited by Ricardo Urgoiti, a producer of commercial films, to work as a producer for his company, Filmófono, and in this capacity produced a total of eighteen films in two years, including four which he directed himself: *Don Quintín, the Embittered One* (*Don Quintín el Amargao*), *The Daughter of Juan Simón* (*La hija de Juan Simón*), *Who Loves Me?* (*¿Quién me quiere a mí?*) and *Sentinel, On Guard!* (*¡Centinela alerta!*). In spite of the fact that the quality of these films was not high, they provided Buñuel with useful practical experience, and he might well have gone on to produce much better work – future projects included his adaptation of *Wuthering Heights* – were it not for the outbreak of the Spanish Civil War in July 1936.

Although Buñuel remained in Spain during the first few months of the war, his sympathies with the Republican side, he left for Geneva in early September, despatched there by the Republican minister for foreign affairs and, on his arrival, was sent to Paris where he remained for the next two years. Officially responsible for cataloguing Republican propaganda films made in Spain, Buñuel was also involved in other activities, sometimes taking left-wing tracts to Spain, sometimes doing a little spying, acting as a bodyguard, and supervising the making of two documentaries: *Spain 1936* (*España 1936*) and *Loyal Spain, To Arms!* (*España leal, ¡en armas!*). In 1938, it was suggested to him by the Spanish ambassador in Paris that he return to Hollywood where he could give technical advice on the films then being made there about the Spanish Civil War. Almost immediately, however, the American Motion Picture Producers Association banned the making of such films, and Buñuel found himself struggling to support himself and his family in Los Angeles and afterwards in New York. By pure chance, however, he succeeded in obtaining a job at New York's Museum of Modern Art, cutting and editing anti-Nazi propaganda films and producing two of the Museum's own projects.

The outbreak of the Second World War in Europe in 1939 saw the arrival in New York of a number of Buñuel's former surrealist colleagues – he had left the group in 1932 – who included Breton, Max Ernst, Marcel Duchamp, Yves Tanguy and Salvador Dalí. Since their failure to agree on ideas for *L'Âge d'or* almost ten years earlier, Buñuel had seen Dalí but rarely, not least because, during the Civil War the one-time left-wing Catalan artist had made no secret of his Francoist leanings. Now, however, Dalí was to enter Buñuel's life once again in a quite dramatic fashion, for in his *The Secret Life of Salvador Dalí*, published in 1942, he had stated that Buñuel, creator of the notorious *L'Âge d'or*, was an atheist and a Marxist. It was an accusation that quickly fuelled existing animosity towards the Museum of Modern Art's film unit, leading to Buñuel's resignation at the end of June 1943. When he subsequently met Dalí in New York, Buñuel kept his hands in his pockets in order to avoid punching him, and the self-absorbed Catalan painter responded to his demand for an explanation in characteristic fashion: 'The book has nothing to do with you. I wrote it to make *myself* a star. You've only got a supporting role' (Buñuel, 183). In his autobiography Buñuel would observe that, even though he still had fond memories of his early friendship with Dalí, he could never forgive him 'for his egomania, his obsessive exhibitionism, his cynical support of the Falange, and his frank disrespect for friendship' (Buñuel, 187).

In 1944, by which time he and Jeanne had two sons, Buñuel returned to Los Angeles where he once more worked on dubbing for Warner Brothers, but this soon came to an end, and in 1946, after a year of inactivity, he went to Mexico – a crucial decision in relation to his work as a film-maker – where he made *Gran Casino* in 1946 and *The Great Carouser* (*El gran calavera*) in 1949. Neither proved to be particularly good or successful, but between 1946 and 1964 Buñuel made twenty films in Mexico, some of them quite outstanding. When he made *Gran Casino*, he had not been behind a camera for many years, but, on the other hand, his experience as a film editor and cutter, as well as his observation of American films, which suggested to him how films should not be made, clearly stood him in good stead.

The Mexican film industry imposed on Buñuel restrictions of various kinds. In making *Un Chien andalou*, *L'Âge d'or* and *Las Hurdes*, he had worked very much as he wanted, particularly in terms of subject matter. In Mexican commercial cinema, on the other hand, he was usually obliged to make popular films on an extremely low budget and in weeks rather than months. As far as genre was concerned, Mexican cinema of the 1940s and 1950s embraced, as Peter Evans has noted, family melodramas, *comedias rancheras* [a kind of 'Western'], and comedies.[3] Many of Buñuel's Mexican family melodramas involved, by their very nature, powerful conflicts and relationships, as in the case of *Susana*, made in 1950, *Daughter of Deceit* (*La hija del engaño*) and *A Woman without Love* (*Una mujer sin amor*), both made in 1951. The second of these three films, for example, concerns an unfaithful wife who is sent packing by her husband. Before her departure, she informs her husband, Don Quintín, that he is not the father of their daughter, Marta, and, as a consequence of this, the girl is sent to live with another family. Many years later, Don Quintín learns from his dying wife that Marta is indeed his daughter, and he sets out to find her, a search that is full of suspense but which ends happily when father and daughter are at last reunited in a loving embrace.

As this brief account of *Daughter of Deceit* suggests, melodramatic plots did not exclude happy endings, for cinema audiences wanted to be moved emotionally but also to leave the cinema in a cheerful frame of mind, as was also so often the case in Hollywood films. With this in mind, Buñuel's melo-dramas had as their counterpart numerous farces and comedies, such as *The Great Carouser*, mentioned earlier, *Stairway to Heaven* (*Subida al cielo*) and *The Tram-ride of Dreams* (*La ilusion viaja en tranvía*), the last two made in 1951 and 1953. But if these films adhered for the most part to a popular formula, Buñuel often succeeded in introducing into them touches of his own, be it in terms of social themes, psychological preoccupations, black humour or ironic comment. As for the time-scale involved in making films in Mexico, directors were normally required to complete shooting in two weeks. In this context, *The Great Carouser* was made in sixteen days, *A Woman without Love* in twenty, and *The Forgotten Ones*, one of Buñuel's truly great films, in twenty-one. In his earlier work as a cutter and editor of documenta-ries for Paramount and Warner Brothers, Buñuel had mastered one valuable lesson of film-making – how to be concise and to the point, a quality that became a characteristic of all his major work.

As well as these commercial films, Buñuel was also able, during his years in Mexico, to make a number of films in which he was not so restricted by formula, and to which he could bring many of the themes and preoccupations that particularly interested him. The first of these was *The Forgotten Ones*, made in the same year as *Susana* but entirely different from it. Taking as his subject the slum children of Mexico City, Buñuel produced a film which, far from seeking to please its audience, succeeded in enraging many, for they considered it a betrayal of their country. His aim, as we shall see later, was to suggest, as do so many of his major films, that we do not live in the best of all possible worlds, and that the self-styled progressive forces of our time are

---

[3]   See Peter William Evans, *The Films of Luis Buñuel: Subjectivity and Desire* (Oxford: Clarendon Press, 1995), 39.

ineffective in a harsh and hostile world. But if this suggests that *The Forgotten Ones* is a thesis film, that notion is swept aside by the care that Buñuel devoted to the creation of his characters and, above all, their inner lives. In this respect, the longings and anxieties of particular characters are revealed at crucial moments in their dreams, as in the case of the young boy, Pedro. Buñuel succeeded in this film, which in 1951 was awarded the prize for best direction at the Cannes Film Festival, in combining the narrative element of Mexican commercial cinema with the dream elements of Surrealism that had distinguished his first films, and on which he would draw so heavily in the future. He had discovered a formula that suited him.

In the course of the next dozen or so years in Mexico, Buñuel made at least half a dozen films of high quality: *Robinson Crusoe* (1952), *He* (*El*) (1952), *Wuthering Heights* (*Abismos de passion*) (1953), *Rehearsal for a Crime/The Criminal Life of Archibaldo de la Cruz* (*Ensayo de un crimen/La vida criminal de Archibaldo de la Cruz* (1955), *Nazarín* (1958) and *The Exterminating Angel* (*El ángel exterminador*) (1962). In these films, most of which will be discussed in some detail later, Buñuel, as he had done in *The Forgotten Ones*, explored those issues that interested him in a style that frequently incorporated powerful surrealist elements. In *The Exterminating Angel*, for example, he renewed the ferocious attack on the bourgeoisie that he had first made in *L'Âge d'or*, stripping away its elegant façade in order to reveal its cruelty and hypocrisy, and also, in true surrealist fashion, exposed through dream sequences the anxieties and phobias that lay deep in its unconscious. Similarly, in *Robinson Crusoe*, on the surface a kind of adventure story highly suited to commercial cinema, Buñuel again launched an attack on bourgeois values – in this case by showing how Crusoe, coming from an essentially bourgeois background and thus inheriting its beliefs, initially acted towards the black and socially inferior Friday in a totally exploitative, cruel and inhuman manner. Only later does he begin to learn the trust and comradeship that are essential if men are not to act like savages, though when Crusoe finally returns to civilisation, it seems quite likely that he will revert to his former self. Furthermore, as in *The Forgotten Ones* and *The Exterminating Angel*, Crusoe's deep-seated anxieties, linked to his upbringing, are revealed in his hallucinatory vision of his cruel and domineering father, who refuses to give him water when he is desperate for it, and whose behaviour towards his son is clearly repeated in the latter's treatment of Friday.

Buñuel's preoccupation with the bourgeoisie, its way of life and its twisted values, is seen to be central too to such films as *He* and *Rehearsal for a Crime/The Criminal Life of Archibaldo de la Cruz*, and is frequently interwoven with his exposure of the damaging effects upon the individual of religious indoctrination. In several films, moreover, of which *Nazarín* is a particularly fine example, Buñuel demonstrates not just the narrow-mindedness and hypocrisy of the Catholic Church and its representatives, but also the futility of Christian ideals – indeed, of idealism in general – in a harsh, uncompromising world. The best of the films made in Mexico reveal very clearly, then, that, even when he was provided with only the minimum of money and time, Buñuel was able to produce work of quality and substance. Indeed, *The Exterminating Angel*, in particular, is as original, as powerful and as disturbing as any film he made in more advantageous circumstances.

Buñuel did not return to Spain for twenty-one years after the end of the Civil War. By this time the Franco dictatorship was somewhat less harsh than it had been in the fifteen years or so after the war, though it was still the case that censorship was still strong and that creative works that were thought to criticise the regime were banned. Buñuel went back to Spain for a few weeks in 1960, having been granted a visa to do so, and, during his stay, was introduced to Gustavo Alatriste, a Mexican businessman who wanted to try his hand at the film industry and who suggested that they make a film together. On the boat back to Mexico, Buñuel began work on the script for *Viridiana*, which he completed with the assistance of Julio Alejandro. He returned to shoot the film in Spain, on an estate outside Madrid, in late 1960 and early 1961, and it received its première in May 1961 at the Cannes Film Festival, winning the Palme d'or. In some ways it created a scandal as great as that occasioned thirty-one years earlier by *L'Âge d'or*.

Viridiana is the story of the eponymous young woman who, during her training to become a nun, visits her widowed uncle, Don Jaime. He becomes strongly attracted to Viridiana because of her striking similarity to his former wife. When she refuses to marry him, he drugs her with the intention of possessing her sexually, but draws back at the last moment. She, however, is convinced that he has raped her, and that she cannot therefore return to the convent. She chooses instead to practise her Christian beliefs in the world at large, and, following Don Jaime's suicide, introduces a group of homeless beggars into the barn of her uncle's house. They take advantage of her compassion and, while she and Don Jaime's illegitimate son, Jorge, are away for the day, occupy the house and indulge themselves in food, wine and sex, almost wrecking the dining-room. When Viridiana and Jorge return, one of the beggars attacks Jorge and another attempts to rape Viridiana. She is saved by Jorge and shortly afterwards abandons her Christian way of life in order to enter into a *ménage à trois* with Jorge and the servant, Ramona.

The film, as the above outline suggests, contained a number of sensational and, as far as the Catholic Church was concerned in 1961, unacceptable elements. The Spanish censors therefore demanded that, before it could be shown at Cannes as the official Spanish entry, changes should be made relating to Don Jaime's suicide, the attempted rape of Viridiana and her burning of her crown of thorns, among other things. They had, however, seen the film without dialogue or sound, both of which Buñuel added when, after shooting, he returned to Paris. When it was shown at Cannes, *Viridiana* scandalised the Spanish authorities and the Catholic Church, for the beggars' orgy was now accompanied by the 'Hallelujah Chorus', and, what is more, Buñuel had failed to make all of the changes suggested to him. The Italian newspaper *L'Osservatore Romano* described *Viridiana* as blasphemous and sacrilegious, and in 1963 the Italian police seized copies of the film in Rome and Milan. In Spain, copies were also seized, journalists were not allowed to refer either to the film or the Palme d'or, and it was banned for many years, as indeed happened in Italy and Belgium. Nevertheless, because the film had been largely financed by Mexican money, it acquired a kind of Mexican nationality about which the Spanish authorities could do nothing. *Viridiana* was thus shown in most countries, if not in Spain until 1977, and is now regarded by many as one of Buñuel's most accomplished works. His return to Spain can, however, hardly be described as auspicious, and he would not make another film there for nine more years.

By 1962 Buñuel was dividing his time between Mexico City, Paris and Madrid, and, although he made two more films in Mexico – *The Exterminating Angel* in 1962 and *Simon of the Desert* (*Simón del desierto*) in 1965 – all his other films in the course of the next fifteen years were made in France and Spain, one in the latter, six in the former. As far as the films made in France were concerned, Buñuel's meeting in 1963 with the producer Serge Silberman proved to be crucial, for five of the six French films had Silberman as producer. More importantly, though, Silberman gave Buñuel a relatively free hand, and filming in France also provided him with working conditions he had never enjoyed in Mexico, not least vastly improved budgets, time for developing ideas and for shooting, and, of course, better actors and technicians.

The point is well illustrated in relation to Buñuel's first French film with Silberman as producer, for in *The Diary of a Chambermaid* (*Le journal d'une femme de chambre*), released in 1964, he had Jeanne Moreau as his lead actress and Jean-Claude Carrière, with whom he would work on almost all of his future films, as co-scriptwriter. But if the resources at Buñuel's disposal were now much greater, this in no way affected his work in terms of its themes and preoccupations, or indeed its surrealist character. If his earlier films reflected a fascination with the unconscious and the world of dreams, a desire to expose the empty elegance of bourgeois life, and a concern with religious issues, all these continued to be his principal concerns. Indeed, given vastly improved budgets and technical facilities, Buñuel was able, for example, to create dreams and nightmares even more effectively, to suggest the façade of bourgeois life in greater detail and with greater accuracy, and to employ the very best actors in order to communicate his ideas and his vision.

In *The Diary of a Chambermaid*, based on the novel by Octave Mirbeau and first published in 1900, Buñuel, as we shall see in more detail later, focuses on a provincial bourgeois family whose self-absorption isolates it from the pressing political realities of the outside world in the mid-1920s. The head of the family, Monsieur Rabour, seeks consolation in his sexual fantasies, be it in the form of a collection of dirty postcards or of female boots and shoes. His son-in-law, Monsieur Monteil, has nothing better to do than hunt and pursue the female servants, while his wife, dreading his twice-weekly sexual advances, seems solely concerned with the expensive objects with which she fills the house, and the mysterious experiments in personal hygiene that she conducts in the privacy of her bathroom. This bizarre household is revealed to us through the presence of the chambermaid, Célestine, who takes up employment with the Rabour/Monteil family at the beginning of the film. But Buñuel also shows us how she, even though she finds this household distasteful, is affected by its values, for in the end she settles for a relatively comfortable life by marrying the servant Joseph, despite the fact that he shares his masters' fascist attitudes and despite her suspicion that he is a murderer.

Buñuel's exposure of the bourgeoisie is also at the heart of three of the other films made in France between 1966 and 1977: *Belle de jour*, *The Discreet Charm of the Bourgeoisie* and *That Obscure Object of Desire* (*Cet obscur objet du désir*). *Belle de jour*, made in 1966 and starring Catherine Deneuve, has become one of Buñuel's most famous films. A considerable budget allowed him to capture to the full the elegant bourgeois world of which Séverine and her wealthy surgeon husband, Jean, are a part, be they at home or on holiday in an expensive ski resort. But the elegant surface, as is always the case in a Buñuel film, merely emphasises the darker forces that lie beneath it, which, in Séverine's case, consist of a desire for the kind of sexual satisfaction and abasement that her correct and somewhat repressed husband cannot provide. These desires reveal themselves in her fantasies and become reality when she begins to spend her afternoons at the brothel run by Madame Anais. The difference between the bourgeois world in which Séverine has grown up and the much more seedy world of the brothel could not be more stark, but it is through her exposure to the latter that she succeeds both in making contact with her true feelings and in finally ridding herself of the fantasies that in the past had been her only escape from her buttoned-up bourgeois existence.

Five year later, in *The Discreet Charm of the Bourgeoisie*, for which he won an Oscar, Buñuel substituted food for sex, for the six principal charac-ters of the film, three bourgeois men and three women, spend most of their time in an attempt to find a meal, be it at home or in a restaurant. Their repeated failure to do so on account of circumstances as bizarre and as coin-cidental as the untimely death of a restaurant owner and the sudden commencement of military exercises leads, of course, to much comedy, and it is true to say that, at seventy-two years of age, Buñuel's treatment of the bourgeoisie is often more ironic than scathing. Even so, the Ambassador's urbane manner and the Bishop's apparent compassion are shown to conceal much darker forces. As well as this, *The Discreet Charm of the Bourgeoisie* is notable for its dream sequences, in which Buñuel, as in *The Exterminating*

Angel, delights in exposing his bourgeois characters to the terrors of their own nightmares. The old surrealist is, in this beautifully constructed film, still much in evidence.

Bourgeois frustration here becomes in Buñuel's last film, *That Obscure Object of Desire*, the sexual frustration of a single individual, the ageing Don Juan-like Mathieu. Embodying the old-fashioned macho belief that a woman exists solely for the sexual pleasure of men, Mathieu spends much of his time and money in vainly pursuing the young and beautiful Conchita. She, essentially modern in her belief that she is her own woman, not his, keeps him on a string, teasing and taunting him to distraction but never allowing him to possess her. Once more Buñuel mocks bourgeois values – in this case Mathieu's belief in the power of money to buy Conchita, as well as his entrenched attitudes towards women – and exposes his protagonist to all manner of setbacks and shocks: not merely to the disappointments of Conchita's rejection of him but to the unsettling explosions created by extreme anti-bourgeois groups operating in Paris.

Between *Belle de jour* and *That Obscure Object of Desire*, Buñuel made two other films in France: *The Milky Way* (*La Voie lactée*) in 1969 and *The Phantom of Liberty* (*Le Fantôme de la liberté*) in 1974. His questioning of the effectiveness of Christian beliefs in a harsh and often uncomprehending world, as well as his exposure of the arrogance and hypocrisy of the Catholic Church, runs to a greater or lesser degree through much of his work, but in *The Milky Way* Buñuel placed inflexible Christian dogma at the very forefront of the film, subjecting it to close examination through the intervention of various heretics and, in the process, creating an enjoyable comedy out of unpromising material. As for *The Phantom of Liberty*, its title points to the notion of freedom which, for Buñuel, did not exist except in the freedom of the imagination. The characters of the film, some from the past and some from the present but usually representing the bourgeoisie or the Church, suggest the extent to which their freedom is denied them by social codes of behaviour or religious attitudes, as well as by the demands of sexual desire. *The Phantom of Liberty* is in many ways a comic film but its central concern with man's ultimate lack of freedom is less than optimistic.

After the controversy surrounding *Viridiana* in 1961 and for a number of years afterwards, Buñuel made only one more film in Spain – *Tristana* in 1970. Basing the script on the nineteenth-century novel of the same name by Galdós, Buñuel and his co-scriptwriter, Julio Alejandro, nevertheless made some important changes. The action was now located not in Madrid but in Toledo, a city that Buñuel knew well from his time at the Residencia de Estudiantes, when, as has been mentioned, he, Dalí, Lorca and other members of the so-called 'Order of Toledo' – a student group initially founded by Buñuel – made numerous visits there and indulged in typical student pranks (Buñuel, 71–4). As well as this, the time in which the events of the film take place was updated from the nineteenth century to the years immediately preceding the outbreak of the Spanish Civil War in 1936. And thirdly, the last third of the film differs markedly from the novel. The amputation of Tristana's leg and her revenge upon Don Lope, now her husband but previously her sexually abusive guardian, are elements introduced by Buñuel that greatly contribute to the film's much more bitter ending. In short, *Tristana* is a much darker and more corrosive film than any of those made by Buñuel in France between 1967 and 1977. Tristana's physical deformity becomes a powerful image of the way in which in Spanish society, of which the claustrophobic city of Toledo was for Buñuel more representative than the more cosmopolitan and liberal Madrid, women are the victims of men – diminished by male sexual attitudes and, in Tristana's case, embittered and driven to take revenge. And in locating the film in the early 1930s, Buñuel was also able to evoke the tensions that on a larger scale would erupt into the war itself and then continue for many years during the Franco dictatorship. Though very different in its storyline, *Tristana* has the same final bleakness as Lorca's great play, *The House of Bernarda Alba* (*La casa de Bernarda Alba*), which was completed in 1936, only months before Lorca himself was murdered by fascist sympathisers.

This brief consideration of Buñuel's career suggests quite clearly that, in the course of almost fifty years as a film-maker, his fundamental preoccupations changed very little. The surrealist concern with the unconscious and the world of dreams, expressed initially in the disturbing images of *Un Chien andalou*, is to be found in much later films, notably in *The Exterminating Angel* and *The Discreet Charm of the Bourgeoisie*. Secondly, the more political aspect of Surrealism, which was all to do with a revolution in society, is to be seen in Buñuel's attacks on and exposure of a self-satisfied and unfeeling bourgeoisie from the early *L'Âge d'or* to the later *The Diary of a Chambermaid*, as well as *The Discreet Charm*. And thirdly, Buñuel's preoccupation with religious themes, be it with the abuses perpetrated by the Catholic Church or the ineffectiveness of Christian ideals, runs through his films to a greater or lesser degree from *L'Âge d'or* to *Nazarín*, *Viridiana*, *Simon of the Desert* and *The Milky Way*. In short, like all great artists, Buñuel created a body of work in which, despite the differences between individual films, there is a consistency both in relation to theme and to his own particular vision of the world.

As well as this, however, many of Buñuel's films contain a strong autobiographical element, which writers on his work seem to have ignored and which will be discussed in detail in Chapter 2. In this context, it is important to bear in mind the effect that his eight-year attendance at the Jesuit Colegio del Salvador in Zaragoza had in shaping his attitudes, in particular towards women and sex. Encouraged by his Jesuit teachers to believe that sex and sin were the same thing, Buñuel's sex life before and after his marriage was largely characterised by inhibition, and it is surely no coincidence that in his autobiography references to his marriage to Jeanne Rucar in 1934 and to their subsequent life together are, to say the least, few and far between, while allusions to his anxieties in the presence of available women are plentiful. Sexual anxieties and frustration of this kind also abound in Buñuel's films, from *Un Chien andalou* through to *He*, *Viridiana*, *Belle de jour* and *That Obscure Object of Desire*, while in other films, such as *L'Âge d'or*, *Wuthering Heights*, *Viridiana*, and to some extent *Belle de jour*, some of the characters embody the fierce erotic desire and passion to which Buñuel undoubtedly aspired. As we shall see, he has often stated that some of his films have a substantial autobiographical element.

From a technical point of view, none of Buñuel's films have the self-indulgent effects or the showy over-the-top characteristics of much of the cinema of the late twentieth and early twenty-first centuries. In terms of length, only two films are more than one hundred minutes, a fact that is mainly a consequence of Buñuel's deceptively simple, precise and unfussy shooting style. Because of this, his films – certainly his best films – appear to be seamless and to move forward with absolute logic. Lacking the technical bravura of the modern blockbuster, they may have little appeal for the cinemagoer seeking thrills and entertainment. But, as is often the case, the true artist is the artist whose mastery becomes evident only on close examination – someone whose artistry appears, in effect, to be artless. Such was Buñuel's art, an art which, combined with the universal relevance of his themes, marks him out as one of the truly great film-makers.

1

BUÑUEL AND THE SURREALISTS

Luis Buñuel, without question one of the outstanding film-directors of the twentieth century, has always been regarded, together with such talents as Salvador Dalí, Max Ernst, René Magritte and Paul Éluard, as one of the great surrealist creative artists. In the 1920s his association with Salvador Dalí led to the making of *Un Chien andalou* in 1929, immediately acclaimed by André Breton, leader of the Paris surrealist group, as a true surrealist film. Its combined elements of shock, horror, dream, sex, illogicality and anti-bourgeois sentiments, utterly at odds with conventional film-making and all an essential part of surrealist thinking, are as striking today as they were more than seventy years ago, and the opening sequence of the eye-ball sliced by a cut-throat razor – filmed in close-up – never fails to turn the stomach of an unsuspecting cinema audience. These are elements, moreover, which Buñuel continued to exploit to a greater or lesser degree in a career that extended from his first film to his last, *That Obscure Object of Desire*, in 1977. We need only think of the dream sequences, the sexual preoccupations, and the assaults on conventional moral values in such films as *The Forgotten Ones*, *Viridiana*, *The Exterminating Angel*, *Belle de jour* and *The Discreet Charm of the Bourgeoisie*, in order to understand why Buñuel has always been regarded as a surrealist, even if in the later work his attitude had somewhat mellowed. Nevertheless, the picture is not as simple or as straightforward as it seems. Buñuel's cultural background, as well as his personality, was a complicated one, and this complexity is fully reflected both in his life and his work.

Buñuel's personality – tough, hard-hitting and unsentimental – found a natural affinity in the bold avant-garde movements that swept through Europe in the first decades of the twentieth century. Born in 1900 in the village of Calanda – population less than 5,000 – in the northern province of Aragón, he shared the down-to-earth, no-nonsense view of life of his fellow Aragonese, Francisco Goya. Although Buñuel's home background, unlike Goya's, was extremely comfortable, this did not prevent him from being exposed as a child to the harsh realities of life in Calanda, to which the family frequently returned even after they moved to the nearby city of Zaragoza when Buñuel was barely four months old. For the most part, the lives of ordinary men and women were extremely austere in a region that in winter was bitterly cold, in summer blisteringly hot. Calanda's nearest railway station was eighteen miles away, the journey by horse-drawn carriage took almost three hours, work in the olive-groves was hard and often unrewarding, the observance of traditional religious practices was unrelenting, and luxuries for most people were few and far between. Buñuel has described Calanda as a place where 'the Middle Ages lasted until World War I', and it is easy to see how, even if his family circumstances were much better than those of the other villagers, he was to a large extent the product of the larger environment (Buñuel, 8). His own tough independence of spirit, much like that of the inhabitants of Calanda, expressed itself at the age of fifteen when, after being kicked by a member of staff at the Colegio del Salvador in Zaragoza, he bluntly refused to return to school. In this context, his sister, Conchita, has also described how he waged a daily battle with his mother over his refusal to wear his school cap, and how, after fighting with and beating the toughest boy in the village, he chose to call himself 'the Lion of Calanda' (Buñuel, 34, 36). By the age of seventeen, when he left home and entered the prestigious Residencia de Estudiantes in Madrid, he was already in the process of turning his back on his religious upbringing and of absorbing the teachings of Darwin and Marx. In short, the young rebel was more than receptive to the new ideas to which he was about to be exposed in Madrid.

In the early 1920s the Spanish capital was alive with the kind of 'isms' to which Buñuel, freed from his provincial background, eagerly responded. Although Surrealism had not yet come to the fore, the anti-establishment and anti-tradition movements that preceded it were much in evidence in Spain, as in France, from around 1916. That year saw the publication in Barcelona of Francis Picabia's Dada magazine, *391*. By 1919 a Dada group had been established in the same city, and the influence of the movement was also being felt in Madrid. One of the capital's most influential figures at this time was Ramón Gómez de la Serna, who encouraged his contemporaries to experiment with new forms of writing. An eccentric individual, in some respects not unlike Salvador Dalí, he kept a female dummy as a companion, changing its clothes as he saw fit, while other characteristic activities included the delivery of a lecture from a trapeze or from the back of an elephant. From 1915 de la Serna held court every Saturday night at the Café Pombo, where, after his arrival in Madrid, Buñuel became one of his greatest admirers, his rebellious spirit clearly fired by the master's example.

Buñuel's rejection of traditional literary forms – at this time he had little interest in the cinema – is reflected in his allegiance to the new poetic movement known as *ultraísmo*, which cast aside sentimentality in favour of detachment and advocated the scientific language of the modern world in preference to the vocabulary of the past. Buñuel has observed:

> At this time, I was more or less connected to a movement called the Ultra-ists, which claimed to represent Spain's avant-garde. We were admirers of Dada, Cocteau and Marinetti. (Buñuel, 59)

An example of his writing, clearly influenced by current avant-garde influences, and also pointing to his love of the irrational, can be seen in the following extract from *Downright Treachery* (*Una traición incalificable*), published in the magazine *Ultra* in 1922:

> Delighted by this offer, and, it has to be said, filled with an understandable pride that such an important person [the wind] should take an interest in my work, I agreed to his request. Crying out with joy, he tore up a couple of trees, gave a couple of houses a 25 per cent turn, and rang all the bells of the city as if they were a triumphal band. Not satisfied with this, he then performed some magic. Three priests who were sneaking through the streets were transformed into upside-down umbrellas; the streets and houses were turned into Himalayas capped by clouds, and, through his magic, the café tables sprouted rags, scarecrows, straw, and other objects from the Great Dunghill Jewellery Store.[1]

In addition, it is important to bear in mind that, as well as Madrid in general, the Residencia de Estudiantes was itself a constant ferment of new ideas, for it both contained among its students such talents as Lorca and Dalí, and also welcomed among its visitors many distinguished artists and speakers, not least Louis Aragon, one of the great influences on Surrealism. Little wonder, then, that Buñuel's enthusiasm for the new should have been stimulated.

Buñuel's departure for Paris in 1925 reinforced his earlier exposure to the literary avant-garde and, crucially, exposed him to the most recent developments in cinema. There he was able to see films as innovative as René Claire's *Entr'acte* (1924), Eisenstein's *The Battleship Potemkin* (1925), Fritz Lang's *Metropolis* and Abel Gance's *Napoléon* (both 1926). From 1927 Buñuel also became film editor and critic for the Madrid-based *La Gaceta Literaria*, the Ultraist journal founded by Ernesto Giménez Caballero. In this capacity he kept his Spanish readers informed of the films that he was able to see in Paris and contributed to the journal articles both by himself and by French and Spanish intellectuals and creative artists, including Jean Epstein, Salvador Dalí, Ramón Gómez de la Serna, Ernesto Giménez Caballero, and Rafael Alberti. Between 1927 and 1932 Buñuel's personal contribution consisted of eight articles, all of which reveal his fascination with such new techniques as slow motion, dissolves, superimpositions and, above all, with cinema as the new poetry. In addition, Buñuel contributed literary pieces and poems to this and other journals, among which the following extract from *Palace of Ice* (*Palacio del hielo*), published in *Hélix* in 1929, provides a fine example of his enthusiastic embracing of modern techniques, and contains

---

[1]   See *Ultra*, 2, no. 23, 1 February 1922. Unless stated otherwise, all translations into English, here and subsequently, are my own.

some of the images which would appear in *Un Chien andalou* in the same year:

> The puddles formed a decapitated domino of buildings, one of which is the tower described to me in my childhood, with just one window, as high as the eyes of a mother when she leans over the cradle.
> Close to the window is a man who has been hanged and who swings over the abyss, surrounded by eternity and howled at by space. **IT IS I**. It is my skeleton of which nothing remains but the eyes. At one moment they smile, at another they cross, at another **THEY GO TO EAT A CRUMB OF BREAD IN THE INTERIOR OF THE BRAIN**. The window opens and a woman appears, polishing her nails. When she believes that they are properly filed, she plucks out my eyes and hurls them into the street. My sockets are left, lonely, sightless, without desire, without sea, without baby chicks, without anything. (*Hélix*, no. 4, 1927)

As well as contributing the cinema page to Ernesto Giménez Caballero's journal, Buñuel's influence also led to the former's founding in 1928 of the Cineclub Español, to which Buñuel sent many of the important films he was able to see in Paris, and where lectures were given by many individuals prominent in literature and in cinema. Films included those already mentioned above, as well as the silent films of Charlie Chaplin, Harold Lloyd, Harry Langdon, Buster Keaton and others, whose comic antics contained for Buñuel the essence of the absurd and the irrational. As for visiting speakers, they included Buñuel himself, Giménez Caballero, Gómez de la Serna, the film-director Germaine Dulac, Rafael Alberti and Lorca. Both the film programmes and the speakers, often chosen by Buñuel, point to his aggressive stance in relation to traditional artistic and cultural values – a stance embodied in his physical appearance when, in the following year, he appeared at the Cineclub for the Spanish première of *Un Chien andalou*: 'Luis Buñuel entered like a comet. He arrived from Paris, his head shaven, his face even stronger in features, his eyes rounder and more prominent'.[2] It was an aggression that was seen too in his contributions to other avant-garde journals to which he contributed at this time. Such was the case in an interview in the Catalan journal, *L'Amic de les Arts*, in which he poured abuse on the moral values and most of the films of Chaplin. Not long afterwards, at a Christmas party at Chaplin's Hollywood house in 1930, he was enraged by the reading of a patriotic poem and proceeded to attack the Christmas tree, for him a symbol of bourgeois convention.

Buñuel's impatience with anything he considered conventional is evident too in his first experiences in film-making. Having met the then famous

---

[2]   The occasion was described by Rafael Alberti in *The Lost Grove* (*La arboleda perdida*), trans. Gabriel Berns (Berkeley and Los Angeles: University of California Press, 1959), 272.

French film-director Jean Epstein in late 1925, Buñuel enrolled as an actor at his Académie de Cinema and soon afterwards was invited to become one of his assistant directors on two films: *Mauprat* and *The Fall of the House of Usher*, made in 1925 and 1928 respectively. Although an avant-garde film-maker in many ways – in his use of slow motion, dissolves, superimpositions and the like – Epstein favoured melodramatic subjects and the creation of beautiful, lyrical and romantic effects, as in the case of his adaptation of the Edgar Allan Poe novel with its wind-swept landscapes and its Gothic, candle-lit rooms. Buñuel subsequently observed in his characteristically blunt manner:

> The fact is that I learned very little from Epstein [. . .] When I watched Epstein direct, he frequently made me think – with the temerity of every newcomer – that this was not the way to do it, that the placing of the camera, lights or cast ought to be in such or such another way. Epstein was patient with me. Above all, I learned by mentally elaborating the picture being made, seeing it in a different fashion.[3]

While working with Epstein, Buñuel's outspoken and aggressive manner also revealed itself when the former suggested that he assist the celebrated film-director Abel Gance to audition two actresses. Like Epstein, Gance tended to be melodramatic and grandiloquent in his style of film-making, and Buñuel's reply was uncompromising:

> With my usual abruptness, I replied that I was *his* [Epstein's] assistant and not Gance's, that I didn't much like Gance's movies [. . .] and that I found Gance himself very pretentious. (Buñuel, 90)

Impatient to do things in his own way, he planned, among other things, to make a film entitled *La Sancta Misa Vaticanae*, in which, on the word 'go', priests compete to recite the mass as quickly as possible, achieving such speeds that, one by one, they collapse with exhaustion, the winner receiving a monstrance as his prize. It was a project typical of the mocking Buñuel.

By 1928 his iconoclastic stance was also being fuelled by his ever closer association with Salvador Dalí, himself increasingly intolerant of everything he regarded as traditional. Although both Dalí and Buñuel were close friends of Lorca – in later life Buñuel would describe him as the finest human being he ever met – Buñuel had earlier told Lorca to his face that he regarded his play, *Love of Don Perlimplín* (*Amor de Don Perlimplín*), as 'a piece of shit', while in a letter to José Bello in 1928, he derided Lorca's very successful volume of poetry, *Gypsy Ballads* (*Romancero gitano*), for its traditionalism:

---

3 See Francisco Aranda, *Luis Buñuel: A Critical Biography*, trans. David Robinson (London: Secker & Warburg, 1975), 34–5.

There is drama for those who like this kind of flamenco drama; there is the spirit of the classical ballad for those who want to go on with the classical ballad century after century; there are too some magnificent and very new images, but they are few and combined with a narrative I find insufferable and which keeps Spanish beds full of menstrual blood.[4]

As well as this, while Lorca in 1927 delivered an important lecture in honour of the tercentenary of the death of the great Spanish poet, Luis de Góngora, widely celebrated in Spain on this occasion, Buñuel could only vent his spleen:

> We have to *resist* with all our scorn and anger all traditional poetry, from Homer to Goethe via Góngora – the foulest beast any mother ever gave birth to. . . . (Sánchez Vidal, 36)

And equally and deliberately insulting was the joint letter that Buñuel and Dalí sent in 1928 to another leading poet, Juan Ramón Jiménez, pouring scorn in particular on his story about a donkey, *Platero and I* (*Platero y yo*) (see Sánchez Vidal, 36):

> Our Distinguished Friend: We consider it our duty to inform you – of course, disinterestedly – that we find your work deeply repugnant on account of its immoral, hysterical, and arbitrary character.
>   In particular: **SHIT!** on your *Platero and I*, on your facile and ill-intentioned *Platero and Me*, less than a proper donkey, the most odious donkey we have ever come across.
> **SHIT!**
> Sincerely,   Luis Buñuel
>   Salvador Dalí

The distinguished recipient of the letter was so shocked that he took to his bed for three days, a reaction that would have delighted both Buñuel and Dalí.

Buñuel has denied on many occasions that he knew much about Surrealism and the surrealists prior to the screening of *Un Chien andalou* in 1929:

> During those first years in Paris, when practically all the people I knew were Spanish, I heard hardly any mention of the surrealist. [. . .] To be quite frank, at that time, Surrealism had little interest for me.[5]

---

[4] For Buñuel's reaction to *Love of Don Perlimplín*, see *My Last Breath*, 101. The letter to José Bello was dated 14 September 1928, and is quoted in *Luis Buñuel: Obra literaria*, ed. Agustín Sánchez Vidal (Zaragoza: Ediciones de Heraldo de Aragón, 1982), 30 [hereafter Sánchez Vidal].

[5] See Luis Buñuel, *Mi último suspiro* (Barcelona: Plaza y Janes, 1982), 86. This observation does not appear in *My Last Breath*.

Nevertheless, as we have seen, the avant-garde movements with which he was familiar and with which he identified both during his time at the Residencia de Estudiantes and in the early Paris years, contained many of the elements – irrationality, shock, subversion – that were part of the surrealist movement, and Buñuel, like many others, was clearly in tune with the general thrust of Surrealism if not yet with the 'official' movement as it developed in Paris:

> More than anything else, surrealism was a kind of call heard by certain people everywhere – in the United States, in Germany, Spain, Yugoslavia – who, unknown to each other, were already practicing instinctive forms of irrational expression. Even the poems I'd published in Spain before I'd heard of the surrealist movement were responses to that call which eventually brought us together in Paris. (Buñuel, 105)

André Breton's *Manifesto of Surrealism*, defining the movement, had appeared in 1924, and it seems clear enough that from around 1927 Dalí, to whom Buñuel was drawing ever closer, was becoming increasingly conscious of Surrealism's importance to his life and work. Despite Buñuel's claim that he had little interest in Surrealism, it was inevitable, then, that he would have been influenced by Dalí's thinking. These were the years, after all, when Dalí was beginning to express in a number of significant paintings his deeply rooted sexual anxieties and obsessions. In *Apparatus and Hand*, completed in 1927, a fiery red hand is placed on top of an elongated 'apparatus', to either side of which are a female bather and various naked female forms. Dalí has given expression, in effect, to his obsession with masturbation, the causes of it, and the shame and anxiety – the hand is blushing as well as excited – that such 'self-abuse' provoked. This and other personal preoccupations, centred on his sexuality and on family relationships, would become the predominant motifs of Dalí's paintings during the next decade, including those that have since become so famous: *The Great Masturbator*, *The Lugubrious Game*, *Illumined Pleasures* (all 1929), and, of course, *The Persistence of Memory* with its limp watches. He was, in effect, putting into practice the surrealist belief, expressed in Breton's *Manifesto of Surrealism*, that the aim of the artist should be to give expression to those feelings that are deeply embedded in the unconscious but which the majority of individuals are unwilling to acknowledge.

Given the above, as well as Buñuel's desperate desire to make a film that accorded with his own beliefs, it is no coincidence that he and Dalí should have exchanged ideas on such a project in 1929. Dalí was already interested in film; he had published an article dedicated to Buñuel, 'Artistic Film, Anti-Artistic Film', in *La Gaceta Literaria* in late 1927; and he was particularly fascinated by film's capacity for suggesting transformation and metamorphosis: in other words, for expressing those shifting, dream-like states associated with the unconscious and on account of which the surrealists soon appreciated film's potential. When, therefore, Buñuel and Dalí met at the latter's house in Figueras, it is not surprising to learn that, in Buñuel's words, they 'never had the slightest disagreement' (Buñuel, 104) when they worked on the screenplay for *Un Chien andalou.*

In discussing what they would include in their screenplay, Buñuel has since observed:

> Our only rule was very simple: no idea or image that might lend itself to a rational explanation of any kind would be accepted. We had to open all doors to the irrational and keep only those images that surprised us, without trying to explain why. (Buñuel, 104)

At its deepest level, as we shall see, *Un Chien andalou* can be seen as an expression of the inner life of both Buñuel and Dalí, but on another level it reveals the same intention to surprise, to upset and shock that we have already witnessed in their pronouncements on traditional art forms and in their virulent attacks on particular individuals. As their original title they had at first proposed *Dangerous to Lean In* (*Dangereux de se pencher en dedans*), a witty inversion of the notice to passengers beneath the windows of French railway carriages. It was, of course, intended to confuse cinema audiences. Their final choice, *Un Chien andalou,* had a similar purpose, for, far from having any obvious relevance to the film, it was taken from the title – *Le Chien andalou* – of an unpublished collection of poems by Buñuel. The fact that people seeing the film would waste their time looking for a dog that did not exist made Dalí and Buñuel 'piss themselves laughing'.[6]

If *Un Chien andalou* was intended to disconcert in general, it may also be seen as an extension of the attacks that Buñuel in particular had earlier made on Lorca. In the first place, Andalusians at the Residencia de Estudiantes – and Lorca was by far the best known – were jokingly alluded to as 'Andalusian dogs' ('perros andaluces'). Secondly, Buñuel was well aware, even though he would usually deny it, of Lorca's homosexuality and therefore of his inability to respond sexually to women – something that in the film is embodied in the central character, the young man, who is presented as effeminate and impotent in his relationship with the young woman. Again, there are clear echoes of Lorca's short play, *Buster Keaton's Spin* (*El paseo de Buster Keaton*), in which the protagonist, a reflection of Lorca himself, falls from his bicycle, fails to respond to two women – both things occur in *Un Chien andalou* – and in which the zebra pattern on one of the girl's stockings has its counterpart in the striped box and the tie belonging to Buñuel's young man. Although Lorca did not see *Un Chien andalou* at the time of its release, he was certainly aware of its content and of its likely relevance to himself, for he observed to a friend in 1930: 'Buñuel has made a little shit of a film. It's

---

6   Agustín Sánchez Vidal, *Buñuel, Lorca, Dalí: el enigma sin fin* (Barcelona: Planeta, 1988), 190.

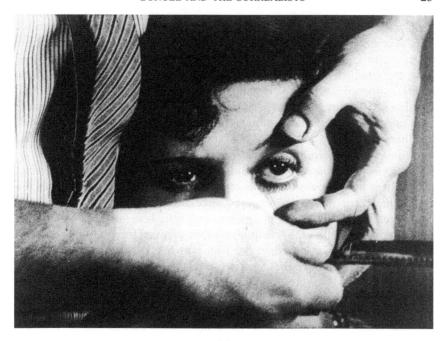

Un Chien andalou: opening one's eyes

called *An Andalusian Dog*, and I'm the dog' (Sánchez Vidal, 32). If the film was indeed about Lorca, it illustrates yet again how uncompromising Buñuel could be in his desire to offend, including on a personal level.

The intention to create a stir in relation to a broader audience and in true avant-garde fashion may be gauged by the efforts made by both Buñuel and Dalí to give their film maximum pre-publicity. In Figueras they invited a local newspaper reporter, Josep Puig Pujadas, to a reading of the screenplay, thus ensuring that he would publish a piece about it. This described the proposed film as creating 'an impression of abnormality', and as being 'deeply disturbing', and Buñuel himself made the point that it was 'something absolutely new in the history of the cinema'.[7] Subsequently, the interview was also published in a Barcelona newspaper, and its essentials appeared too in February 1929 in the influential *La Gaceta Literaria*. By the time Buñuel had completed filming, enormous interest had been created, and this was fuelled even more by the fact that a few days before the film's Paris première, a private screening was arranged for Man Ray and the highly influential Louis Aragon, both of whom were completely amazed by what they saw. The outcome was that Buñuel was invited to meet the surrealist group at

[7] Ian Gibson, *The Shameful Life of Salvador Dalí* (London: Faber & Faber, 1997), 192–3.

the Cyrano, near André Breton's apartment. Those present, according to his own account, were Breton, Max Ernst, Paul Éluard, Tristan Tzara, René Char, Pierre Unik, Yves Tanguy, Hans Arp, Maxine Alexandre and René Magritte (Buñuel, 105). Shortly afterwards, on 6 June 1929, *Un Chien andalou* opened at Paris's leading experimental cinema, the Studio de Ursulines. The surrealists, as well as other distinguished individuals, were astounded by the seventeen-minute film. Buñuel soon became an official member of the group and at the end of the year the screenplay was published in the journal, *La Révolution surréaliste*.

Un Chien andalou represents Buñuel and Dalí at their most aggressive. Indeed, it is no coincidence in this respect that the character who wields the eye-slicing razor in the opening sequence should be Buñuel himself, the committed opponent of all things conventional, here assaulting the cosy expectations, as well as the sensibilities of the viewer. Henry Miller's description of audience reaction when the film was later shown in Madrid fully reveals the effect of this initial episode:

> Afterwards they showed *Un Chien andalou*. The public shuddered, making their seats creak, when an enormous eye appeared on the screen and was cut coldly by a razor, the drops of liquid from the iris leaping onto the metal. Hysterical shouts were heard.[8]

Such is the power of the image, it is as if our own eyes were being threatened, which is, of course, the purpose of this moment: to make us look anew, to shake us out of the complacency that might have been awakened by the fairy-tale promise of the preceding title, *Once upon a time*, and by the appearance of a rather romantic moon in a sky that contains only one thin cloud.

This initial, sickening shock proves to be the first of many. Our introduction to the film's male protagonist, the young man, is, to say the least, bizarre, for as he mechanically rides his bicycle along a deserted street, he is seen to be wearing on his head and around his shoulders and waist what appear to be baby clothes. When he then falls from the bicycle and lies totally inert in the road, our first glimpse of the film's female protagonist introduces another surprise, for she suddenly throws aside her book, rushes downstairs into the street, and, for no apparent reason, passionately embraces and kisses the young man. Equally strange and unexpected incidents follow: an androgynous young woman uses a stick to prod a dismembered hand lying in the road and is killed by a passing car, observed from an upstairs window by the young man and the young woman. The former is then seen staring at a hole in his hand from which ants are beginning to emerge, after which he approaches the young woman and fondles her breasts and buttocks, which are first depicted clothed, then naked. She attempts to escape, he grasps the end of

---

8   Henry Miller, *The Cosmological Eye* (London, 1945), 57.

two ropes with which to capture her, but is held back by a great weight attached to the ropes, which, as it comes into view, is seen to consist of grand pianos, rotting donkeys draped over them, and two priests, astonished but still praying. Subsequently, the young man reverts to his initial baby-like state, prostrate on his bed, only to be surprised by another, much more energetic young man who pulls him to his feet, forces him to remove the baby clothes, and, as a punishment, orders him to stand in the corner and to hold two books above his head. The books are suddenly transformed into revolvers, upon which the young man shoots the newcomer. He falls to the ground in the bedroom which, in a flash, become a park from which a group of onlookers carry the corpse. The young woman then reappears in the bedroom, looking for the young man, but when his mouth disappears and the hair from her arm-pit appears on his chin, she abandons him, exiting the room not into another but on to a beach where a second young man waits for her. They embrace and walk away into the distance. The film ends with a title, *In the Springtime*, which seems to promise a rosy future for the young couple, but this at once becomes a shot of the lovers buried to their waist in sand beneath a blazing sun, their eyes eaten away by insects.

This bald account of the sequence of events that constitute *Un Chien andalou* suggests very clearly its unusual and disconcerting character. As far as form is concerned, the film undoubtedly has a sense of progression, a certain narrative structure, but it also seems to consist of a series of disjointed episodes, which in a way parallel the jerky rhythm of the tango with which it begins. In addition, the sense of disorientation is reinforced by the use of titles – *Eight years later, Towards three in the morning* – and by sudden changes in location – a room into a park, a room into a beach. Again, the characters are often driven by an aggression that for the viewer becomes disturbing: the young woman rushing to caress and embrace the young man; the latter lustfully fondling the girl's breasts and buttocks, then pursuing her around the room; the newcomer upbraiding the young man before being shot by him; the young woman aggressively sticking out her tongue at the young man before abandoning him. These, in short, are not rounded characters but individuals driven by impulse, rejecting reason in favour of instinct, particularly in relation to sexual matters. The sexual implications of the film will be examined in detail in Chapter 2. Suffice it to say for the moment that *Un Chien andalou* struck out in both its themes and its form at conventional film-making.

The reactions of the critics reveal both their astonishment at and their appreciation of such an unusual film. Writing in the Brussels magazine *Variétés*, André Delons concluded: 'One forms the impression of being present at some authentic return of truth, of truth skinned alive.'[9] Robert

---

9   *Variétés*, Brussels, 15 July 1929, 22.

Desnos observed: 'I do not know of any film which affects the viewer so directly, which has been made so specifically for him, which engages him in conversation, in such an intimate relationship.'[10] And Eugenio Montes, reviewing the film for *La Gaceta Literaria*, emphasised its Spanish directness: 'Do not look here for French roses. Spain is not a garden, and the Spanish are not gardeners. [. . .] Nothing decorative here. Spain expresses the essential, not the refined. Spain does not refine, nor falsify.'[11] *Un Chien andalou* had achieved all that Buñuel and Dalí could have hoped for.

Buñuel, we recall, had stated that he knew little about Surrealism prior to the making of *Un Chien andalou*. Many years later, however, he was in no doubt that 'my connection with the surrealists in many ways determined the course of my life' (Buñuel, 105). What, then, did Buñuel encounter in the ideas of the Paris surrealists that appealed to him so much? In 1924 André Breton's *Manifesto of Surrealism*, influenced in no small degree by Freud's investigations into the unconscious mind, had defined the aims of Surrealism in the following way:

> SURREALISM. *n.masc.* Pure psychic automatism through which it is intended to express, either orally, or in writing, or in any other way, the actual way thought works. The dictation of thought, free from all control exercised by reason, without regard to any aesthetic or moral concern.[12]

If it seems unlikely that Buñuel was not familiar, especially through Dalí's influence, with the general thrust of surrealist thinking, it is perfectly clear that his entry into the Paris surrealist group consolidated his ideas in a variety of ways, not least in terms of his political leanings. Breton's *Second Surrealist Manifesto*, published in the journal *La Révolution surréaliste* in December 1929, both coincided with Buñuel's official entry into the official surrealist group and represented an increasing emphasis on the political aims of Surrealism, in which Breton saw a clear link with those of the Communist Party.[13] The surrealists were, after all, as committed to changing society as it existed as were the communists, as Buñuel has indicated:

> All of us were supporters of a certain concept of revolution, and although the surrealists didn't consider themselves terrorists, they were constantly fighting a society they despised. Scandal was a potent agent of revelation, capable of exposing such social crimes as the exploitation of one man by another, colonialist imperialism, religious tyrrany – in sum, all the secret

---

10 *Le Merle*, Paris, 28 June 1929.
11 *La Gaceta Literaria*, Madrid, 15 June 1929, 1.
12 See *Manifestoes of Surrealism*, trans. Richard Seaver and Helen R. Lane (Ann Arbor: University of Michigan, 1972), 3.
13 See *La Révolution surréaliste*, 15 December 1929.

and odious underpinnings of a system that had to be destroyed. The real purpose of Surrealism was not to create a new literary, artistic, or even philosophical movement, but to explode the social order, to transform life itself. (Buñuel, 107)

This loose alliance with the communists was one that would result in serious dissension within the surrealist group itself. Louis Aragon, originally one of Surrealism's prime movers, would embrace Communism and abandon the surrealist group because he considered it not to be sufficiently revolutionary, and Dalí would eventually be expelled from it on account of his love of making money. As for Buñuel, he was, by his own admission, a communist sympathiser and remained so until the 1950s when he became disillusioned with the regime in the Soviet Union. Whether or not he joined the Communist Party remains unclear – he has denied it (Buñuel, 138) – but there can be no doubt that the ideals of Communism, like those of Surrealism, appealed to his aggressive and rebellious character:

We all felt a certain destructive impulse, a feeling that for me has been even stronger than the creative urge. The idea of burning down a museum, for instance, has always seemed more enticing than the opening of a cultural centre or the inauguration of a new hospital. (Buñuel, 107)

In short, his absorption into the Paris surrealist group brought together his fascination with the irrational and his anti-bourgeois tendencies, offering him a coherent philosophy:

For the first time in my life I'd come into contact with a coherent moral system. [. . .] When I ask myself what Surrealism really was, I still answer that it was a revolutionary, poetic, and *moral* movement.

(Buñuel, 107, 109)

Given the success of *Un Chien andalou*, Buñuel and Dalí were naturally eager to begin work on another film, a project made much more likely as a result of the friendship Buñuel had formed with Vicomte Charles de Noailles and his wife Marie-Laure, sophisticated and wealthy patrons of the arts, both of whom had been so impressed by *Un Chien andalou* that they had helped to secure a licence for its public screening. Indeed, the Noailles assured Buñuel that he would have complete freedom over the new film, and so he and Dalí met in Cadaqués in the summer of 1929 in order to exchange ideas, which they worked on in the autumn in Paris and later in Cadaqués. Initially, the new film was to be called *La Bête andalouse* (*The Andalusian Beast*), its title a clear indication that it was to be a follow-up to *Un Chien andalou*. As for the respective contributions made by Buñuel and Dalí to the screenplay, the evidence is in some ways confusing. Buñuel has claimed that the screenplay was entirely his:

Dalí and I went to his house in Cadaqués, where we began work. After a couple of days, however, it was obvious that the magical rapport we'd had during *Un Chien andalou* was gone. [. . .] In any case, we couldn't agree on anything; we found each other's suggestions impossible, and the vetoes were fast and furious. In the end we separated amicably, and I wrote the screenplay alone, at the de Noallies' in Hyères. (Buñuel, 115)

For his part, Dalí undoubtedly made many suggestions for improvements to the screenplay, as a number of his letters suggest.[14] They included a suggestion that in the love scene in the garden the young man, instead of merely kissing the young woman's fingers, should rip out one of her nails with his teeth, and that a shot of the young woman's trembling lips should dissolve into a shot of a vagina. In the end Buñuel either rejected or modified Dalí's ideas, for, regarding the first, the film shows the lovers sucking each other's fingers, while the lips–vagina transformation was abandoned. In short, in the process of filming, at which Dalí was not present, Buñuel made his own decisions about what was to be included in what was now to be called not *La Bête andalouse* but *L'Âge d'or*. Even so, both men seem to have agreed that the theme of the film was to be the confrontation between sexual instinct and the social and religious forces that seek to repress it.

Although nothing in *L'Âge d'or* matches the shocking opening sequence of *Un Chien andalou*, it contains many incidents which, in true surrealist fashion, are intended to surprise and disconcert its audience. The beginning of the film, part of a documentary that Buñuel used because he was unable to film the real thing, depicts the activities of scorpions pursuing each other, and a struggle in which a scorpion kills a rat. The images are also accompanied by titles that give out information about these creatures and their habits. The relationship of the sequence to the rest of the film will be discussed later, but initially it seems bizarre, and this impression is sustained when the scorpions give way to a group of bandits who, delirious, dying and exhausted, witness the arrival by boat of a large number of people among whom civic dignitaries, nuns, priests and military men are prominent. One of the company, a pompous individual, then proceeds to lay a foundation stone, but is interrupted by the ecstatic cries of two lovers who, oblivious to the ceremony, are passionately embracing on the ground. When they are pulled apart by the onlookers, they are dragged away, and the young man, in sheer frustration, kicks out at a dog, sending it flying through the air. The focus of the film, again somewhat bizarrely, then opens out from the rocky coastline to reveal the grandeur of Rome, its magnificent buildings, its traffic and its milling crowds, and finally reveals the male lover, still in the clutches of two policemen but now in the city itself. He soon secures his release and sets out to find his beloved, knocking aside a blind man who is about to enter a taxi.

14 See *The Shameful Life of Salvador Dalí*, 245–9.

The young woman, meanwhile, is seen at home, where a cow lies on her bed. She is, with her mother, in the process of organising a lavish dinner-party.

The dinner-party at the home of the Marquis of X occupies the longest section of the film and, like the preceding episodes, contains a succession of arresting incidents. While the bourgeois guests are absorbed in their conversation, a horse and cart full of drunken peasants lumbers through the drawing-room; a servant runs from the smoke-filled kitchen and falls unconscious; and the gardener shoots his son when he steals one of his cigarettes and runs off. Soon the young man arrives, eager to get his hands on the girl, but he is distracted by her mother, and, when she accidentally spills wine on his suit, he slaps her across the face. Later, when he and the young woman are alone in the garden, desperate to make love, he is summoned to take a telephone call from the Minister of the Interior and so abuses him that the minister commits suicide. And then, when the young woman abandons him and returns to the bosom of her bourgeois family, the young man vents his anger on her bedroom, hurling through the window a fir-tree, a giraffe, a plough and an archbishop.

L'Âge d'or concludes with a sequence in which there are further and greater surprises. A series of titles, taken from the Marquis de Sade's novel, *One Hundred and Twenty Days of Sodom*, describes the activities within the Chateau de Selliny of four debauched criminals, including their leader, the Duke of Blangis, and announces their emergence from the castle after their orgy with 'eight lovely young girls' and 'four depraved women'. The last of the four men to leave the castle is the Duke himself, whose bearded face, pious gestures and long white robe at once bring to mind the traditional image of Jesus Christ. As he leaves, a young girl crawls after him, her breast covered in blood. He turns, picks her up and carries her into the castle. A piercing scream is heard, the Duke reappears, this time without a beard. The four men walk away and the film ends with a close-up of female scalps nailed to a cross.

Although *L'Âge d'or* contains the same element of surprise and shock as *Un Chien andalou*, it also has a greater political emphasis, for Buñuel's aggression is directed at those institutions – bourgeois society and the Church – that both he and the surrealists considered to be repressive, materialistic and destructive in relation to the natural instincts and desires of mankind. Buñuel's dissection of the bourgeoisie will be discussed in detail later on, but for the moment we can at least mention its complacency and its indifference to those outside its tightly closed circle. When, for example, the rustic cart with its drunken peasants rolls unnoticed through the drawing-room, it does so because the bourgeois guests are so absorbed in their own conversation that they take no interest in anything else. Similarly, when the female servant collapses in front of them, they are indifferent to her fate, and even the gamekeeper's shooting of his son awakens in them only a mild curiosity before they return to the drawing-room and the more important matter of their empty social chit-chat. Buñuel's assault on this privileged group frequently takes the form of mockery of bourgeois manners, but his principal instrument of assault in this film is, of course, the love-obsessed young man, played by Gaston Modot, who, in his pursuit of the young woman, Lya Lys, sweeps aside like nine-pins every bourgeois obstacle in his path, including the blind man – a favourite object of bourgeois sentimentality – and the young woman's prattling mother.

Buñuel's attack on the Church will also be discussed later, but in this second film he already pinpoints its lasting influence and its double standards. In the sequence concerning the bandits, the archbishops intoning in the rocks are later turned into skeletons, but even as they die they give way to other representatives of the Church who are arriving by boat. And when in his rage the young man hurls an archbishop from the bedroom window, the latter merely gets up and scuttles away to continue his work, shaken but not dead, a pointer to the indestructible nature of the Church and its lasting hold over so many men and women. In the episode involving the orgiasts, Buñuel savagely exposes the Church's hypocrisy, for here the Christ-like figure embodying piety and compassion murders the suffering girl – comment enough on the Catholic Church's suppression of and intolerance towards women, who, of course, have been among its most faithful followers throughout the ages.

While *L'Âge d'or* perfectly illustrates the political dimension described by Breton in the *Second Surrealist Manifesto*, it embodies in the form of the passionate lovers the earlier *Manifesto of Surrealism*'s emphasis on the role of instinct 'free from all control exercised by reason, without regard to any aesthetic or moral concern'. Oblivious to all social and moral impediments, the two young people live for each other. When they are set upon by the enraged onlookers and dragged away, their physical separation cannot obliterate their thoughts of or feelings for each other, for the young man sees his beloved everywhere: in advertisements for hand cream and silk stockings, and in the portrait of a girl in a window. And when she sits in front of a mirror in her bedroom, she sees not her own reflected image but a beautiful sky and passing clouds, the image of her romantic thoughts. In the extended sequence in the garden where they attempt to make love, their ecstasy is conveyed to us in ways which are often quite startling. When, for example, they begin to bite each other's hands, a close-up of the young man reveals that his beloved has, in her rapture, devoured his fingers. Shortly afterwards, when he has unexpectedly been called away to take a telephone call, she maintains the level of her passion by sucking the toe of a nearby statue. And when he returns and his excitement grows even more, his face is suddenly seen to be covered with blood, Buñuel's way of indicating the intensity of his emotions.

In the behaviour of the lovers there is, then, a ferocity that ignores the narrow-minded propriety demanded by the society in which they live. They exist only for the fulfilment of their sexual longing for each other, the part of the garden in which they make love an image of their self-contained world, separated by hedges from the buttoned-up world of the young woman's parents and their guests. In its exaltation of passion, *L'Âge d'or* is very different from *Un Chien andalou*, particularly in the sense that its male protagonist reveals not the slightest sign of sexual anxiety. It is, in contrast, a celebration of *amour fou*, the wild passion championed by the surrealists, even if in the end it is defeated by bourgeois restraints. As Ado Kyrou once observed:

> Buñuel is the most honest and sincere man that I know. [. . .] He has expressed himself, expresses himself and will continue to express himself simply, freely and valiantly. He has spoken and will always speak of love and the enemies which love must fight.[15]

Although initially disconcerting and apparently disjointed in a way that, as in the case of *Un Chien andalou*, strikes out at conventional film-making, *L'Âge d'or* is quite cunningly constructed. As we have seen, the opening documentary sequence depicting the activities of scorpions becomes in turn the bandits and the people arriving by boat. The location then moves to Rome and its grandeur, the focus narrows to the extended episode of the dinner-party, and the film ends with the sequence set in the Chateau de Selliny. The film consists, in effect, of five sections, corresponding to the structure of the scorpion's tail, which the documentary opening informs us is formed of 'five prismatic joints', and a further one which is the deadly sting. Furthermore, although the various sections of the film may appear to be unconnected, they are in fact linked in significant ways. The titles describing the nature of the scorpions inform us that they are aggressive, unsociable, and intolerant of any creature or person who seeks to disturb them. In this respect, their behaviour anticipates that of the bourgeois guests at the dinner-party, for when the young man's behaviour becomes unacceptable to them, they imme-diately eject him. On the other hand, the aggressive nature of the scorpions is embodied in the young man, who, fired by his single-minded passion for his beloved, attacks the obstacles in his path. And finally, Buñuel himself is a scorpion, the bourgeoisie his chosen enemy, as much the object of his sting here as of the razor in *Un Chien andalou*. The opening sequence can already be seen to have a clear relevance to the rest of the film.

The bandits of the second section are the scorpions in another form, and it is no accident that some of the bandits were played by surrealists: Max Ernst, for example, played their leader, and Paul Éluard did the voice-over in the love sequence in the garden. Like the bandits, the surrealists were considered by the bourgeoisie to be undesirable outsiders, for they launched their attacks on bourgeois society and values with similar ferocity. This said, the bandits are portrayed as being in a state of collapse in the face of the arrival of the

---

[15] Quoted in Aranda, *Luis Buñuel: A Critical Biography*, 73.

bourgeois group and their companions – the dignitaries, the priests, the military – who arrive by boat. It is as if Buñuel recognises the uphill and ultimately futile battle that the surrealists face in their efforts to transform society, though the defeat of the bandits is accompanied by music from Beethoven's Fifth Symphony, which is, of course, heroic.

The third section of *L'Âge d'or* develops directly from the second in the sense that the laying of the foundation stone now gives way to the city of Rome, symbol of both ancient and modern civilisation, the focal point of the Catholic Church, and the meeting place of bourgeois and religious values. Furthermore, impressive panoramic shots of Rome's grandeur are interposed with close-ups of decaying and collapsing houses, and various bizarre incidents – a passer-by crushing a violin beneath his foot, a man emerging from a restaurant and brushing plaster dust from his clothes – which point to cracks in the initial façade, and which, by extension, anticipate less salubrious realities beneath the glittering façade of bourgeois elegance. In this sense, the fourth section of the film – the dinner-party at the elegant home of the Marquis of X, which reveals to the full bourgeois self-centredness and indifference to others – stems directly from the third, while the arrival of the young man at the dinner-party, where he proves to be a disruptive influence, also links the fourth section to the second, where his love-making with the young woman disrupts the laying of the foundation stone. As well as this, the fourth section reinforces the links between the bourgeoisie and the Church already suggested in sections two and three, for, as they arrive at the home of the Marquis, the guests are seen to have religious objects in their cars, and the orchestra that entertains them in the garden contains priests.

The last section of *L'Âge d'or*, the sting in the tail, links with all that has preceded it in several significant ways. The orgy is a debauched form of the dinner-party in section four, the lust and cruelty of the aristocrats who emerge from the castle a savage parallel to the indifference of the Marquis of X's guests to the fate of their employees. In addition, the identification of Christ and the Duke of Blangis links the Church and the socially privileged, and also reveals the way in which, throughout the ages, both have degraded and abused the dignity of women by using them for their own selfish ends and relegating them to a position of inferiority. The end of the film also echoes the beginning, for if Buñuel is the aggressive scorpion there, he here launches his final, venomous attack on the institutions he despises.

If *L'Âge d'or* has the structure outlined above, which suggests that it possesses the kind of coherence associated with conventional film-making, how can this be reconciled with the surrealist aim of undermining all things conventional? The explanation lies in the fact that in the *Second Surrealist Manifesto* Breton had suggested that psychical or psycho-neurotic material, the stuff of automatic writing synonymous with the previous stage of Surrealism, was no longer sufficient, and that the movement was in need of greater conceptual substance. In this context he praised the method then being employed by Dalí, which became known as the 'paranoia-critical method', whereby the painter claimed he was able to participate in the events of his unconscious as actor and spectator simultaneously, deeply involved but able to maintain an essential critical detachment, which allowed him to transfer his neurosis to canvas in an artistic way.[16] Strictly speaking, this process is more directly relevant to *Un Chien andalou*, given its structuring of motifs deeply embedded in the unconscious, but the sense of overall control in relation to material that at first seems unconnected, even if it is more 'political', is also true of *L'Âge d'or*. Beneath its apparently chaotic events, there is certainly the greater conceptual substance that Breton had called for.

Given that *L'Âge d'or* had been made with the financial backing of Charles and Marie Laure de Noailles, it was appropriate that the film should have had its first screening in their private cinema on 30 June 1930. During the next ten days the Vicomte arranged several more screenings for friends and critics, and, on 22 October, an important private screening at the Cinéma du Panthéon, attended by 300 guests. They included Jean Cocteau, Picasso, Gertrude Stein, André Gide, Alberto Giacometti, George Bataille, Marcel Duchamp and, of course, the 'official' surrealists. Buñuel, however, was not present. He returned to Paris a few days later, but he would have been pleased to learn that many of the aristocrats invited to the screening by the Vicomte were so shocked by *L'Âge d'or* that they left in silence, refusing to thank their host or to attend the reception that followed. This reaction, as well as an attack on the Noailles in the following day's *Paris-Soir*, anticipated the outrage that followed the public première.

This took place at Studio 28 on 28 November, once more in Buñuel's absence, for he had been invited to Hollywood by Metro-Goldwyn-Mayer and did not return to France until 1 April 1931. As might have been expected, right-wing reaction to *L'Âge d'or* was extremely hostile. On the evening of 3 December, Studio 28 was attacked by members of the League of Patriots and the Anti-Semitic League, the latter incensed by the fact that such a subversive film had been financed by Marie Laure de Noailles, whose father was a wealthy American-Jew, the former enraged by the film's onslaught on the bourgeoisie and traditional values. Shouts of 'Death to the Jews' and 'You'll soon see if there are still Christians in France', were accompanied by the throwing of ink at the screen and smoke and stink bombs into the audience, which was also attacked with clubs. In addition, surrealist paintings on display in the cinema foyer – by Dalí, Max Ernst, Hans Arp, Yves Tanguy and Man Ray – were slashed. The police took half an hour to arrive, evidently allowing the right-wing agitators sufficient time to do as much damage as possible. But they did not completely ruin the occasion, for the screen was

---

[16] See André Breton, 'The Dalí Case', in *Surrealism and Painting*, trans. Simon Watson Taylor (London: Macdonald, 1965), 133.

repaired, the film shown, and more than sixty of the audience, as they left the cinema, signed a protest against what had occurred.

In the days that followed the attack, many right-wing newspapers expressed their opposition to the film in no uncertain fashion. Writing in *Le Figaro*, Richard Pierre Bodin concluded:

> A film called *L'Âge d'or*, whose non-existent artistic quality is an insult to any kind of technical standard, combines, as a public spectacle, the most obscene, disgusting and tasteless incidents. Country, family and religion are dragged through the mud.[17]

Another, less up-market newspaper, *L'Ami du Peuple*, considered the film to have been made by a couple of 'dagos' and thought it should have been called, more appropriately, *L'Âge d'ordure* (*The Age of Shit*).[18]

Many others, of course, rallied to support the film against its right-wing opponents. In the Communist daily newspaper, *L'Humanité*, Leon Moussinac praised *L'Âge d'or* for its uncompromising attack on the bourgeoise:

> Never before in the cinema, or with such power, such disdain for 'conventions' and for bourgeois society and its trappings – the police, religion, the army, morality, the family, the State – has there occurred such a violent assault, such a kick up the backside.[19]

And Paul Rejac, in *Cinémonde*, was similarly full of praise:

> *L'Âge d'or* presents an obsessive vision of sexual love which embraces and will not release the viewer. There has never been anything to compare with this in the cinema.[20]

Such plaudits did not appease the Right. *Le Figaro* urged the authorities to ban the film. The Paris Chief of Police, Jean Chiappe, received hundreds of complaints. The Italian Embassy complained that one of the couples at the dinner-party – a short man and his tall wife – was a deliberate parody of King Victor Emmanuel and his queen, and that the Roman setting was an insult to Italy itself. Punitive action quickly followed. On 5 December Jean-Placide Mauclaire, the owner of Studio 28, was told to remove from the film the two early episodes portraying archbishops, and three days later to cut from the programme notes the statement that 'The Count of Blangis is obviously

---

17 *Le Figaro*, 7 December 1930.

18 See Jean-Michel Bouhours and Natalie Schoeller (eds), *L'Âge d'or. Correspondance Luis Buñuel–Charles de Noailles. Lettres et documents* (Paris: Centre Georges Pompidou, Les Cahiers du Musée National d'Art Moderne, 1993), 176.

19 *L'Humanité*, 7 December 1930.

20 *Cinémonde*, 11 December 1930.

Christ'. On 9 December he was instructed to take the film to the Censorship Office; on the following day it was banned; on the 11th legal proceedings were taken against him; and on the 12th two of the three existing copies of the film were confiscated. Fortunately, the Vicomte de Noailles succeeded in preserving the negatives, but, as a direct consequence of his financial support of *L'Âge d'or*, he was forced to resign from the Jockey Club, snubbed by his own social circle, and only saved from excommunication by his influential mother's connections with the powers-that-be at the Vatican. It was an unhappy outcome for someone who had backed Buñuel so wholeheartedly.

The surrealists were, of course, delighted by the scandal *L'Âge d'or* had provoked and enraged by right-wing reaction to it. They produced a four-page account of all that had happened, including photographs of the damage inflicted on Studio 28 and a series of questions as to the right of the police to ban the film, to limit free speech, to allow property to be damaged and to encourage fascist activities. In the event, *L'Âge d'or* would not be seen by the general public for another fifty years, but this, of course, merely drew attention to the fact that Buñuel and the surrealists were totally justified in launching their attacks against a bourgeois society that they considered to be repressive and authoritarian.

Buñuel's third film, *Las Hurdes*, also known as *Terre sans pain* (*Land Without Bread*), is at first sight very different from both *Un Chien andalou* and *L'Âge d'or*, for it has none of the former's erotic associations nor the latter's concern with sexual desire in conflict with bourgeois restrictions. On the contrary, *Las Hurdes* proclaims itself as a documentary set in the mountainous region of that name in the province of Extremadura, near the Portuguese border to the west, and sixty miles from the university town of Salamanca to the north-east. The film begins in La Alberca, a town outside Las Hurdes, and then proceeds to the valley of Las Batuecas before moving on into Las Hurdes proper and the village of Aceitunilla where we are shown the way of life of its inhabitants and the activities of the children in the schoolroom. Later, in the villages of Martilandrán and Fragosa, Buñuel focuses in some detail on the housing conditions of the people who live there and on the way in which their lives are affected by illness. As well as this, we learn something of the farming methods and of the diet of the inhabitants of Las Hurdes as a whole.

Given the apparent difference between *Las Hurdes* and the two earlier films, one has to ask the question: in what sense, if any, is Buñuel's third film surrealist? One year before he made it, Buñuel had in fact left the Paris surrealist group for the following reasons:

> In 1932 I separated from the surrealist group although I remained on good terms with my ex-companions. I was beginning not to agree with that kind of intellectual aristocracy, with its artistic and moral extremes, which isolated us from the world at large and limited us to our own company.

Surrealists considered the majority of mankind contemptible or stupid, and thus withdrew from all social participation and responsibility and shunned the work of the others.[21]

Disagreements about the aims of Surrealism and the extent to which the surrealists should ally themselves with the Communist Party had affected the movement from the outset. By 1932, Breton, Louis Aragon, Georges Sadoul, Pierre Unik and Maxime Alexandre had left the surrealist group in order to join the Party. Buñuel did not do so, but his communist sympathies remained strong and were closely bound up with the belief that one of the principal aims of Surrealism was to transform society. *Las Hurdes* is a surrealist film, therefore, in the sense that it has a political motive: to open the eyes of the powers-that-be to the reality of the region the film portrays in the hope that the lives of its people will be improved.

The early 1930s was a time of significant political upheaval in Spain. The seven-year dictatorship of General Miguel Primo de Rivera had come to an end in 1930 and been replaced in the following year by the left-wing Republican Government with its promise of fundamental social change, of which a huge amount was certainly needed. Spain at this time was an extremely backward country in many ways. As far as education was concerned, just over 11,000 schools had been built in thirty years, and almost 33 per cent of the entire population of the country was illiterate. Social conditions in both the cities and the countryside were often very poor, unemployment high, work hard when it was available, and pay extremely low, not least in southern Spain where vast areas of land were owned by absentee landlords and the workers were little better than slaves. In addition, of course, diet, housing and hygiene were often very poor indeed, and, in consequence, malnourishment and disease were inevitable. They were conditions that the Republican Government attempted to improve by means of a variety of social and economic measures put into effect in its first two years of office, but the problems were so extensive that by 1933, the year in which the Left lost its majority to the Right and Buñuel made *Las Hurdes*, vast areas of Spain remained untouched by reform.

Las Hurdes had already been for very many years a symbol of Spain's isolation and backwardness. In the early part of the twentieth century it was the subject of various articles and studies: in 1906 *La Semana Ilustrada* had described it as the abode of primitive, wolf-like creatures; in 1911 Blanco Belmonte's *Por la España desconocida, La Alberca, Las Hurdes, Las Batuecas y Peña de Francia (Through Unknown Spain, La Alberca . . .)* had provided an illustrated account of the region's primitive customs; in 1913 Miguel de Unamuno's essays on agrarian reform, published in the newspaper *El Imparcial*, had drawn attention to Las Hurdes; and in 1927 there appeared

21 *Luis Buñuel: A Critical Biography*, 88.

Las Hurdes, étude de géographie humaine, by the French scientist Maurice Legendre, a detailed study of the region that resulted from an earlier visit and on which Buñuel drew in making his film.[22]

During the ten years preceding it, Las Hurdes had also become a political issue, for in 1922 Dr Gregorio Marañón was despatched to write a report on sanitation in the region. This in turn led to a debate in the Spanish Parliament and also to a two-day visit to the area in June of that year by King Alfonso XIII, who was appalled by the spectacle of human misery and degradation. Seven years later, a series of articles and photographs in the journal *Estampa* focused attention once more on Las Hurdes, and in March 1930, not long before his abdication, King Alfonso made a second visit. In this context it is easy to understand the political purpose of Buñuel's film.

Although Buñuel was no longer a member of the Paris surrealist group, many of those who worked with him on *Las Hurdes* were revolutionaries. Financial backing for the film came from Ramón Acín, a committed anarchist and regional organiser – shot by the fascists in 1936 – who, according to Buñuel, had earlier promised to fund the project when he won the lottery (Buñuel, 139). Acín may, though, have been merely the channel through which the anarchist group as a whole financed the project, for they would certainly have had a vested interest in producing a film that drew attention to the terrible conditions of the rural poor. As for Buñuel's other colleagues, the assistant director, Rafael Sánchez Ventura, was an anarchist who had organised a general strike in Zaragoza as a protest against the execution of Republican officers in the town of Jaca in December 1930. Eli Lotar, the cameraman, was a committed Trotskyist who had already been arrested and imprisoned for attempting to make a documentary about anarchist groups in southern Spain. And Pierre Unik, who worked on the script with Buñuel, was, as we have seen, one of the Paris surrealists who had joined the Communist Party, disillusioned by his former colleagues' lack of political commitment. In short, Buñuel's team was markedly political in character, and its purpose in making *Las Hurdes* was, in the true spirit of this aspect of Surrealism, to shock, to explode a bomb, as *Un Chien andalou* and *L'Âge d'or* had done, among a complacent public.

Buñuel's shock tactics at the beginning of *Las Hurdes* are reminiscent of those employed in his first two films. In *Un Chien andalou* the opening title, *Once upon a time*, followed by the shot of a full moon in an almost cloudless sky, has the effect of creating in the viewer a certain expectation and complacency, which the slicing of the eye-ball immediately transforms into horror and revulsion. In *L'Âge d'or* the initial documentary sequence of the scorpions, accompanied by explanatory titles, similarly gives little idea of what is

---

[22] On this point, see Robert Havard, *The Crucified Mind: Rafael Alberti and the Surrealist Ethos in Spain* (London: Tamesis, 2001), 201, n. 20.

to follow. In much the same way, the title of Buñuel's third film, *Las Hurdes*, is immediately followed by its description as a documentary: *Documentaire de LUIS BUÑUEL*, and this by titles that describe Las Hurdes:

> This cinematographic essay in human geography was made in 1933 shortly after the inauguration of the Spanish Republic. In the opinion of geographers and travellers, the region which you are going to visit, called Las Hurdes, is a barren and inhospitable place where man is obliged to struggle constantly in order to survive. Until 1922, when the first road was built there, Las Hurdes was practically unknown to the rest of the world, Spain included.[23]

The information arouses in the spectator a sense of curiosity, puts him or her off guard, and even, by means of the reference to the struggle for survival, hints at admiration for the people of Las Hurdes, a feeling reinforced by the inspiring music from Brahms's Fourth Symphony that accompanies the titles. As well as this, a voice-over's address to the audience – 'which **you** are going to visit' – has the effect of creating a shared experience and of drawing the spectator into a journey that will be interesting and, perhaps, enjoyable.

This effect is continued when the titles give way to a map – firstly of Europe, then of Spain, and then of the region including Las Hurdes – and the voice-over enlarges on the information provided by the titles, and now subtly changes the second person 'you' of the opening titles to the more familiar 'we', thereby ensuring that, as we watch the journey unfold, we are indeed fellow travellers:

> Before **we** reach Las Hurdes, we have to pass through La Alberca, a relatively rich town, feudal in character, and which greatly influences life in Las Hurdes, whose inhabitants are for the most part its dependants.

Furthermore, our initial impression of La Alberca is a favourable one, for a series of shots reveals white-washed houses, narrow, winding streets through which men ride on mules, an impressive church, and women having their hair arranged and dressed in their traditional costumes in preparation for a traditional ceremony.

The first indication that these pleasant images are about to give way to something more disturbing comes with the commentator's revelation that the ceremony alluded to is 'strange and savage' and requires that the recently married men in the town rip the heads off cockerels. The first cockerel is seen in close-up, suspended upside down from a rope strung across the street. A man on horseback rides up to it, grasps its neck and tears off its head. The

---

[23] The commentary is reproduced in Mercé Ibarz, *Buñuel documental: 'Tierra sin pan' y su tiempo* (Zaragoza: Prensas universitarias de Zaragoza, 1999).

camera closes in to reveal a fluttering, headless cockerel. Thereafter, the six men pour wine for the crowd of onlookers and the camera picks out some of the townspeople and a small child dressed up for the occasion. But these more pleasant moments cannot erase from our mind's eye the images of struggling, decapitated cockerels, of an episode whose horror and cruelty seem even greater in the light of the commentator's calm description of it and his cool reminder to us that 'In spite of the cruelty of this scene, our duty to be objective obliges us to show it to you.' Buñuel has in effect exploded his first bomb. This is to be no ordinary documentary.

From the town of La Alberca we are taken to the valley of Las Batuecas before moving on to Las Hurdes itself. Again there is a kind of reassurance, for the commentary refers to the 'splendid valley of Las Batuecas' and describes the vegetation as extremely rich. The camera focuses on lush trees and rushing water, as well as on a frog and a snake, evidence of the abundant wildlife in the valley. The monastery that was once active is now, we are informed, deserted, for 'only the ruins remain in an area of magnificent and savage beauty'. It is a point that seems almost insignificant here but one that acquires a subversive edge as the film unfolds.

The calm of the preceding sequence is short lived, for Buñuel now plunges us into the harsh and inhospitable land of Las Hurdes, in which the village of Aceitunilla is one of the poorest. The houses are small and built of rough, dry walls, the inhabitants are shabbily dressed, and through the village there is only a rough track. Buñuel's principal focus is, though, on the stream and the village school. In contrast to the river, which rushes through the lush but uninhabited valley of Las Batuecas, the stream in Aceitunilla is a mere trickle. Furthermore, the initial shot of a woman washing what seem to be vegetables in the water becomes that of a pig drinking from it, of a young girl giving a baby a drink, of a boy kneeling to quench his thirst, of a mother washing a baby's head, of a woman washing her clothes, and of children softening crusts of bread before eating them. The commentator's observation that 'In summer this is the only water the village has,' and that 'it serves all purposes', merely adds to the repugnance of what is, in effect, a sequence that Buñuel has orchestrated for maximum effect.

In the austere primary school the children are seen to be dressed in clothes which, the commentator informs us, 'have been repaired so often that hardly a trace of the original garment remains'. Many of them are orphans whom the local women have accepted from the orphanage in the town of Ciudad Rodrigo because they are paid fifteen pesetas a month to bring them up. They have no shoes, their faces display few signs of joy, many have shaven heads – no doubt to rid them of lice – and yet, we are told, they enjoy the same education as all other children. The irony of the situation is further underlined when the camera reveals on the wall a picture of an elegant and evidently wealthy young lady, and a pupil writes on the blackboard a sentence from a schoolbook: 'Have respect for the property of others.' The children write the sentence in their exercise books, practising their penmanship and oblivious to the lack of concern shown towards them by the world at large. It is a telling moment whose meaning would not have been lost on those who for so long had chosen to ignore Las Hurdes and its wretched inhabitants.

From Aceitunilla we proceed quickly to the village of Martilandrán where, if anything, human suffering is even greater. Pigs wander freely through the streets, the people are dressed in rags, the sights that greet us are 'of utter wretchedness'. The necks of the inhabitants, in particular that of a thirty-two-year-old woman holding her child in her arms, reveal that the illness prevalent here is goitre. Just afterwards, the camera focuses on a young girl lying against a rock and so weak that she has not moved for three days. A close-up of her open mouth reveals extensive inflammation of gums and throat, which, the commentary informs us, led to her death two days later.

Before we move on to the village of Fragosa, the voice-over concentrates for a while on the poor diet and the almost total lack of fertile land in Las Hurdes. Potatoes and green beans are the normal sustenance of poor families, but in June and July there are none. Only better-off families own a pig, but when it is slaughtered – one pig each year – the meat lasts only three days. The milk of the goat, the animal most suited to the rocky terrain, is given only to the gravely ill, and while honey is one of the main products of the region, the hives are owned by people in La Alberca and the honey is therefore transported away from Las Hurdes itself. As for cultivation, the people attempt to use land near the river and try to prevent flooding by building dry walls, but such is the poor quality of the soil and the harshness of the climate that their efforts come to nothing. In an effort to fertilise the land, they are obliged to use the leaves of the strawberry plant, but the area in which it grows is also inhabited by vipers, and efforts to neutralise their bite, which is not in itself fatal, lead to infection that often causes death.

In a way the *hurdanos* seem to be as much at the mercy of an impassive fate as the animals that live in the region. At one particular point during the commentary on goats, a goat is seen to lose its footing on a steep slope and falls to its death, and when a mule is shown transporting honey, several hives fall from its back, the bees escape and sting the animal to death. The commentary notes that one month earlier eleven mules and three men had died in the same way. In short, men and beasts are linked in their helplessness to resist a fate that is indiscriminate. The *hurdanos* are not merely a little lower than the angels; they are on a par with the pigs that rummage in the streets and the mules which transport their deadly burdens. And yet, in the end, although fate and chance may play their part, the ultimate responsibility for the wretchedness of these people lies with those who, in positions of power over many years, have done little to help.

Buñuel saves his most savage attack until the film's final sequences. The camera reveals in detail the conditions in which people live in the village of Fragosa. The primitive houses have no chimneys or windows, which means that the smoke from the fire in the small living-room cannot easily escape, thereby damaging the health of those who live there. The whole of the region is also ravaged by disease of various kinds, among which malaria is widespread. A cool, factual account of the presence and nature of the mosquito, illustrated by slides and diagrams and typical of Buñuel's objective and often scientific manner, effectively gives way to a close-up of a trembling victim of malaria, and this to a girl so affected by the disease that she is unaware that she is being filmed. But there is even worse to come, announced by the commentator's matter-of-fact observation that 'Dwarfs and cretins abound in the Upper Hurdes' because of 'hunger, poverty and incest'. Three stunted men come into shot, close-ups revealing their mindlessly grinning, bony faces. Another, his eyes close together and half shut, suddenly pops up from behind a bank of earth, and yet another sits inside his house, staring vacantly and hopelessly into space. The commentator notes pointedly that the realism of the painters Zurbarán and Ribera fall far short of this reality.[24]

The dwarfs and cretins presumably die quite young, but there are those who die even younger, as the next section of the film informs us. A close-up reveals a dead child whose funeral is about to take place. Its mother sits in the house, staring impassively ahead. But in many of the villages of Las Hurdes there is no cemetery and, as in this case, the body has to be transported many miles for burial. Initially, the father carries the body – there is no coffin – for several days through thick undergrowth, then floats it on a wooden trough across a river until, finally, he reaches the cemetery where, for the most part, a rough wooden cross is all that marks the graves. This symbol of religion leads logically but ironically to a shot of a cross on the altar of a church which, the commentary informs us, is the only sign of wealth to be found in Las Hurdes as a whole, this particular one in one of the poorest villages. We are reminded at once of the cross with its scalps, which is the closing shot of *L'Âge d'or*, and here the complacency and indifference of the Church to the misery of its poorest followers contrasts pointedly with the stoical efforts of the father to provide his dead child with a Christian burial.

The final sequences of *Las Hurdes* focus on the living conditions of its inhabitants. In what is described as one of the better houses, the family sit around the fire in the middle of the room, but even here they live in this one area. Many houses do not have a bed, but where there is one the whole family sleep together. In winter, moreover, they sleep fully dressed, wearing the same clothes until they fall to pieces. The film ends with a shot of an old, toothless woman intoning the words 'There is nothing that can keep you more alert than the thought of death,' and a statement that 'After a stay of two months in Las Hurdes, we abandoned the region.' There is a pointed irony in

[24] Francisco de Zurbarán (1598–1664) and Jusepe de Ribera (1588–1652) were two of the great painters of the Spanish Golden Age. Both painted in a broadly realistic style, many of their paintings depicting the pain of martyrdom or deformity.

both the old woman's and the commentator's observations. The latter points clearly to the Government's abandonment of Las Hurdes, and it implies too that, even if the film crew has also abandoned it, it has at least created a permanent reminder of the inhabitants' desperate plight.

The preceding discussion of the film's content has already suggested how Buñuel's political objective determines its structure. Initially, the audience is led to expect something quite pleasant, then presented with its opposite, early expectations undermined. Again, we are led, as if by a guide, on a tour where horror piles upon horror in a carefully structured pattern that leaves the worst to last, ensuring that we will not forget the things to which we have been witness. But if there is horror, there is nothing sensational, for if the material of the commentary is carefully selected in order to highlight hunger, poverty, malnutrition, disease and death, it also has an objectivity and a calm delivery that make the horror an inescapable fact of life, and, reinforced by telling close-ups of suffering faces and diseased bodies, all the more terrible for it. As well as this, there are allusions to the Church cunningly placed throughout the film – a church, a religious inscription above the door of a house, a ruined convent, a cemetery with wooden crosses – which show how the Church has influenced the lives of the people of Las Hurdes but has now abandoned them.

In addition to this element of selectivity and structuring, it is also clear that certain situations in the film were 'staged' in order to obtain the maximum effect. When, for example, the goat falls to its death, a puff of smoke to the right-hand side of the frame suggests, as Robert Havard has pointed out, that the animal has been shot and that its dramatic fall is not therefore accidental.[25] Similarly, the baby who, towards the end of the film, is presented as dead, was in reality merely asleep, in which case her mother's grief was merely acted.[26] It seems more than likely that other episodes were also staged, but this is not to say that such things did not happen in Las Hurdes or that the suffering of its inhabitants was not as great as the film portrays. Buñuel, like all great artists, shaped his material – sometimes staging events in the interests of time and money – in order to capture and hammer home an essential truth.

As far as public screenings were concerned, *Las Hurdes* had a difficult time. The first screening was a semi-private one at the Palacio de la Prensa in Madrid in December 1933, attended by many of the capital's intellectuals. At this time the film had no sound-track, and Buñuel himself read the commentary and played a recording of Brahms's Fourth Symphony. The reaction of the audience was decidedly cool. Furthermore, Buñuel was hoping to persuade Dr Gregorio Marañón – the same Marañón who had accompanied the King on a visit to Las Hurdes in 1922 and who was now not only Presi-

---

[25] Havard, *The Crucified Mind*, 207.
[26] Ibarz, *Buñuel documental*, 121.

dent of the Council of Las Hurdes but also an extremely influential figure in Spanish cultural life – to grant the film a licence for public screening. To that end he arranged a private performance, but Marañón's reaction was one of hostility, for he complained that Buñuel had failed to include 'the most beautiful dances in the world' and 'the carts loaded with wheat', which regularly passed by on the roads of Las Hurdes. Needless to say, the film was banned – a somewhat ironic outcome in view of the Republic Government's enlightened social policies, despite the swing to the Right in 1933. But opposition to the film at least proved that Buñuel's uncompromising attack had hit its target. Not until the Left, in the form of the Popular Front, regained power in early 1936 did *Las Hurdes* obtain a licence for public screening, but once more Buñuel's hopes were dashed, for the summer of that year saw the beginning of the Civil War. But although the film was not released in Spain, the sound-track – in French and English – was added in the same year. Even so, problems of various kinds – cuts demanded by censorship and the like – continued to affect *Las Hurdes* until 1965, when a version restoring cuts and improving the sound finally appeared.

This consideration of Buñuel's first three films reveals to the full the aggressive nature of his character both as a man and a film-maker. His pugnacious nature is suggested by the fact that during his years at the Residencia de Estudiantes he was extremely proud of his muscular physique and took part in a variety of physical sports. He went out running every morning, barefoot, regardless of the weather. He showed off the strength of his stomach muscles by having fellow students jump on him. He enjoyed throwing the javelin, arm-wrestling, doing press-ups, working with a medicine ball, and boxing, even claiming to have become an amateur boxing champion of Spain, though this was a blatant untruth. His essentially combative approach to life also ensured that, as far as his cultural interests and background were concerned, he was drawn to cultural movements and individual artists characterised by toughness, an uncompromising realism and a vigorous questioning of accepted social and moral values. The Spanish picaresque novel of the seventeenth century, marked by its ruthless exposure of the ills of Spanish society and its unsentimental view of life as a whole, appealed to him greatly. He loved the paintings of his fellow countryman, Goya, in particular that aspect of his work that stripped away the surface gloss of his age in order to reveal beneath it the true reality of hypocrisy, cruelty and superstition that the disillusioned painter saw all around him. For similar reasons he was attracted to the aggressive exposure of Spanish life in the 'esperpento' plays of the twentieth-century dramatist, Ramón del Valle-Inclán, and, as we have seen, to those modern movements in the arts, such as *ultraísmo*, which had sprung up in Madrid in the 1920s and which advocated the rejection of the traditional in favour of the new.

Given Surrealism's aim to shock, disconcert and ultimately transform society – and of course, its links with Communism – it had an immediate appeal for Buñuel, as his first three films suggest. Each of them reveals his hard-hitting character: the razor-wielding Buñuel in the eye-slicing sequence of *Un Chien andalou*; the driven young man of *L'Âge d'or*, sweeping aside the obstacles in his path; the sickening realities of life in *Las Hurdes*. And each, of course, had its effect. The beginning of *Un Chien andalou* made its audience gasp; *L'Âge d'or* caused a scandal; *Las Hurdes* was banned by the government of the day. Little wonder, then, that after the screening of *Un Chien andalou*, Buñuel was embraced by the Paris surrealists as a true brother. But was Buñuel a true surrealist in every way, a champion of all the unconventional values the movement stood for? The evidence suggests that, in matters of love and sex, he was not.

2

A SURREALIST IN CHAINS

Given that the surrealists advocated freedom from the restrictions of conventional social and moral values, it is hardly surprising that sexual freedom should have been high on their list of priorities. To exercise this kind of freedom was, after all, to be true to one's instincts and to oneself, as well as to strike out at the stifling restrictions of bourgeois society and the narrow-minded moral instruction of, in particular, the Catholic Church. Buñuel, in describing his attraction to Surrealism, drew attention to the importance the surrealists placed on passion as part of their opposition to traditional values: 'It was an aggressive morality based on rejection of all existing values. We had other criteria: we exalted passion' (Buñuel, 107). In this respect, the surrealists championed *amour fou*, wild love, the kind of passion that in *Wuthering Heights* forever links Heathcliff and Cathy, and which Buñuel embodied in the lovers of *L'Âge d'or*, in which, as we have seen, they are obsessed with each other to the exclusion of all else. This said, the question arises as to whether *amour fou* was a surrealist ideal rather than a reality that affected their personal lives; something that they lived out in their creative work rather than in their amorous relationships – in short, whether it was merely a passion in the head.

The surrealist group that Buñuel joined in 1929 was, in spite of its common philosophy, made up of individuals whose temperament and personality were often very different, but many of them seem to have practised what they preached in terms of their sexual relationships. André Breton, leader of the Paris surrealists, was in most respects an extremely disciplined, intellectual and formal individual, not much given to the more outrageous sexual indulgence of some of his colleagues, but even so his sexual life was far from ordinary. His marriage to Simone Kahn was, for example, an open one in which both partners did as they wished. In 1927 Breton had spent some of the summer in Normandy, where Louis Aragon and his mistress, Nancy, were also staying. Breton took advantage of the situation to sleep with Nancy. By 1928 he had become obsessed with Susanne Muzard, who had previously worked in Paris as a prostitute and who was now living with Emmanuel Berl. She left Berl in order to become Breton's mistress but suddenly abandoned him at the end of the year and married Berl.

Louis Aragon was a very different kind of person from Breton. Emotional and uninhibited, he led an extremely colourful sexual life. He had many mistresses, one of whom was an American, Elisabeth (Eyre) de Lanux. His relationship with her was complicated by the fact that she was married, a lesbian, and also the mistress of Aragon's good friend, Drieu La Rochelle. This complication, needless to say, did not deter him, and when the relationship ended, he turned to Nancy Cunard, daughter of the shipping magnate. Rich and beautiful, she had a string of good-looking men in tow, but she was also an exhibitionist and given to drink. Consequently, Aragon sought consolation with other women, and when Nancy took up with the black American jazz pianist Henry Crowder, Aragon began an affair with a Viennese dancer, Lena Amsel. She too had many male admirers, and when Elsa Kagan, the Russian daughter of a rich Jewish merchant, set her sights on Aragon, Lena agreed to give him up. Subsequently Elsa and Aragon married and their relationship lasted for forty years. Then, after her death, Aragon revealed that he was homosexual.

The Franco-Cuban painter Francis Picabia was a man given to every kind of excess. The son of a wealthy Cuban father, he was married to a rich French woman, Gabrielle, but in 1918 became obsessed with Germaine Everling, who was then in the process of a divorce. Both women became pregnant by Picabia at more or less the same time. In the autumn of that year Gabrielle gave birth to her child, and Germaine produced hers at the beginning of 1919. The same midwife attended both women but only realised that Picabia was the father of Germaine's child when she saw his car parked outside her apartment. She is reported to have said: 'Really, what a household! [. . .] He wasn't even living with her, it turns out he has a mistress, and she's pregnant too! Artists, I ask you!'[1] It was not long, though, before Picabia had moved on to another girlfriend, the singer Marthe Chenal.

The poet Paul Éluard had married Helena Diakonova, better known as Gala and subsequently the wife of Salvador Dalí, in 1917. In 1922 she began an affair with the painter Max Ernst during a holiday that several of the surrealists enjoyed together, and subsequently Ernst moved into Éluard and Gala's home to form a *ménage à trois*. Although he was deeply in love with Gala, Éluard was also attracted to group sex and therefore accepted the situation. As for Gala, her sexual appetite proved to be enormous, and the open marriage she had with Éluard allowed both of them to entertain a number of willing partners. In this context, her relationship with the timid, sexually inhibited and probably impotent Dalí seems very strange indeed, and whether or not they ever made love in the full sense remains unclear. What is clear, though, is that Gala continued to enjoy sexual relations with Éluard and many others, including Giorgo de Chirico and Man Ray, after her marriage to Dalí.

As far as sexual matters were concerned, even those surrealists who were

---

[1]   See Ruth Brandon, *Surreal Lives: the Surrealists 1917–1945* (London: Macmillan, 1999), 123.

by nature reticent and given to asceticism were tempted by and accepted the opportunities that came their way. Such was Marcel Duchamp, a quiet, highly disciplined man not easily given to pleasure. Yet he too, constantly surrounded by female admirers, eventually proved willing enough to satisfy them sexually while refusing to commit himself to any one woman. A contemporary has described him sliding his hands under women's bodices and whispering: 'Madame, I'm sure you have the cunt of a filthy whore.'[2]

In general, then, most if not all of the surrealists practised what they preached, allowing themselves in their sexual lives that licence and freedom they advocated in life in general. Submission to one's instincts was to cast aside the layers of good manners and moral behaviour that they believed had enslaved men and women over the centuries; to strike out at those bourgeois and religious values that the surrealists despised. But there were also some surrealists, of course, who at some point were so exposed to those values that they could never fully escape them, who were chained to certain aspects of their background and upbringing. Buñuel is a case in point. It is no coincidence that he should have believed that, for all his efforts, man is not free.[3]

The world in which Buñuel grew up was one in which few children could escape the influence of Catholicism. Although his family left Calanda when he was only four months old, they returned there, as we have seen, for many years during the summer, and Buñuel has vividly evoked the way of life he encountered there, not least the emphasis on religious practices:

> Life unfolded in a linear fashion, the major moments marked by the daily bells of the Church of Pilar. They tolled for Masses, vespers, and the Angelus, as well as for certain critical, and more secular, events.
>
> (Buñuel, 8)

But if life in general was steeped in religious practices, it was undoubtedly Buñuel's schooling in Zaragoza that marked him most profoundly. There, as we have seen, he attended the Colegio del Salvador, a school run by the Jesuit Order, where he remained for seven years, a crucial period in his emotional and psychological development. Among other things, the Jesuits instilled in their pupils the notion that sex, be it in thought or in action, was sinful and deserving of punishment. Indeed, Saint Thomas Aquinas, such an important influence on Catholic doctrine, had asserted that the sexual act between husband and wife was a venal sin because it implied lust, and suggested too that, if it were to take place, it should be devoid of desire and focused entirely on producing more and more servants of God. As for Buñuel's teachers, they invariably kept a close eye on their charges, ensuring that there was never any

---

[2] See Brandon, 70.
[3] The idea runs through most of his films, be the limitations placed on human beings social, economic, moral or religious.

physical contact between them. When the pupils went to the toilet, they were watched every step of the way, and it was common practice for them to have to urinate without touching their penis. In addition, they were constantly warned that the sin of masturbation would be punished with eternal damnation, and at night they were obliged to sleep with their arms across their chest, thereby avoiding the temptation of touching their genitals.

Given such indoctrination, it is easy to imagine the conflict that was bound to take place in adolescent young boys as they became aware of their sexuality, as well as of the attractions of the opposite sex. Buñuel has vividly described their awakening:

> Wicked pleasures like these [visits to brothels], all the more to be savoured because they were mortal sins, transpired only in our imaginations. We played doctor with little girls; we studied the anatomy of animals [. . .] During the summer siesta hour, when the heat was at its fiercest and the flies droned and buzzed in the empty streets, we used to meet secretly in a neighbourhood dry goods store. When the doors were closed and the curtains pulled tight, one of the clerks would slip us some so-called erotic magazines – heaven only knows how he got hold of them – the *Hoja de Parra*, for instance, and the *KDT*, whose photos, I distinctly remember, were somewhat more realistic. These forbidden delights, devoured in secret, would seem divinely innocent today. At most, all we could make out was an ankle or the top of a breast, but this was sufficient to inflame our ardour and wreak havoc with our fantasies. (Buñuel, 15)

Sexual curiosity and experiment are, of course, normal adolescent activities, but in the case of Buñuel and many of his Spanish contemporaries who attended similar educational institutions, they were coloured in two important ways. Firstly, the belief that sexual activities were sinful made them more tempting, a point that Buñuel repeatedly makes in his autobiography. Secondly, however, the deeply ingrained notion that sex was equated with sin led to inevitable conflict and a profound feeling of guilt. Salvador Dalí, who attended the Christian Brothers' School in Figueras, subsequently experienced both pleasure and shame in the act of masturbation: 'I was vaingloriously proud of being able to know and live this phenomenon and also full of consternation at what I was doing, realizing how reprehensible it might be considered.'[4] Lorca, whose schooling was less strict but who was, nevertheless, exposed to traditional Catholic teaching, was both confused by and ashamed of his homosexual feelings, anathema to the Church. And his contemporary, the poet Rafael Alberti, who was educated at the Jesuit Colegio de San Luis Gonzaga in El Puerto de Santa María, has described the violence with which his teachers condemned the act of masturbation: 'If you

---

4   See *The Unspeakable Confessions of Salvador Dalí, as told to André Parinaud*, trans. Harold J. Salemson (London: Quartet Books, 1977), 68.

could see your soul, you would die of horror. Yours is filthy [. . .], because if the soul is darkened by lustful behaviour, lying makes it even blacker. You sin and refuse to admit your error. You are thus committing a double sin.'[5]

As for Buñuel, he has described the effect of Jesuit indoctrination both on himself and on others:

> [. . .] 'they' [the Jesuits] never ceased to remind us that the highest virtue was chastity, without which no life was worthy of praise. [. . .] In the end, we were worn out with our oppressive sense of sin, coupled with the interminable war between instinct and virtue. (Buñuel, 14)

Furthermore, in a conversation with Max Aub in 1971, some sixty years after his Jesuit schooling, he made a remarkable confession: 'For me, throughout my life, coitus and sin have been the same thing.'[6] And if this were not enough: 'And although I'm not sure why, I also have always felt a secret but constant link between the sexual act and death' (Buñuel, 15). Like many others, Buñuel was, then, irreparably damaged in terms of his relationship with women, 'a victim of the most fierce sexual repression in history'.[7] In Carlos Saura's film, *La prima Angélica* (*Cousin Angelica*), made in 1973, Luis Hernández, a man in his forties, returns to Segovia where, as a child, he had been educated at a Salesian school and made to believe that sex and sin were to be equated. In adult life that conviction remains with him and, even though he loves Angélica, his childhood sweetheart in Segovia, he is unable to commit himself to her. As much as anything, Saura's film is a powerful condemnation of the ferocity of religious indoctrination, and, in watching it, it is easy to understand the lasting effect it had on so many of those who were subjected to it, not least Buñuel himself.

The evidence that, unlike most of his surrealist colleagues, he was sexually inhibited is overwhelming. Escape in 1917 from the provincialism of Zaragoza to the much more liberal atmosphere of Madrid and the Residencia de Estudiantes meant that opportunities for sexual adventures were much more frequent, particularly visits to brothels. In his account of his stay at the Residencia, Buñuel, however, refers to brothels only in passing, and, when the opportunity arose to dance with a young woman to whom he was attracted, he succeeded – extremely rudely – in getting rid of her male partner, but then had cold feet in relation to the girl:

---

5 See Alberti, *The Lost Grove*, 56.
6 Max Aub, *Conversaciones con Buñuel* (Madrid: Aguilar, 1985), 160.
7 See Luis Buñuel, *Mi último suspiro*, 23. In *My Last Breath* this sentence is translated incorrectly as 'the powerful sexual repression of my youth reinforces this connection' (15).

'Please forgive me,' I begged. 'What I just said was inexcusable. My dancing is even worse than his!' Which was true; but despite my apologies, I never did get up enough courage to dance with her. (Buñuel, 66)

This lack of initiative would become, as we shall see, a recurring aspect of Buñuel's behaviour with women both before and after marriage.

When he became acquainted with the even more liberal habits of Paris in 1925, he admitted to being shocked by the sexual behaviour of young men and women:

I was shocked, in fact disgusted, by the men and women I saw kissing in public, or living together without the sanction of marriage. Such customs were unimaginable to me; they seemed obscene. (Buñuel, 48–9)

Again, he has described how, shortly after arriving in Paris, he and some student friends had dinner together before moving on to a ball, Le Bal des Quat'zarts, which had the reputation of being the most original orgy of the year. At the dinner, Buñuel was astonished when one of the students 'placed his testicles delicately on a plate, and made a full circle of the room', while later, outside the venue for the ball, he was 'dumbfounded' by the spectacle of 'a naked woman [. . .] on the shoulders of a student dressed as an Arab sheik. (His head served as her fig leaf.)' (Buñuel, 82–3). It seems almost inconceivable that someone whose films would prove so shocking and subversive in relation to traditional morality should himself display such a conventional reaction.

More revealing still were Buñuel's responses to the opportunities for sex that regularly seem to have come his way. A few weeks into his stay in Paris, he visited the Chinese cabaret next to his hotel and was quickly engaged in conversation by one of the hostesses. The expectation on her part was clearly that Buñuel would pay her to go to bed with him, but he insists that he did not and that he was more interested in her conversation (Buñuel, 79). Some five years later, during a visit to the United States, he became attracted to a friend of the film actress Lya Lys, and was so taken with her that he postponed an eagerly awaited trip to the Polynesian islands. But, however strong Buñuel's feelings may have been, he makes the significant point that 'I fell in love (platonically, as usual) (Buñuel, 79). Furthermore, in the course of the return voyage to France, he encountered an eighteen-year-old American girl who was travelling alone, who declared her love for him, and who, to prove the point, ripped up a photograph of her fiancé. Buñuel went to her cabin on two occasions but resisted temptation, describing his relationship with her as 'once again perfectly chaste' (Buñuel, 136).

The same kind of sexual inhibition characterised his behaviour with two other women. In 1933 Buñuel accompanied the conductor, Roger Desormiére, to Monte Carlo where he was to conduct the first performance of the new Ballets Russes. After the performance, Desormiére went off with his girlfriend, leaving Buñuel in the company of an attractive ballerina, but once more he found himself incapable of any kind of amorous advance:

> [. . .] but, true to form, I was seized by that awkwardness which seemed an inevitable part of my relationships with women. Suddenly, there I was, launching into an intense political discussion about Russia, communism, and the revolution. The dancer made it perfectly clear that she was vehemently anti-Communist; in fact, she had no hesitation in talking about the crimes committed by the current regime. I lost my temper and called her a dirty reactionary; we argued for a long time until finally I gave her money for a cab and left in a turmoil. Later, of course, I was filled with remorse, as I had so often been in the past. (Buñuel, 120)

The second incident, even more extraordinary, took place in 1935, when Buñuel had been married to Jeanne Rucar for about a year. In Madrid he met a young actress called Pepita, with whom he fell in love and in whose company he spent an entire summer. The relationship, he claims, remained chaste, but one day a friend informed him that she was not what she seemed and that he was sleeping with her. In order to test the truth of this revelation, Buñuel suggested to Pepita that she become his mistress and that she make love only with him. His account of the affair continues:

> She seemed surprised, but accepted readily enough. I helped her off with her clothes and held her naked in my arms only to find myself paralysed with nervousness. I suggested we go dancing; she got dressed again, and we got into my car, but instead of going to Bombilla, I drove out of Madrid. Two kilometres from Puerta de Hierro, I stopped and made her get out. (Buñuel, 148)

Buñuel's numerous chaste relationships could, of course, be seen as evidence of his virtue and integrity, as well as, during courtship and after marriage, of his fidelity to his wife. But his allusion to being 'paralysed with nervousness', and his frequent habit of resorting to some kind of discussion or argument in order to put off intimate contact with a female surely point to something deeper. The suggestion that he wished to remain faithful to his fiancé, later to become his wife, is also seriously weakened when we consider his behaviour with her both before and after marriage.

Buñuel first met Jeanne Rucar, the daughter of a French accountant, in 1926 and married her in 1934. After his death she published an account of their life together which, read in conjunction with his own autobiography, is extremely revealing. Asked by her sister-in-law about their relationship during their courtship, she admitted that Buñuel 'respected' her.[8] It seems almost inconceivable that a man who could be so passionate and aggressive

---

[8] Jeanne Rucar de Buñuel, *Memorias de una mujer sin piano* (escritas por Marisol

in other respects should have had no sexual contact with his bride-to-be during a courtship of eight years. But the likelihood that such was the case is certainly suggested by subsequent events. After a civil marriage ceremony in Paris – Buñuel was passionate enough to reject a Catholic church wedding – he and Jeanne had a meal with two friends in a restaurant, but he then took the train to Madrid, leaving Jeanne behind and the marriage evidently unconsummated. When, a month later, she followed him to Madrid, the sexual act so condemned by the Jesuits evidently took place, for Jeanne produced her first child in Paris in November 1934, roughly ten months after the wedding. But when she returned to Madrid with the baby in March 1935, she must have been shocked both by Buñuel's failure to meet her at the station, and by his bluntly proposed sleeping arrangements:

> The apartment was large. Luis told me: 'This is your room, mine is next door.' From that moment we always slept in separate rooms.
>
> (Rucar de Buñuel, 54)

Sexual passion was certainly not Buñuel's forte.

It is no coincidence, given the above, that for Buñuel true sexual satisfaction was more easily achieved in the form of dreams or daydreams, for they are, after all, free from the constraints of reason and conscience. His sexual reticence in relation to the dancer from the Ballets Russes has already been described, but in the preceding train journey to Monte Carlo he was able to indulge in a fantasy in which there were no such inhibitions:

> During the two-hour trip, I lapsed into my habitual fantasies – this time of a bevy of dancers in black stockings sitting side by side on a row of chairs, facing me, like a harem, awaiting my commands. When I pointed to one, she stood up and approached meekly, until I suddenly changed my mind. I wanted another one, just as submissive. Rocked by the movement of the train, I found no obstacle to my erotic daydreams. (Buñuel, 119)

The phrase 'my habitual fantasies' is significant here, for Buñuel experienced vivid dreams and daydreams throughout his life, many of a sexual nature. At the age of fourteen he fantasised that he had sex with the Queen of Spain, the beautiful wife of Alfonso XIII, having first put her to sleep with a narcotic (Buñuel, 97). Nevertheless, there were also dreams, one of them particularly vivid and recurring, in which, as in reality, Buñuel found the sexual act to be either difficult or impossible:

Martín del Campo) (Madrid: Alianza Editorial, 1990), 51 [hereafter Rucar de Buñuel]. Translations into English are my own.

[. . .] one of the strange things about dreams is that in them I've never been able to make love in a truly satisfying way, usually because people are watching. They're standing at a window opposite our room; we change rooms, and sometimes even houses, but the same mocking, curious looks follow us wherever we go. Or sometimes, when the climactic moment arrives, I find the woman sewn up tight. Sometimes I can't find the opening at all; she has the seamless body of a statue. (Buñuel, 97)

The people at the window are clearly reminiscent of the Jesuit priests who, at the Colegio del Salvador, kept a close and constant watch over their pupils in order to make sure that there were no misdemeanours, sexual or otherwise, and who in the classroom instructed them that sex was sinful. Even in some of his dreams, therefore, it seems that Buñuel could no more escape the shackles of his childhood years than he could in reality. The conflict between sexual desire and the fear and guilt he associated with it haunted him even in sleep.

Imprisoned and inhibited in this way, Buñuel was also the prisoner of a deep-rooted and extreme possessiveness whose origins appear to lie in a sexual fear, largely if not entirely associated with Latin peoples. In this case the fear in question is not one of sexual inhibition but of the dangers posed by other males to one's girlfriend, partner or wife, in particular the possibility of her being either seduced or lured away. Extreme caution and possessiveness, as well as obsessive jealousy, are therefore the reaction to such possibilities. In Spanish literature the theme of the fearful, jealous and possessive husband has been for centuries the subject of both comedy and tragedy. A classic example in this respect is Cervantes's comic tale, *The Jealous Extremaduran (El celoso extremeño)*, published in 1613, in which the old man, Carrizales, goes to absurd lengths to safeguard his thirteen- to fourteen-year-old wife against the attentions of the Don Juans of Seville, denying her any freedom in so doing. Calderón's *The Surgeon of Honour* (*El medico de su honra*), is, in contrast, an extremely dark tale in which a husband, Don Gutierre de Solís, is so haunted by irrational fears of his wife's infidelity that he has her murdered when he suspects her of betraying him. And in the story of Carmen, Don José murders Carmen rather than lose her to another man, thereby depriving her not merely of her freedom but also of her life. These examples are, of course, the inventions of creative writers, but there is no doubt that they reflect a reality that existed then and that still exists, even though in the twenty-first century Spanish women have more freedom than they once did. As far as Buñuel is concerned, we are, moreover, dealing with someone who spent his formative years in the early twentieth century not in a liberal-minded environment but in the provincial atmosphere of Calanda and Zaragoza where the attitudes to women described above undoubtedly prevailed. When he left his native province for Madrid in 1917, he remembers 'being paralized [sic] by my provincialism' (Buñuel, 51). The paralysis was not something that could easily be eradicated.

In his autobiography, Buñuel barely mentions his married life with Jeanne Rucar, but in her own account of it she describes a possessiveness on his part that can truly be described as paranoid. In the early days of their eight-year courtship, for example, she worked as a gymnastics or movement teacher at an academy in Paris run by a Mme Poppart. When Buñuel accompanied her one day and noted what she wore in the class – a blouse and a short, loose skirt over knickers with elasticated legs – he became preoccupied, and shortly afterwards made her give up the activity: 'It's not respectable, Jeanne. People can see your legs. I don't like my fiancé displaying herself' (Rucar de Buñuel, 38). Again, when she began to take piano lessons, Buñuel soon discovered that they involved her being alone with a middle-aged man. Not long afterwards, he informed her that she played very badly and that she would be wise not to continue (Rucar de Buñuel, 38). During their courtship, Jeanne worked in a bookshop, but noticed one day that her name did not appear on the pay-roll with the other employees. Puzzled by this apparent omission, she was informed by the owner that her wages were being paid by Buñuel himself. Quite clearly, he wished to keep her occupied during the day, fearful of the attentions that might be paid to her by other men if she were free to do as she pleased.

The examples mentioned above relate to situations in which Jeanne Rucar might have become involved, so it is not surprising that Buñuel should have reacted even more strongly when real threats presented themselves. During the filming of *Un Chien andalou* in 1929, three years into the courtship, he noticed that the lead actor, Pierre Batcheff, was beginning to take an interest in Jeanne whenever he was in the studio. Buñuel therefore decided that there was work for her in the office, where, he explained, she would not be interrupted (Rucar de Buñuel, 40). Other men, moreover, fully aware of his extreme possessiveness, were very cautious about their behaviour towards her. When, on one occasion, one of Buñuel's friends, Pepe Moreno Villa, flirted with her, she asked him why he didn't take her out. His reply was revealing: 'Don't even think of it, my little Jeanne. I wouldn't dare when you are with a man like Luis. If I asked you out, he'd kill me' (Rucar de Buñuel, 43). And when, in 1930, she asked the advice of Jean Epstein about Buñuel's proposal of marriage, his reaction was unequivocal: 'Jeanne, you are making a mistake. [. . .] It's not right for you, don't marry him' (Rucar de Buñuel, 43). When he was away from Paris, Buñuel issued strict instructions to Jeanne's mother that she was to keep an eye on her, and that she was only to be allowed to go out with the two Spanish friends he could trust completely: Salvador Dalí – clearly no sexual threat at all – and Rafael Sánchez Ventura. Jeanne subsequently commented: 'I'm glad I wasn't born in the Middle Ages. Luis would certainly have made me wear a chastity belt' (Rucar de Buñuel, 41).

This situation did not change after their marriage. As we have seen, they slept in separate rooms. Furthermore, his new wife later observed that he was very puritanical in matters of love, even to the extent of placing a sweater over the keyhole of the bedroom door on the occasions they indulged. Despite their new situation and, presumably, their greater closeness, Buñuel remained intensely possessive and jealous, as an incident almost twenty years after their marriage reveals. Now living in Mexico, Jeanne one day dropped in unannounced on Ana María Custodio and her husband, Gustavo Pittaluga, who had written the music for Buñuel's film of 1951, *Stairway to Heaven*. Because his wife was not at home, Pittaluga invited Jeanne in and she chatted with him for a short while. When she returned home and informed Buñuel of these facts, he flew into a terrible rage:

> 'What do you mean, Jeanne? Did you go to bed with him?'
> 'Of course not, calm down. How can you even think it!
> I went to say "hello",
> Ana had gone out, so I spent a few moments with Gustavo.'
> 'So why did you have to see him?'
> 'Luis, if what you think had really happened, would I be dressed like this, in my everyday clothes? Would I have told you where I'd been?'
>   Luis didn't answer. He went up to his room to look for a gun. He came back down with it. In my presence he phoned Gustavo.
> 'Gustavo, I'm coming over to kill you. This minute.'
> Gustavo managed to calm him down, but it took a lot of effort. Luis was as jealous as that. (Rucar de Buñuel, 104)

The episode is certainly worthy of one of Calderón's more paranoid protagonists, as well as of one of Freud's more interesting cases.

    Yet another aspect of Buñuel's character and therefore of his relationship with his wife was what she has described as his extreme *machismo*: 'Luis was a jealous macho. His wife had to be a kind of child-woman who had not matured' (Rucar de Buñuel, 130). *Machismo* is, of course, often regarded as a typical characteristic of Latin men, though it is by no means limited to them, and is to do with the notion of masculinity and male superiority in relation to the inferiority of women. Furthermore, even if it contains an element of sexual superiority, it also extends to a domination of the female in a more general and all-embracing sense. In this respect, Buñuel reveals himself to be what we would now describe as a total 'control freak'. When, for example, he and his wife lived in Madrid before the commencement of the Civil War, Jeanne used to take their first child, Juan Luis, to the Retiro Park on a daily basis, and so became friendly with a French woman who invited her to her home for coffee. But when Jeanne wished to return the invitation, Buñuel refused to allow it, causing his wife such embarrassment that she avoided seeing her new friend again. He, in contrast, invited his own friends, exclusively male, to his house where they shut themselves away in the 'bar'. And on these occasions, as well as on others, Buñuel excluded Jeanne from his conversations and discussions, or, if she was ever able to offer an opinion, as once occurred at the home of Louis Aragon, he curtly dismissed it: 'Be quiet,

Jeanne. You know nothing. You are talking rubbish' (Rucar de Buñuel, 44). Instead, he encouraged her to take up domestic activities such as cooking and knitting, reinforcing the traditional role of woman encapsulated in the Spanish saying: 'A reputable woman, a damaged leg, and at home' ('La mujer honrada, pierna quebrada, y en casa'). In Lorca's famous play, *The House of Bernarda Alba* (*La casa de Bernarda Alba*), five daughters are confined to the house by their mother, engaged in and embittered by the traditional tasks imposed upon them. One can imagine that Jeanne Rucar often felt much the same.

Perhaps Buñuel's most reprehensible act in relation to his wife involved her beloved piano, a gift from Jeannette Alcoriza, wife of the scriptwriter, Luis Alcoriza. This was an instrument that Jeanne enjoyed playing every day, as Buñuel well knew, but one evening, after dinner and after drinking a copious amount of alcohol, the daughter of a family friend suggested that Buñuel give her the piano in exchange for three bottles of champagne. Jeanne initially thought that this was a joke, but to her horror the exchange took place on the following day (Rucar de Buñuel, 106). Despite her feelings of outrage at such a thoughtless act, she remained silent, as she invariably did when her husband treated her in the ways described earlier. Later, he regretted what he had done and, as compensation, bought her – typically – a sewing machine and – more thoughtfully – an accordion, but such gifts can barely excuse Buñuel's inconsiderate behaviour. The bitterness that Jeanne must have felt surely remained with her for the rest of her life, for when she produced her autobiography she chose to call it *Reminiscences of a Woman Without a Piano* (*Memorias de una mujer sin piano*).

As far as domestic affairs were concerned, Buñuel, in true chauvinist fashion, exercised total control. He kept financial matters strictly to himself, never discussing them with Jeanne and obliging her to ask him for money if she wished to buy something. He made all the decisions concerning the household: meal-times, trips, the children's education, the furnishing of the house. In short, although Jeanne refers to the fact that Buñuel could often be tender and loving, the picture that emerges from her account is that of a cold, unfeeling, inconsiderate, sometimes quite cruel man. She notes at one point that he hated seeing anyone cry, including herself, and that when he died she shed no tears because she had 'forgotten how' (Rucar de Buñuel, 111). Buñuel apparently cried only on three occasions: when his mother died, when his dog died, and when he was ill and Jeanne had to leave the house (Rucar de Buñuel, 111, 131).

Looking back after Buñuel's death on the things he had done to her against her will – giving away her piano, stopping her teaching gymnastics, and, much later on, obliging her to abandon book-binding classes on the pretext that finishing at seven o'clock in the evening was far too late – Jeanne regretted the fact that she had done so little to assert herself. Buñuel, in effect, stifled her potential, in particular putting paid to the possibility of her setting up a gymnastics or movement school in Mexico (Rucar de Buñuel, 108). Indeed, many of her female friends wondered how she could possibly live with such an authoritarian husband, and, even though Jeanne defends her position on the grounds that she loved him, there does seem to be some reservation in her statement that 'If we balance out our long life together, I can see that we were happy most of the time' (Rucar de Buñuel, 111). Undoubtedly, what happiness there was lay in the fact that she did little to upset the marital boat, for, as she admits, what Buñuel wanted in a wife, in a typically conventional Hispanic manner, was 'a wife who would never question him' (Rucar de Buñuel, 44).

In the latter part of her reminiscences, Jeanne observes that late in life, and especially when he became ill, Buñuel formed a close friendship with a Mexican priest, Father Julián, whom many considered to be 'odd', implying that he was gay. If that were true, she adds, she might as well believe that Buñuel too was gay, given his preference for male company and his close friendships with Saldador Dalí and Lorca (Rucar de Buñuel, 129). She emphatically denies such a possibility, arguing that he always liked good-looking women, but does not the fact that the thought should have occurred to her not seem rather strange? To all appearances Buñuel was strongly homophobic, for while he was at the Residencia de Estudiantes he frequently attacked homosexuals as they emerged from public toilets. And when a rumour went around the Residencia that Lorca was homosexual, Buñuel bluntly asked him if it was true that he was a queer. In the emphasis he placed on physical exercise and fitness, he was also, of course, extremely *macho*, but so are many sportsmen who, beneath the façade, turn out to be gay, or to have gay tendencies. Furthermore, although Buñuel never admitted to it, his younger brother, Alfonso, was markedly homosexual, while he himself, like many men who later prove to be gay, had attended a purely male educational institution. In the end, there is no solid evidence to suggest that Buñuel was homosexual. The most that can be said is that he may have had homosexual leanings, but if that were the case, they would certainly have been suppressed, as was his sexual life in general.

The relationship between a creative artist's life and work cannot be denied, and even if a knowledge of the former does not necessarily improve the quality of the latter, it nevertheless adds to our understanding of it, and, in the case of the greatest creative artists, reveals how their obsessions and neuroses not only become the raw material of their work, but also – because we all share them to a greater or lesser degree – allow us to recognise and, perhaps, understand all the better our common humanity. Dalí was certainly a strange human being, but it is perfectly clear that the often bizarre and haunting images of his paintings were rooted in his personal anxieties. And both the poetry and the plays of Lorca become even more moving when we understand how their material stems from his homosexuality and the anguish that it caused him. As for Buñuel, he observes in his autobiography that he doesn't believe 'a life can be confused with a work' (Buñuel, 198), but others have certainly seen a strong personal element in many of his films. Knowing him as well as she did, his wife compares his possessiveness and extreme jealousy to that of the protagonist of *He*, made when he was fifty-three (Rucar de Buñuel, 108), while Peter Evans has concluded that 'Buñuel nevertheless manages to surround *Cet obscur objet*, as almost all his other films, with an autobiographical aura even more emphatic than usual.'[9] Buñuel's admission that some of his films were personal favourites – *He* was one of them – may, indeed, be seen as an implicit acknowledgement of their autobiographical element. Furthermore, given the fact that he placed so much emphasis on the unconscious, it would be extraordinary if his own deep-rooted desires, obsessions and fears did not rise to the surface in his films. In this respect his comparison between film and dream, in which the unconscious expresses itself, is extremely revealing:

> The creative handling of film images is such that, among all means of human expression, its way of functioning is most reminiscent of the work of the mind during sleep. A film is like an involuntary imitation of a dream. Brunius points out how the darkness that slowly settles over a movie theatre is equivalent to the act of closing the eyes. Then, on the screen, as with the human being, the nocturnal voyage into the unconscious begins. [. . .] The cinema seems to have been invented to express the life of the subconscious.[10]

As we have seen earlier, Buñuel experienced vivid dreams and fantasies throughout his life. In some of them he was able to achieve the sexual satisfaction he was so often denied in reality; in others his sexual fears haunted him. In many respects his films can be seen as an extension of that process.

The earlier discussion of *Un Chien andalou* focused largely on its power to shock, but the film can be seen too as a clear expression of the inner life of both Dalí and Buñuel. It is highly significant in relation to their preparation of the shooting script that they should have discussed and compared their dreams, of which Buñuel mentions two in particular as their main inspiration:

> When I arrived to spend a few days at Dalí's house in Figueras, I told him about a dream I'd had in which a long, tapering cloud sliced the moon in half, like a razor blade slicing through an eye. Dalí immediately told me that he'd seen a hand crawling with ants in a dream he'd had the previous night.
> 'And what if we started right there and made a film'? he wondered

9   Evans, *The Films of Luis Buñuel: Subjectivity and Desire*, 125.

10 Quoted from Buñuel's essay, 'Poetry and Cinema', reprinted in Joan Mellen (ed.), *The World of Luis Buñuel: Essays in Criticism* (New York: Oxford University Press, 1978), 105–10.

aloud. Despite my hesitation, we soon found ourselves hard at work, and in less than a week we had a script. (Buñuel, 103–4)

Dalí's 'hand crawling with ants' combines the images of the hand and ants that are often seen separately in his paintings, or else ants are seen crawling around or close to a mouth that is clearly his own. The hand is a dominant motif in *Apparatus and Hand* (1927) and *The Lugubrious Game* (1929), and the ants covering or near a mouth are evident in *The Great Masturbator* (1929) and *The Dream* (1931). Invariably, the hand motif was related to masturbation, which Dalí practised regularly, but which, as we have seen, the priests who taught him regarded as sinful. It therefore became in his work an image of his sexual guilt and deep sense of shame, as well as suggesting a habit which, if performed alone, involves fantasy and the avoidance of contact with a woman of flesh and blood. As for Buñuel's dream, the thin cloud piercing the moon and the razor the eye both suggest penetration, this involving a passive woman violated by an aggressive and misogynistic male who, in the film's opening sequence, is, significantly, played by Buñuel himself. At all events, both these dreams and the images associated with them were clearly to do with Dalí's and Buñuel's sexuality. Furthermore, the other key images in *Un Chien andalou* are of a similar kind. And if some of them may be thought to be particularly associated with Dalí rather than Buñuel, it is important to remember that the two men were in total agreement over their choice of material, which means, in effect, that the images in the film were as meaningful to the one as to the other, for they expressed the sexual obsessions and anxieties of both.

Un Chien andalou's male protagonist, played by Pierre Batcheff, is first seen riding a bicycle along a deserted street. He stares blankly ahead and rides the bicycle in a stiff, mechanical manner, as if he were an automaton, while over his suit and tie and on his head he wears what seem to be frilly baby clothes. The image as a whole suggests a baby-like arrested development and emotional immaturity, while the suit identifies a bourgeois individual. In one sense he is the kind of bourgeois character who, emotionally crippled by his upbringing, appears in many of Buñuel's later films, but he is also very clearly Dalí and Buñuel, both, as we have seen, emotionally and sexually damaged by their respective education and Catholic background. The point is reinforced shortly afterwards when the young man falls from his bicycle and lies completely motionless in the road, even when the young woman, the film's principal female character, rushes to his assistance and begins to kiss and embrace him. His inability to respond to her at once brings to mind Buñuel's own reaction to women prior to the making of the film, as well as his reticence with Jeanne Rucar during their courtship. If Lorca thought that the film's male protagonist was a form of himself, it is now perfectly clear that he was also a projection of Buñuel.

Shortly afterwards, the young man is again seen to be motionless, staring

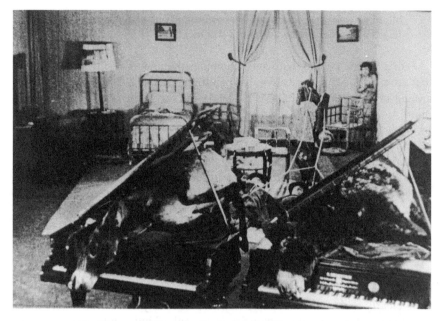

Un Chien andalou: the dead weight of bourgeois values

at his hand in the centre of which there is a hole from which ants are emerging. The hand motif, as we have seen, is prominent in Dalí's paintings and has to do with masturbation and its associated sense of shame, but it is equally central to the work of Buñuel, Lorca and others who were similarly indoctrinated about the sinfulness of what was generally described as self-abuse. In *Un Chien andalou*, moreover, the hand is both frozen and mutilated, pointing to emotional paralysis and damage, while the crawling ants, often seen close to a mouth and indicative of emotional putrefaction and death in what are, in effect, Dalí self-portraits, appear here to announce the beginnings of sexual energy, or perhaps, through the juxtaposition of putrefaction and awakening, the conflict that raged in the mind of men who had been taught that sex equalled sin.

The young man has in this sequence been aroused by what he and his female companion have seen in the street below: a young woman using a stick to prod an amputated hand, the latter pointing not so much to masturbation on this occasion as to male impotence or even castration. At all events, the young man advances on the girl, his previously motionless hands reaching out to caress her breasts and buttocks, suddenly naked in his imagination. Arousal is, though, short lived, for the girl resists him, running away and holding him at bay with a tennis-racket. And when she runs out of the room and slams the door on his hand, the camera focuses on it in close-up, stilled and motionless once more. Not long afterwards, we see him once again reverting to what he was originally: a lifeless, inert figure lying on his bed and dressed in his baby clothes, the very embodiment of infantile sexuality.

The causes of this sexual inertia are suggested in the witty and startling sequence that follows the young woman's attempt to escape. The young man picks up two ropes that lie close at hand. He is evidently intent on securing the girl, but, as he seeks to move towards her, he is held back by an almost immovable weight, which, as we have seen, consists, among other things, of two grand pianos on top of which are two dead and rotting donkeys, and two priests. The rotting donkey was, like the ants, a favourite Dalí image – as in *Honey is Sweeter than Blood* (1927) – but it was also meaningful for Buñuel, for he has described how, when he was a child, the sight and smell of a dead donkey,

> swollen and mangled, serving as a banquet for a dozen vultures, [. . .] both attracted and repelled me. [. . .] I stood there hypnotized, sensing that beyond this rotten carcass lay some obscure metaphysical significance. (Buñuel, 11)

When we also bear in mind that, as a result of his schooling, he subsequently equated death with sex, and that in the film sequence the donkeys are not only dead but their eyes have been mutilated, the image as a whole taking on a sexual resonance that is linked to the earlier motif of the hand. Furthermore, the two priests are clear reminders of the Colegio del Salvador, where Buñuel's sexual guilt had its origins. As for the grand pianos, they clearly suggest the refined world of bourgeois culture in which Buñuel, who had played the violin as a child, had been brought up.

There are also echoes of education in a later sequence in which the camera picks out a school desk with its inkwell and pen, and some exercise books. Furthermore, the young man is obliged at one point to stand in a corner of the room holding books above his head – a clear reminder of the kind of punishments handed out by Buñuel's Jesuit teachers in response to any misdemeanour:

> At the merest infraction, a student would instantly find himself on his knees behind his desk, or in the middle of the classroom, arms outstretched, under the stern eye of the proctor, who surveyed the entire room from a balcony flanked by a ramp and a staircase. (Buñuel, 27–8)

But more important still, as we shall soon see, is the moment when the books mentioned above are transformed into guns.

The theme of sexual inhibition is developed further when the young woman appears once more in search of the young man. Initially, she sees a moth on the wall, its head, seen in close-up, resembling a skull. When the moth, known as the 'Death's Head Moth', is then transformed into the young man, standing motionless before the young woman, the association between death and sex, so deeply felt by Buñuel, is perfectly clear. The young man's sexual anxiety is made even more obvious when his mouth, representing an early stage in sexual contact, disappears, thus preventing the girl from kissing him, and the hair beneath her arms is suddenly transferred to his mouth, further underlining his effeminacy. Finally appreciating that the lover she has sought is incapable of responding to her, she walks out on him in the hope of finding a more sexually active man.

The male protagonist of *Un Chien andalou* fits perfectly the sexually repressed, guilt-ridden Buñuel who emerges from his autobiography, as well as from his wife's memoirs. But if this is the case, what are we to make of the two other young men who figure prominently in the film? The first arrives after a title, *Towards Three in the Morning*, bounds up the stairs to the young man's room, vigorously rings the doorbell, confronts him, pulls him off the bed where he has lain motionless, strips him of his baby clothes, and hurls them out of the window. The second active young man appears immediately after the young woman has abandoned her inadequate lover. Waiting for her on a beach, he is dressed in a striped sweater and plus-fours. He walks away with her, kissing her from time to time, and at one point his clenched fist in front of her face, the very opposite of the maimed and amputated hands seen earlier, points to his aggressive masculinity. If, then, the film's repressed male protagonist is a form of Buñuel as he was in reality, the other two men are the kind of sexually motivated man he would like to have been, as well as projections of his uninhibited surrealist companions in Paris. In this context the transformation into guns of the books held aloft by the film's angst-ridden protagonist is significant, for with them he shoots and kills the first aggressive young man who has, by removing the baby clothes, attempted to bring him to some kind of sexual maturity. The two men here are, in a sense, the two sides of Buñuel, the books that become guns suggesting the destructive effect of his schooling, and it is therefore no coincidence that, of the two young men, it is the sexually inhibited one who lives on, as did Buñuel, forever marked by his time with the Jesuits.

His deep-seated fear of women is expressed very clearly in the film's female protagonist. Initially, we see her sitting quietly in her room, reading a book on painting in which an open page reveals Vermeer's *Lacemaker*. The image is one of quiet domesticity, of the kind that Buñuel recommended to his wife, and which in the painting itself is symbolised in the woman making lace. A moment later, however, the apparently calm and composed girl throws the book aside and, responding to a sudden impulse, rushes down to the street where, as mentioned earlier, she begins to kiss and embrace the motionless cyclist. Buñuel and Dalí, both familiar with Vermeer's painting – it hung on one of the walls of the Residencia de Estudiantes – were highly conscious of and disturbed by the fact that female tranquillity could well conceal powerful and aggressive sexual appetites, and in *Un Chien andalou* this is precisely the kind of woman the protagonist proves to be.[11] When, later on, she searches for the young man and becomes aware of his inability to respond to her – the sequence in which his mouth disappears – she underlines the complete contrast between them by ostentatiously lipsticking her mouth and sticking out her tongue at him before turning on her heel and marching off. She is indeed the sexually aggressive woman Buñuel feared, an echo no doubt of the various women who had displayed amorous intentions towards him and from whom, as we have seen, he so often succeeded in escaping. In addition, her aggressive sexuality is embodied in the earlier scene in which the androgynous female prods the amputated hand with the stick. This episode, witnessed by both the film's male and female protagonists, is in effect a projection or exteriorisation of their thoughts and desires, the amputated hand the equivalent of the emotionally damaged male who at this point wants to be aroused, the stick the aggressive woman who seeks to do the arousing. When she is finally killed by a passing car, her death can be seen in a variety of ways, one of which could well be linked to Buñuel's desire, as the all-powerful film-maker, to put an end to the kind of woman he was afraid of.

This deep-seated anxiety was also embodied in an image common to both Dalí and Buñuel: that of the female praying mantis who, after mating, devours the male. Buñuel's fascination with insects is to be seen throughout his work. During his student days at the Residencia de Estudiantes, he had embarked on a course in Agricultural Engineering but had abandoned it in order to study at the Museum of Natural History under the guidance of the celebrated entomologist, Ignacio Bolívar. Furthermore, *Souvenirs entomologiques*, by the famous French entomologist, J.H. Fabre, would always figure among Buñuel's favourite books. As for the praying mantis – and the black widow spider – they fitted in perfectly with his association of sex and death, and he doubtless discussed the matter with Dalí, for whom Jean-François Millet's famous painting, *Angelus*, had a similar meaning. In the painting, a young man and a young woman stand facing each other in a field at the end of their day's work. Both are praying. The young man's head is bowed and he holds his hat in front of him, more or less at waist level. The woman too has her head bowed in prayer and her hands are clasped in front of her breast. For Dalí the young man's hat concealed his erection, while the apparently passive and demure female was the virgin in waiting, about to pounce on and devour him, emotionally if not physically. So obsessed with Millet's painting was Dalí that he produced a number of variations on it, as in *Homage to Millet* (1934), in which a mantis-like female holds a knife in her right hand and is clearly about to attack the man's exaggeratedly erect penis. There can be no doubt that Buñuel shared Dalí's ideas in this respect, and it is

---

[11] On this topic, see Agustín Sánchez Vidal, *El mundo de Buñuel* (Zaragoza: Caja de Ahorros de la Inmaculada de Aragón, 1993), 157–66.

no coincidence, therefore, that *Un Chien andalou* should end with a shot that echoes the couple in Millet's painting. After a title, *In the Springtime*, which seems to promise a happy future for the girl who has at last found her virile lover, the film's epilogue reveals them to be positioned opposite each other and half buried in sand beneath a fierce sun, their eyes devoured by insects. It is a final and powerful image of the extent to which, for Buñuel, sex and death were synonymous.[12] Indeed, the film as a whole, in terms of its portrayal of the male–female relationship, in which the male is overwhelmed by sexual guilt and inhibition, is his first exercise in autobiography.

The themes of sexual inhibition, guilt and frustration still preoccupied Buñuel many years later in such films as *Viridiana, Belle de jour* and *That Obscure Object of Desire*. In two of these films the male character who embodies these preoccupations – Don Jaime in *Viridiana* and Mathieu in *That Obscure Object* – is, significantly, an older man, played by the experienced Spanish actor Fernando Rey, who has himself observed that in both cases the character is a form of Buñuel.[13] Given the fact, however, that all three films were made when Buñuel was himself much older, it is hardly surprising that there should be a marked change of tone in the presentation of the issues mentioned above. In his sixties and especially during his seventies, the sexual hang-ups that had plagued him as a young man, and which found such powerful expression in *Un Chien andalou*, proved to be less pressing, as he has observed:

> [. . .] lately, my own sexual desire has waned and finally disappeared, even in dreams. And I'm delighted; it's as if I've finally been relieved of a tyrannical burden. (Buñuel, 49)

The consequence was that, in channelling personal experience into his films, Buñuel was able to adopt a cooler, more ironic and even mocking tone in relation to the portrayal of sexual behaviour, much as Cervantes had done when, at the age of almost sixty, he poked fun at the idealism of his youth in the comic figure of Don Quixote.

In *Viridiana* Don Jaime is a widower whose wife died on their wedding night some twenty years before. Since that time, racked by a sense of guilt as well as loss, he has sought in a variety of ways to keep her memory alive, playing on the harmonium music that she liked, and keeping her clothes, including her wedding-dress, in a large wooden chest. In an attempt to get closer to her, he even puts her shoes on his feet and her corset around his waist. His worship of his wife's memory has, in effect, become his religion, to the exclusion of all else, including the maintenance of his estate, which has

---

12 See Sánchez Vidal, 109–20 on the image of the praying mantis in Dalí and Buñuel.
13 See Bruce Babington and Peter William Evans, 'The Life of the Interior: Dreams in the Films of Luis Buñuel', *Critical Quarterly*, 27, no. 4 (1985), 13.

fallen into serious decline. But Don Jaime's devotion to his dead wife inevitably includes, of course, a deep sense of sexual frustration, for it has
demanded of him two decades of abstinence, relieved only by the moments
when he is able to watch the little girl Rita skipping, his eyes fixed on her
quickly moving legs. He is not, though, a paedophile – simply a man
deprived of the sexual pleasure unexpectedly removed by his wife's death.

The arrival at the house of Viridiana, his beautiful niece who is about to
take her vows, and who is a virtual replica of his dead wife, proves to be a
terrible temptation, made worse as each day goes by. Firstly, Don Jaime's
servant, Ramona, having seen Viridiana in her nightgown, comments on her
beautiful skin. Later, Don Jaime encounters Viridiana sleepwalking and,
when she sits by the fire, sees the lower part of her thigh uncovered. So
tempted by her is he that he persuades her to wear his dead wife's
wedding-dress, and afterwards asks her to marry him. Rejected by her, he
then has Ramona introduce a sleeping-draught into her coffee and, when she
has become unconscious, he and Ramona carry her to the bedroom, placing
her on the bed where his wife died. Unable to resist, he touches her hair, lifts
her towards him, kisses her, and begins to unbutton her dress, half exposing
her breasts. But then, on the point of fulfilling his overwhelming desire, he
draws back, overcome by guilt, unable to go any further. Although the
circumstances are different from any experienced by Buñuel in his personal
life, Don Jaime undoubtedly embodies the sexual guilt and inhibition that his
creator felt in his encounters with desirable women, as in the case of the
actress Pepita, whom he held naked in his arms, only to find himself paralysed by nervousness. Furthermore, guilt so haunts Don Jaime subsequently
that he hangs himself with the skipping-rope he had given Rita, the handles
of which have a markedly phallic shape. In other words, sex and death are
equated in the way Buñuel believed them to be. But if Don Jaime is presented
as an essentially good man who, in his twenty years of celibacy and his
current predicament, merits our compassion, there is in the way he is
portrayed and played by Fernando Rey a good deal of irony, of which the
character himself seems aware, not least when he decides, before hanging
himself, to leave his estate to his illegitimate son, Jorge. He draws up his will
with a smile, knowing full well the shock that such a decision will create in a
narrow-minded community.

The theme of sexual inhibition is also embodied in Viridiana herself, for,
as we shall see, Buñuel did not limit its expression to male characters.
Furthermore, as in Buñuel's case, Viridiana's sexual reticence is clearly part
and parcel of the religious teaching to which, as a novice nun, she has been
exposed. When she visits Don Jaime, she takes a variety of religious objects
with her – a crucifix, a crown of thorns, a hammer and nails. They are, in
effect, the religious baggage of which she cannot initially be free, not unlike
the great weight which in *Un Chien andalou* holds back the male protagonist,
and its effect can be seen on a variety of occasions. Shortly after her arrival at

her uncle's house, she is invited by one of the servants to milk a cow, but the sensation of the teat in her hand and the prospect of squeezing it until the milk spurts make her feel uncomfortable and oblige her to draw back. Much later, after the beggars' drunken banquet, one of them attempts to rape Viridiana. She puts up a fight, but in the course of the struggle her hand grips the phallic-like handle of the skipping-rope, which the beggar wears around his waist, and she faints. Both instances highlight a deep-seated sexual fear and inhibition which, if they are entirely understandable on the second occasion, are clearly always with her – a fact suggested by her discomfort in the presence of Don Jaime's good-looking and virile son who has taken over the estate after his father's death. When, for example, he enters her room, tests the hardness of her bed, deliberately runs his eyes over her body, and blows smoke from his cigar towards her, she is much put out.

Another sexually inhibited and frustrated female is Séverine in *Belle de jour*. She, of course, comes from a very different background from Viridiana, for, married to the wealthy Pierre, she is the very embodiment of the bourgeois elegance represented by their Paris apartment and her immaculately tailored clothes. In one way her sexual attitudes have been influenced by the moment when, at the age of eight, she was roughly abused by a workman. Subsequently, she has come to associate sex with roughness and brutality, but this is at the very opposite extreme from her adult married life, which is distinguished by its cool bourgeois formality. Indeed, at one point in the film, Pierre suggests that for him there are two kinds of women: the prostitute on whom he can expend his lust, and the elegant woman, like Séverine, who decorates his life. In other words, if Viridiana is sexually inhibited as the result of her education in the convent, Séverine has become so in relation to her husband and the demand for propriety imposed by the bourgeois society of her adult life, in which, of course, Catholic values also play their part.

Significantly, Séverine is sexually liberated, precisely like Buñuel, in her dreams and daydreams. In the first of these she appears with Pierre in an open landau, with liveried coachman and footman. He refers to her coldness towards him and she to his failure to arouse her, but his manner then changes and he and the coachman tie her to a tree. Pierre tears her clothes from her back, orders the servants to whip her, and allows them to make love to her. Her reaction is seen to be a mixture of apprehension, indicative of the feelings she experiences in her daily life, and the pleasure she can experience only in her fantasies. But if this first daydream reflects her suppressed longings, a second one emphasises her guilt. It is, in effect, a variation on the former, for Séverine's hands are again tied, and the coachman and the footman have become Pierre and one of his bourgeois friends, the ageing playboy Husson, both of whom pelt her with mud and pour abuse on her. Furthermore, Husson observes that the bulls in the background are frequently called Remorse, and one of them Expiation. It is no coincidence that this daydream should occur after Séverine's first day of work at the brothel run by

Madame Anais, for the sexual liberation she seeks to achieve by doing so is accompanied by feelings of terrible wrongdoing. Later still in the film, she has yet another daydream in which, after Husson has discovered her working in the brothel, she envisages two carriages, one containing Husson, the other Pierre. They prepare to fight a duel and, as they fire, Séverine, wearing the same clothes and tied to the same tree as in the film's opening sequence, is killed by a bullet, her initial vision of erotic pleasure transformed into one of social disgrace and a wronged husband's revenge.

The parallels between Séverine and Buñuel are not, of course, precise, but they are certainly suggestive. If, for example, her sexual attitudes were shaped by childhood abuse and subsequent exposure to bourgeois correctness, his were strongly marked by the equally lasting but different abuse – that of religious indoctrination – which he endured at the hands of his Jesuit teachers. Buñuel's relationship with his wife certainly suggests the sexual reticence that was the outcome of that teaching and which Séverine, for other reasons, experiences with her husband. And, as in her case, Buñuel, as the earlier examples suggest, appears to have found much more sexual satisfaction in dreams and daydreams than in reality.

Buñuel's last film, *That Obscure Object of Desire*, is a portrayal of frustrated desire strongly coloured by his view of passion seen from the perspective of old age. Throughout the film, Mathieu, an ageing and wealthy bourgeois, is consumed by his passion for the young and beautiful Conchita. His is clearly, then, not a case of sexual inhibition, but one of desperate longing thwarted at every step, a process that Buñuel presents ironically, subjecting Mathieu to a series of increasingly humiliating indignities. Conchita's name is itself highly suggestive, for it is a shortened form of Concepción ('conception') and also the diminutive of 'concha', one of whose meanings is 'cunt'. It suggests, therefore, even though the name Conchita is common enough, the way in which for Mathieu she is a pure sex object. Fascinated by her from the outset when she is employed as his maid, Mathieu's first setback occurs when she leaves his service after one day. Desperate to find her, he next encounters her three months later in Switzerland, and she gives him her address in Paris. There he visits her daily and is further captivated by her provocative manner – she dances for him in her underwear, kisses him to thank him for his gifts – and by her claim that she is still a virgin. Unknown to Conchita, he bribes her mother to allow her to live with him, and at great expense redecorates his apartment to that end, only to receive a farewell letter from her in which she accuses him of trying to buy her. Later, he meets her once more at a restaurant where she works as a cloakroom attendant. She agrees to become his mistress and he takes her to his country house in great anticipation of a night of love, only to discover, when they are in bed, that she wears a chastity belt. Persuaded by her to wait a little longer, Mathieu subsequently finds a young man in her room, an argument develops, and Conchita and the young man leave. Finally, he follows her from

Paris to Seville where she once more declares her love for him. He buys her a house where they can meet, but when he arrives there at the agreed time, he finds himself locked out and is obliged to watch her making love with a young man. Driven to distraction, he beats her up and they part, but they meet again on the train to Paris. When they arrive, they walk past a shop window where they see a woman sewing a tear in a piece of lace – a sure indication that, as far as Mathieu is concerned, Conchita's vagina will remain intact.

Although Mathieu could not be more different from Buñuel in his active pursuit of Conchita, his failure to possess her physically suggests certain similarities. There is, for instance, a clear parallel between Mathieu obstructed by Conchita's chastity belt and Buñuel's dream, mentioned earlier, in which, 'when the climactic moment arrives, I find the woman sewn up tight'. As well as this, the chastity belt, invariably associated with a female, can be interpreted metaphorically and applied to Buñuel himself in his encounters with women, when his sexual reticence proved to be as much of an obstacle as any garment. And when Mathieu fails to possess Conchita after she has danced provocatively for him, Buñuel could well have had in mind, as a basis for the episode, the occasion on which he found himself alone with the ballerina from the Ballets Russes, even if his failure to make love to her was less her fault than his. At all events, in presenting a story in which frustration follows on frustration, it seems quite likely that Buñuel, at the age of seventy-six, was looking back on his own sexual failures and poking fun at himself.

It is also the case that in Buñuel's work the theme of frustration takes other forms. The relationship between sex and food – both involving hunger and fulfilment – is, after all, a common one, and so it is no coincidence that in *The Discreet Charm of the Bourgeoisie*, which preceded *That Obscure Object* by five years, the pursuit of a meal is the principal concern. Six bourgeois individuals, bent on eating, are frustrated at every step. When they enter a restaurant, they discover that the owner has just died. When they arrive at the Sénéchal household for lunch, their hosts disappear into the garden, overcome by an erotic impulse. In an elegant tea-room they are informed that there is no tea and, later still, no coffee. Again, when they arrive at the Sénéchal home for dinner and are on the point of eating, they are interrupted by the arrival of soldiers, and, when these have departed, by the commencement of army manoeuvres. Later on they visit the same house for lunch and are interrupted by the appearance of the police. And while all these incidents and their attendant frustrations occur in reality, there are also in the film a number of dream sequences in which the characters' pursuit of a meal is similarly thwarted. In short, although the emphasis on frustration is usually of a sexual nature in Buñuel's films, its appearance in other forms, often comic, suggests the extent to which he was preoccupied by it.

Conversely, the theme of the sexually inhibited and frustrated individual is contrasted in a number of films with the virile and passionate male, of which,

L'Âge d'or: love's sweet rapture

as we have already seen, there are two examples in *Un Chien andalou*. Another is the protagonist of Buñuel's second film, *L'Âge d'or*, in which the young man is the embodiment of sexual passion to the exclusion of all else. When we first see him, he is locked in a passionate embrace with a young woman, totally oblivious to the formal ceremony of the laying of the foundation stone nearby. When he is seized by the outraged onlookers and dragged away, his eyes are still on her, '*half-closed, and he seems to be contemplating an ineffable vision*'.[14] Later, although in the clutches of two brutal policemen, he thinks only of her, transforming images on posters and sandwich-boards into her hands and legs, and a photograph in a shop window into her enraptured face. Finally freed by the police and desperate to find her, he knocks aside a blind man in order to appropriate a taxi. At the dinner-party arranged by the girl's parents, he has eyes only for her and scant regard for the distracting and trivial conversation of others, including the young woman's mother whose face he slaps in sheer annoyance. The intensity of his passion – as well as that of the girl – expresses itself fully in the garden scene where, alone at last, the two lovers live only for each other, kissing, embracing, deaf to the concert taking place in another part of the garden.

[14] References are to Buñuel's screenplay in *Un perro andaluz/ La edad de oro* (Mexico: Ediciones Era, 1971). The translation here and subsequently is my own.

In the end, the young man's pursuit of his beloved ends in failure when she, overcome by a sudden feeling of guilt, abandons him and returns to the bourgeois fold. Furthermore, the lovers are, throughout the film, seen to be battling against bourgeois restrictions of good taste and decorum, for the theme of the film is the confrontation between passion, the *amour fou* beloved of the surrealists, and the social and moral forces that oppose it. But if the young man is the embodiment of a surrealist idea, of the kind of blazing passion that was never part of Buñuel's personal experience, he is, like the virile characters of *Un Chien andalou*, the kind of man he may well have wanted to be, who in the dream mentioned previously was able to choose whichever of the black-stockinged dancers he fancied, as they sat facing him, awaiting his command.

The same kind of man appears too in later films. Although Buñuel did not make *Wuthering Heights* until 1953, he had originally intended to make the film after *L'Âge d'or*, so it is not surprising to discover that its two lovers, Catalina and Alejandro, the equivalents of Cathy and Heathcliff, should once more embody *amour fou*. Eight years later, in *Viridiana*, the virile male appears again in the form of Don Jaime's son, Jorge, though on this occasion he is less passion-driven than sexually calculating. A pragmatist in relation to the improvements he makes to his father's run-down estate, he is also a pragmatist in terms of sexual relationships. When, for example, his female companion Lucía becomes bored and decides to leave, his reaction could not be more matter-of-fact: 'That's life. Some people come together, others separate. What can we do if that's how it is?' As far as Jorge is concerned, no woman is irreplaceable, and in no time at all the servant Ramona takes Lucía's place. In the sense that for him women are little more than sex objects, he is the opposite of the passionate protagonist of *L'Âge d'or*, but, in his total lack of sexual reticence, he is very much the man that Buñuel was not. Time after time Buñuel describes his own relationships with women as 'chaste', even when their amorous intentions towards him were perfectly clear. Can we imagine Jorge resisting the eighteen-year-old American on the ship, the Russian ballerina, or the naked young actress, Pepita? By the end of *Viridiana* he is enjoying not only the favours of Ramona; he is also about to include Viridiana herself in a cosy *ménage à trois*, for by this time she has, like Jorge himself, abandoned what has proved to be futile idealism in favour of more worldly pleasures. The chaste woman has literally let her hair down – it now falls over her shoulders – and cast aside the crown of thorns, the cross, the hammer and nails, just as Buñuel would have shaken off, had he been able to, the emotional and psychological burden of his Jesuit education. In Jorge, and in Viridiana too, he embodies what he could only imagine or dream about.

Yet another sexually aggressive male appears in *Belle de jour*. At the brothel where she works in the afternoons, Séverine meets Marcel, a newcomer to the establishment. From the outset he proves to be the rough, dominant male who is capable of breaking through the sexual coldness she feels towards her husband. He is not, with his gold teeth, the most handsome of men, but they – replacing those previously knocked out in a fight – together with the mark on his shoulder-blade, mark him out as a man of action who wears his scars like medals. When, later in the film, Séverine is away from Paris with Pierre, she is clearly longing to see Marcel, and, when he learns of her return, he rushes off to Madame Anais' to meet up with her once more. In their eager pursuit of each other, they bear a certain similarity to the lovers of L'Âge d'or. In the end Marcel is killed, shot by a policeman after he has shot Pierre and made his escape from Séverine's apartment. But the effect of Marcel's intervention in her life is to reawaken her love for Pierre, who has been left paralysed after the shooting. The virile, sexually uninhibited man has made her aware once more of her own sexuality.

A very different kind of character who appears in a number of Buñuel's films is the extremely possessive and/or pathologically jealous male. The examples quoted earlier reveal Buñuel to have been precisely this kind of man, above all in his relationship with his wife, Jeanne, whom he always kept on a tight leash, fearful of the attentions of other men and determined to exercise control over her activities. Indeed, the Mexican actress, Silvia Pinal, who starred in three of Buñuel's films and knew him well, once commented: 'At home he was like Hitler. Like Othello.'[15] Two films in particular embody such attitudes: He and Tristana. Buñuel's wife, describing his treatment of her, significantly mentions He, in which 'Luis deals with the theme of extreme jealousy' (Rucar de Buñuel, 108). As for Buñuel himself, he has observed of the protagonist, Francisco, that 'he increasingly perceives reality according to his own obsession, until everything in his life revolves around it. Suppose, for instance, that a woman plays a short phrase on the piano and her paranoid husband is immediately convinced that it's a signal to her lover who's waiting somewhere outside, in the street' (Buñuel, 203). The husband's jumping to conclusions here is little different from Buñuel's immediate assumption that, when his wife spent five minutes with Gustavo Pittaluga in his home, she must have gone to bed with him. But to be blind to one's own shortcomings is clearly characteristic of the paranoid individual, and it is not therefore surprising that Buñuel should draw a parallel not between himself and the film's protagonist but between the latter and another man who lived near Buñuel in Mexico City: 'An officer who closely resembled the character in the film. He too used to tell his wife that he was leaving on manoeuvres, then sneak back that same evening, fake a voice, and call to his wife: "Open up, it's me! I know your husband's gone" ' (Buñuel, 204). The attribution of one's faults to another is in effect a kind of psychological self-defence.

In He Francisco is a well-to-do bachelor who is attracted to Gloria when

---

[15] See John Baxter, Buñuel (London: Fourth Estate, 1994), 225.

he catches a glimpse of her feet in church. At the time she is the girl-friend of Raúl, but she abandons him in order to marry Francisco, his best friend. The initial promise of the marriage soon vanishes during the honeymoon, however, when in their hotel Gloria encounters a male friend, an incident that so provokes Francisco's jealousy that he insists on their finishing their meal in private. Even in the seclusion of their room, he is convinced that the friend is watching them through the keyhole, through which he sticks a long pin, and, just afterwards, when both men meet in a corridor, Francisco punches him in the face. After the honeymoon, they entertain friends at home, but when Gloria dances with her husband's young lawyer, Francisco suffers another violent attack of jealousy and locks her in her room. The following day, when she returns from her mother's, he produces a gun, which he fires at her, though later we learn that the bullets were blanks. Gloria finally makes her escape after a horrific night when Francisco creeps into the bedroom armed with cotton, string, a razor blade, scissors and a rope. He is evidently bent, in a desperate attempt to prevent any other man possessing her, on sewing up her vagina, and is only prevented from doing so when his efforts to tie her hands fail, and she wakes up screaming. At the end of the film we see Francisco in a monastery where he is visited by Gloria and Raúl, now happily married and with a child.

The most bizarre and horrific incident in the film involves, clearly, Francisco's plan to close Gloria's vagina. Its extreme nature is self-evident, and Buñuel undoubtedly delighted in its capacity to shock, without perhaps being aware of how it related to himself. In this respect, though, the following comment by Jeanne Rucar is surely revealing: 'I'm glad I wasn't born in the Middle Ages, or Luis would certainly have made me wear a chastity belt' (Rucar de Buñuel, 41). In a sense, of course, he did, encouraging her to stay at home and to devote herself to domestic chores, which would obviously have included sewing and, as we have seen, knitting. Such activities were in the past a traditional part of women's lives not only in Spain but elsewhere, though it is probably true to say that in those countries where *machismo* was strong, even greater emphasis was placed on them. In Lorca's *The House of Bernarda Alba*, for example, Bernarda draws a clear distinction between the roles of men and women: 'A needle and thread for women. A whip and a mule for men.'[16] Furthermore, as far as Bernarda is concerned, her five daughters are still virgins, in the light of which the act of sewing, in which they are frequently engaged in the play, can be seen as a parallel to their being sewn up sexually. As for Buñuel, we have already seen that at the end of *That Obscure Object of Desire*, a shop assistant sews a tear in a piece of lace, indicating that for Mathieu Conchita will forever be sewn up. Whether or not

---

[16] See Lorca, *The House of Bernarda Alba*, trans. Gwynne Edwards (London: Methuen, 1998), 21.

Buñuel was aware that his encouragement of Jeanne to take up sewing and knitting had similar connotations, ensuring that she would be safe from other men, can never be known, but the thought may well have lurked in his subconscious, which in his case would have been perfectly appropriate.

Buñuel's own experiences found expression in the character of Francisco in other ways too. The Church plays a significant part in shaping Francisco's attitudes. In the film's opening scene, he assists a priest in washing the feet of some of the faithful. He frequently asks Gloria to regard him as her confessor. After she has left him, he imagines himself pursuing her to the church where he first saw her. And he enjoys standing in the bell tower, looking down on the people below as though he were God. In effect, erotic desire is for him strangely interwoven with religious devotion, though, as far as the latter is concerned, what we witness in him is not so much Christian love and charity as the anger and retribution of the Old Testament. In this respect the parallel with Buñuel is not, of course, precise, for Francisco is not someone in whom religious teaching has led to sexual inhibition. But he is, clearly, someone who, like Buñuel, has been damaged in his sexual relationships with women by the influence of religion.

If Francisco embodies extreme jealousy, Don Lope in *Tristana* is the perfect example of male possessiveness. Following the recent death of Tristana's mother, Don Lope, a bourgeois gentleman of about sixty years old, has become the guardian of the young woman, who is barely twenty. From the outset he is clearly attracted by her beauty, and when she has a nightmare, he hurries to her room, and is somewhat disturbed by her relatively low-cut nightdress. Before very long, she submits to his advances and becomes, in effect, his mistress, doubtless influenced by his frequent proclamations that love and passion must be free of the restrictions imposed by the Church and society: 'It is the natural law. No chains, no signatures, no blessings.' But Don Lope is a man of contradictions, to some extent a hypocrite, and if he often tells Tristana that love must be freely given and that people can choose to do what they wish with their lives, he does not mean that she is free to love or be with someone other than himself. On the contrary, he keeps her at home as much as possible, and when she is allowed out, either to mass or for a walk, he ensures that she is accompanied by his housekeeper, Saturna. Furthermore, when he takes her to buy new clothes, he does so for his own gratification, so that he, not some other man, can feast his eyes on her maturing beauty.

Don Lope's hold over Tristana begins to weaken as she tires of him and gradually realises that he denies her the freedom that he advocates in general. Things come to a head when she meets the young painter Horacio and, greatly attracted to him, starts to meet him secretly. Eventually, Don Lope learns the truth, he and Horacio have a confrontation during which the latter strikes Don Lope, and, as a result of this, Tristana decides to move in with Horacio. Two years later, however, she falls ill, suffering from a tumour in the

leg, and, in the belief that she is dying, returns to Don Lope in order to end
her days in the house that she still regards as her home. Saddened by her
illness, Don Lope is, nevertheless, delighted by the fact that it will allow him
to reassert his control over her life:

> DON LOPE: Saturna, now she can't escape. If she comes back to this
> house, she'll never leave it!

This conviction is then reinforced when the doctor informs Don Lope that
only amputation of the leg will save Tristana's life. His earlier advice to her,
'A reputable woman, a damaged leg, and at home,' has ironically come true in
the most unexpected way. Furthermore, he cunningly ensures that Horacio
will lose all interest in her by inviting him to visit her at home, knowing full
well that he will be repulsed by the spectacle of his crippled lover. When the
tactic succeeds, Don Lope is delighted. His possession of Tristana seems
complete.

For all his apparent control of her, Don Lope fails to take into account the
reality of the aggressive and potentially destructive female that Tristana
becomes, a theme that, as we have seen, Buñuel had already explored in some
depth in *Un Chien andalou*. In later films females of this kind continue to
appear, as in *The Brute* and *The Temperature Rises in El Pao*. In the former
Pedro is a powerful brute of a man who carries out the orders of his boss, the
landlord Cabrera, especially in evicting tenants late with their rent. Paloma,
Cabrera's wife, is attracted by Pedro's physical prowess and embarks on an
affair with him, but he is forced to flee after he has killed a fellow worker. He
is hidden by Meche, a much more innocent character than the exploitative
Paloma, and she opens Pedro's eyes to the way in which he has been used by
Cabrera. Paloma, however, resentful of Meche's interference, informs her
husband, and through him the police, of Pedro's whereabouts. He is finally
shot, but not until he has strangled Cabrera. In *The Temperature Rises in El
Pao*, the destructive female is Inés Vargas, widow of the assassinated
governor. After his death, control of the island El Pao is seized by the unscrupulous Alejandro Gual, who is opposed in his treatment of the inhabitants by
the idealistic Ramón Vázquez. He is in love with Inés, who, hungry for
power, urges him to take action against Gual and at the same time offers
herself to Gual if he will allow Vázquez, accused of involvement in the
governor's murder, to remain free. Eventually, Vázquez manages to gain
control of the island and Gual is arrested and executed. Even so, his
conscience is troubled by the thought that, through Inés's influence, he has
become as unscrupulous as Gual, while she, as greedy for power as ever, sees
him as essentially weak, and finally witnesses his death at the hands of his
enemies. In both films, therefore, men are seen to be the victims of women
who are stronger and more controlling than themselves: the first driven by
sexual jealousy, the second by a mixture of sexual desire and a hunger for

power. The most powerful presentation of the theme of the manipulative woman is, though, to be found in *Tristana* and *That Obscure Object of Desire*.

Tristana's attitude to Don Lope becomes rebellious even before the amputation of her leg, but afterwards it is quickly transformed into bitterness. Although she has an artificial limb, her ventures, be it to church or elsewhere, require a wheelchair that is usually pushed by the deaf mute Saturno, with Don Lope in close attendance. But, far from being a helpless victim, Tristana is in complete control, issuing orders and instructions to both males as to where she wishes to go and what she wants to do, and banging her walking-stick on the floor in order to make the point. She is, in short, a changed woman, embittered by her misfortune, as the filmscript suggests: **TRISTANA** *is dressed with an excessive severity which contrasts with her former appearance. Her face is extremely pale and displays an equally unaccustomed harshness.*[17] At times, moreover, her immobility has that stillness which, as we have seen in *Un Chien andalou*, conceals a female's powerful feelings, and which also characterises the praying mantis when it is about to strike.

Tristana's sexual control over Don Lope and Saturno is evident in a number of powerful sequences. The early part of the film suggests a closeness between Tristana and Saturno, which stems from the fact that they are both young and exposed to misfortune: she is an orphan, he a deaf mute. After the amputation of her leg, however, that initial closeness has disappeared and given way to Tristana's cold and deliberate sexual domination of her one-time friend. At one point he enters her bedroom, clearly in the hope of going to bed with her. She angrily dismisses him, but having done so, she then, a few days later, stands on her balcony – Saturno is below her, at the edge of the garden – and opens her dressing-gown so that he can see her completely naked body. Nothing could better express either her control or her manipulation of the young man.

As for Don Lope, her control over him, already evident in her brusque commands from the wheelchair, becomes total after he proposes marriage and she accepts. He, of course, assumes that marriage will guarantee him the sexual rights of a legal husband and tie her to him for the rest of his or her life, reinforcing the lack of physical freedom imposed on her by her disability. In anticipation of the wedding night, Don Lope has gone to the lengths of buying a new bed, and on the night itself we see him in his pyjamas, looking at himself in the mirror, and spraying his mouth with an atomiser. Imagine his shock and disappointment, then, when Tristana coldly informs him that she intends to spend the night alone in her own bedroom. It is an assertion of her independence that Don Lope did not expect and a firm

---

[17] See Buñuel's screenplay *Tristana* (Barcelona: Aymá, 1971), 118.

indication both of her manipulation of him and of the revenge she intends to take on him for his abuse of her when she was younger.

Later on, Tristana's harshness of heart and spirit is powerfully suggested in a sequence in which, while the quickly ageing Don Lope is closeted in the dining-room with three priests, Tristana walks up and down the corridor outside, hauling herself along on her crutches. She is dressed entirely in black and the crutches produce a monotonous creaking and dragging sound on the floor of the corridor. As the camera focuses on her in medium shot and then close up, she reminds us of some threatening beetle, if not a praying mantis, perhaps a black widow spider about to consume her male partner. It is no coincidence, therefore, that this is what happens next. During the night Don Lope falls ill and calls out to Tristana to telephone the doctor immediately. She appears to her husband to do so, for she speaks into the mouthpiece, but she does not in fact dial the number. And when Don Lope's breathing grows more faint, she opens the window, allowing the bitter wind and snow to enter the room and help Don Lope on his way to the next world. The avenging woman has achieved her goal in a literally chilling manner.

Tristana echoes Buñuel's life in a variety of ways. As we have seen, Don Lope is the possessive man that Buñuel was in relation to his wife, but he also echoes Buñuel in his views on freedom. At one point he mocks a married couple and informs the young Tristana that 'Passion must be free. It's the natural law.' And later on, when she has matured somewhat, he reinforces the point: 'Tristana, make your own decision about the limits of your freedom.' In his advocacy of freedom, Don Lope is Buñuel the surrealist. On the other hand, practising what he preaches where his own freedom is concerned, Don Lope denies Tristana hers, for, before she leaves him for Horacio, he does his best to keep her indoors, away from the eyes of other men. He is, in short, an almost exact reflection of Buñuel himself, the surrealist who at every stage limited his own wife's freedom: physically, in restricting her movements outside the home; and spiritually and emotionally, in curtailing her involvement in such creative activities as gymnastics, piano playing and book-binding.

As far as the avenging Tristana of the film's final third is concerned, there were no such women in Buñuel's life. Indeed, Jeanne accepted her husband's possessiveness, often to the amazement of her female friends. But this being so, it is quite easy to see how, when at the age of seventy he looked back on his life and realised what a tyrant he had been towards her, he was able to create in the character of Tristana a woman who takes revenge on a person very similar to himself. Buñuel doubtless counted his blessings that he did not in reality suffer the same fate as Don Lope, and so took the easier option of punishing himself, and other men like him, on the cinema screen. Jeanne's revenge came after Buñuel's death in the form of her autobiography.

The female protagonist of *That Obscure Object of Desire* can be seen as the avenging or punitive woman in a somewhat different form. *Tristana* is set

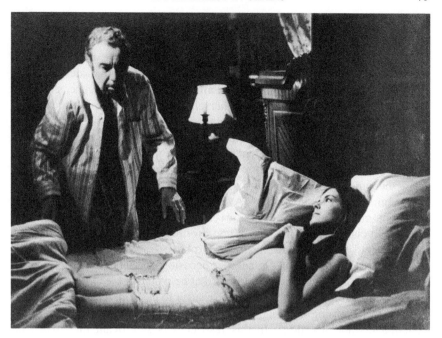

That Obscure Object of Desire: passion thwarted

in the early 1930s in a Spain that was highly traditional and conservative, in which men considered women to be inferior, as well as fair game for their attentions. *That Obscure Object*, on the other hand, is set in Paris and Seville in the late 1970s, by which time sexual attitudes had changed a great deal. Mathieu is, though, still of the old school, a man who believes that a woman whom he finds attractive exists only to be seduced. In this particular sense he is not, of course, a reflection of Buñuel, who was no Don Juan, but it is perfectly possible to see him as a projection of the film-director in terms of his desire to possess Conchita and keep her solely for himself. It is as if Buñuel, as rooted in the past as Mathieu in relation to his possessive attitude towards his wife, is imagining how he would have fared at the hands of a modern, liberated woman, or, indeed, how Jeanne would have made him suffer had she been more resolute. To this extent, Mathieu's frustrations and punishments become his own, though Buñuel, in the twilight of his life, presents them much more light-heartedly than in *Tristana*, as if passion itself is no longer to be taken seriously.

The avenging woman, in complete contrast to the icy Tristana, is presented in *That Obscure Object* as a mixture of innocence and voluptuousness, opposing qualities which are embodied in the two actresses – Carole Bouquet and Angela Molina, who play Conchita – and which serve to attract and frustrate the ever-eager Mathieu. When, for example, he visits her in her flat in Paris, she sits on the sofa in the most provocative manner – arms behind her head, legs apart – but with a cool, composed and even innocent expression on her face. Between her thighs she holds a box, from which she takes a sweet, placing it and her fingers in Mathieu's mouth. Later, when he visits her again, she dances for him and afterwards, in his presence, she strips to her underwear in order to wash herself. She kisses him provocatively, which he takes to be an invitation to make an advance, but when he puts his hand on her thigh, she pushes it away, claiming that the kiss was merely an expression of her gratitude and that she is still a virgin. In this case, then, the avenging woman is the teaser *par excellence*, and Mathieu's ever-growing desire becomes an increasingly comic spectacle. The temptations placed before him become even greater. At his country house she undresses in the bathroom, enters the bedroom in a revealing nightdress, exposes her breasts to him, but claims she is not in the mood for love. When he then attempts to force himself on her, he discovers, as we have seen, that the chastity belt prevents sexual intercourse. On another occasion she gets into bed, removes her nightdress, lies with him, but argues that he would cease to love her if she gave herself to him. Mathieu is indeed a martyr to passion, made to suffer and exposed to increasing humiliation for his misplaced belief that he can make Conchita his and his alone. In this respect it is significant that, when he follows her to Seville, he walks past a bar called 'Las cadenas' ('The Chains'), a name that encapsulates the obsession by which he is imprisoned. But if he is a martyr to desire and he is made to suffer for it, his fate is not that of Don Lope who dies at the hands of the woman he has abused. Rather is it the comic spectacle of the bucket of water that at one point Conchita throws over him when he is on the train to Paris. In short, *That Obscure Object* represents Buñuel's view of passion that, in old age, seems farcical, as does the extreme possessiveness that for so many years dominated his own married life. In addition, as has been suggested earlier, it seems quite possible that in the sexy and provocative Conchita Buñuel was recalling his own sexual failures with the tempting young women he had encountered many years ago – failures for different reasons than Mattieu's, but failures all the same, and to be smiled at from the perspective of the autumn of his life.

   Buñuel, the great champion of Surrealism and therefore of freedom in all its forms, was thus, in sexual matters, a very different man from what we might expect. He was, in short, someone who believed fervently that one should be free from the moral and emotional restrictions imposed by bourgeois values, by culture and by religion, yet he remained throughout most of his life imprisoned by the very things he railed against, inhibited in particular by his Jesuit schooling. It is not surprising, therefore, that a conflict of such opposites should have expressed itself both in his personal life and in his work, or that sexual dilemmas should have become so important a focus in films as varied as *Un Chien andalou, L'Âge d'or, He, Viridiana, Tristana* and *That Obscure Object of Desire*. In their characters Buñuel embodied his own problems which, over a period of forty-eight years, evidently changed, demanding in the end to be viewed comically where once they were seen very seriously. His films are, in effect, a kind of autobiographical graph, and provide incontrovertible proof of the close relationship between the life of a creative artist and his work.

3

BUÑUEL AND THE BOURGEOISIE

Dadaism, the revolutionary artistic movement that emerged in different European countries around 1916 and that preceded Surrealism, was, in effect, an angry and outraged reaction to the values of contemporary society, and was fuelled even more by the senseless destruction of the First World War, which many saw as the consequence of those values and beliefs. The fate of millions of young men dragooned into fighting for their country and exposed by their superiors to the most terrible conditions – clinging mud, stinking trenches, endless shelling, mustard gas, disease, hunger and, in many cases, death or chronic illness and injury – intensified a fundamental questioning of all those hitherto sacred cows that had led to and were manifest in the course of that catastrophic conflict: patriotism, honour, and self-sacrifice among them. These were, of course, ideals that were identified with those groups that exercised power and control, that enjoyed position and wealth, and in which the bourgeoisie figured prominently. In relation to the French social structure in particular, the word 'bourgeois' covered a broad economic spectrum, which included those families that were extremely rich, as well as those that were salaried or self-employed but not necessarily very well off. Wealthy or not, they nevertheless shared similar views, those at the lower end of the scale aspiring to the status of those above, and therefore embracing all those things that the latter believed in, be it decency and propriety, the importance of money, good name, respect or love of one's country. In short, these were the traditional and essentially conservative principles that had been at the heart of French and European society for many years and which the Dadaists made every effort to undermine.

The extent to which Dadaism struck out at everything conventional may be gauged by the activities of one of its founders, Tristan Tzara, who in 1916 was also one of the founders of the Cabaret Voltaire in Zurich, and the co-editor of a new magazine of the same name. The Cabaret Voltaire was in reality a room in a milk bar, the Meierei, in one of the more disreputable parts of Zurich, an area inhabited by many foreign exiles then in neutral Switzerland. A different programme was offered every night and was invariably anarchic. Richard Huelsenbeck, a medical student and poet, read his poems to the beat of a big drum. Tzara accompanied his poetry readings with bells, screams, sobs and whistles. Emmy Hennings, an actress and nightclub performer, sang songs in a shrill voice. And Hugo Ball, a theatre-director dressed in strange cardboard costumes, intoned his sound-poems. As far as the magazine was concerned, Ball and Tzara were initially its joint editors, but Tzara became its sole editor in 1917 when its name changed to *Dada*. Using the magazine to attack all conventional art forms and to make himself known to a wider audience of like-minded people, Tzara moved from Zurich to Paris in 1920 and soon met up with André Breton and Louis Aragon, two of his greatest admirers.[1]

Breton and Aragon soon became involved, with Tzara, in Dada events in Paris. In one of them, for example, Tzara cut up an article by Léon Daudet, dropped the pieces into a hat, and then proceeded to read the individual snippets as though they were a poem. As he did so, Breton and Aragon stood in the wings of the Palais des Fêtes, ringing bells and drowning out Tzara's words. On another occasion, Tzara made it known to the press that Charlie Chaplin had joined the Dada movement and would be participating in a poetry reading at the Salon des Indépendentes in the Grand Palais des Champs-Elysées. He did not, of course, appear, much to the disappointment of the packed audience, and the session ended in complete uproar. Many similarly outrageous events followed, but it was not long before the more serious-minded Breton became weary of Tzara's purely iconoclastic form of Dada and, influenced by the writings of Freud and the work of Pierre Janet, a leading French authority on the unconscious, began to move in a different direction: one that in its initial stages involved automatic writing and that came to be known as Surrealism.

Surrealism was in general, even though shock was one of its elements, a much more sophisticated and constructive movement than nihilistic Dadaism. Its aim, after all, was not so much to destroy as to change man's priorities, and, in its first manifestation, embodied in Breton's *Manifesto of Surrealism*, it emphasised, as we have seen, the importance of the inner life, unrestricted by logic and reason, as the true reality, the opposite of those rational and conventional values on which western civilisation had previously been based and which many believed had led only to war and catastrophe. In its attempt to put forward an alternative to long-held principles, Surrealism was clearly a revolutionary movement, and it is not therefore surprising that quite soon it acquired a political dimension that led it and its supporters to an alignment with Communism. Indeed, Breton soon realised that if Surrealism in its initial form were not to end up in the same cul-de-sac as Dada, it needed to be something more than just a literary and cultural movement. By 1926 Breton, Aragon, Paul Éluard and Pierre Unik – with Buñuel he later co-scripted *Las Hurdes* – had officially joined the Party. Significantly, in 1929, the first issue of the new magazine, *Surréalisme au service de la révolution*, contained an exchange of telegrams between the Surrealists and the International Revolu-

---

[1]   See Brandon, *Surreal Lives: the Surrealists 1917–1945*, 93–169.

tionary Bureau in which Breton and Aragon declared their allegiance in the event of an imperialist war on the Soviets.

Buñuel considered that most of the surrealists with whom he associated in Paris were themselves essentially bourgeois: 'Like the *señoritos* I knew in Madrid, most surrealists came from good families; as in my case, they were bourgeois revolting against the bourgeoisie' (Buñuel, 107). The truth of the matter was not, however, as clear cut as he suggests, for the individuals who formed the surrealist group in Paris came from a variety of social and economic backgrounds. Louis Aragon and Paul Éluard, in particular, belonged to families that laid little claim to wealth. Éluard was born in the industrial suburb of Saint-Denis in the north of Paris and always remembered his working-class background, while Aragon spent the first twenty-six years of his life in a family of very modest means in which he, an illegitimate child, was passed off as his mother's youngest brother in order to avoid any possible scandal.

André Breton and Max Ernst were the sons of parents a little higher up the social scale. Breton's father, by the time the boy was in his teens, was assistant manager of a glassworks in the outskirts of Paris, and Ernst, born in the small town of Brühl, six miles south of Cologne, was the son of a schoolteacher. In economic terms, Salvador Dalí's background was even more favourable. His father, Salvador Dalí y Cusí, was a notary – a public servant authorised to draw up contracts, deeds and wills – a position that earned him good money and allowed him to purchase very comfortable apartments and offices in the town of Figueras. When his son, the future painter, was eight years old, for example, the family lived in spacious accommodation on the top floor of a new building designed by the best architect in the town. But if Dalí came from a privileged background, he could not match Francis Picabia in this respect. The only son of a wealthy and well-connected Cuban, Picabia's private income allowed him to enjoy a lifestyle that involved alcohol, drugs, women and fast cars, and to move freely in the highest levels of Parisian society. Influential contacts also allowed him to avoid being conscripted into the French army on at least two occasions.

Although the economic circumstances in which all these individuals grew up varied a great deal, most of the families to which they belonged shared what may fairly be described as conventional attitudes. Breton's father wanted him to become a doctor so that he might become a comfortably off and well-respected member of the middle class. Aragon's family attempted to direct him towards a medical career for similar reasons, and Ernst's parents encouraged him to study at the University of Bonn so that he too could take up a respectable profession. In addition, many of the future surrealists came from families in which traditional moral values were very strong. Breton's mother was extremely strait-laced and puritanical, his background strongly Catholic. The parents of Ernst were staunchly religious, his father a serious and solemn man, the household in general very disciplined and orderly. But it is risky to generalise in this respect, for Dalí's father, to all appearances a typical bourgeois, was in reality something of a rebel: a declared atheist, a strong supporter of Catalan nationalism, and a free thinker with anarchist leanings.

In the light of the above, it seems more than likely that many of the surrealists adopted an anti-bourgeois stance as an act of rebellion against their background and the pressures placed upon them by their families, though in some cases other personal motives also played their part. Forced by his family to study medicine in order to become respectable, Breton had no interest either in that career or the material wealth that it promised. Much more preoccupied with his inner life, he chose to pursue his long-held ambition to write poetry. Similarly, despite family pressure not to do so, Aragon abandoned his medical studies in order to devote himself to a literary career, even if this meant taking low-paid jobs in order to survive. And Ernst, the son of strict parents, evidently reacted against that background, both in relation to women, of which there were many in his life, and to his dedication to artistic trends that were decidedly unconventional. As for Dalí, his father was, as we have seen, the very opposite of bourgeois in his political beliefs, but even so the young Salvador was determined to upset his parents as much as possible, as well as to be fundamentally different from them. In short, many of the surrealists were, like many young people, rebels against an older generation, though it is clear enough too that the narrow-minded nature of middle-class life sharpened the desire to rebel even more so than it does today.

Buñuel's background was, by his own admission, extremely bourgeois; much more so than that of many of his surrealist companions. His father, Leonardo, had joined the army at the age of fourteen and later took part in Cuba in the Spanish–American War, even though his was only a desk job. When the war ended, he remained in Havana where he opened a hardware store, which proved so successful that, as the business expanded, he went into partnership with two associates. In 1899 Cuba acquired its independence and Leonardo Buñuel decided to sell his share of the business and, now that he was a rich man, to return to his birthplace of Calanda in order to settle down. There he bought a sizeable estate and, at the age of forty-three, married a local girl of eighteen, María Portolés. One year later, no doubt bored by the prospect of living in a small town with fewer than 5,000 inhabitants, Leonardo moved the family to the nearby city of Zaragoza where he rented a large apartment. But this by no means ended his association with Calanda, for he soon rebuilt his original house, as well as another house called La Torre near the river, three kilometres away (Buñuel, 17). For many years the family spent Holy Week and the summer months in Calanda, away from the bustle of the city.

The extent of Leonardo Buñuel's wealth may be gauged both by the character of the properties in Calanda and Zaragoza and by his way of life. In his autobiography, Buñuel gives a clear impression of both Calanda houses. The house in the town was 'a monument to art deco, that "bad taste" which art historians now praise and whose most brilliant practitioner was the Catalonian Gaudí. Whenever we opened the front door, there was a cluster of poor children staring open-mouthed into our "luxurious" interior' (Buñuel, 16). Although Buñuel does not go into detail, we can well imagine a house filled with expensive furniture, ornaments and pictures. As for the house outside the town, it was even more lavish, and 'surrounded by a superb garden and clumps of fruit trees, which led down to a small pond, where we kept a rowboat, and finally to the river itself' (Buñuel, 17). When the Buñuel family spent the summer in Calanda, living in the town house, they went by horse-drawn cart every day to La Torre where they 'often dined, copiously, in the garden [. . .] under the soft glow of acetylene lamps, returning to Calanda only late at night' (Buñuel, 17). In Zaragoza, the apartment rented by Leonardo Buñuel consisted of the entire second floor of a building that had once been a police headquarters and had ten balconies. The Buñuels also employed domestic staff. A gardener looked after the grounds at La Torre, and, as Buñuel notes, there were servants to carry out any menial task that his father considered below his or his family's dignity:

> The only thing my father would carry in the street was his elegantly wrapped jar of caviar. According to social convention, men of 'rank' were never supposed to carry anything; that's what servants were for. Even when I went to my music lesson, my governess always carried the violin case.
>
> (Buñuel, 25)

In this context it is not surprising to learn that Leonardo Buñuel was the fourth or fifth richest man in Zaragoza – sufficiently wealthy to rescue the local Hispano-American bank when it was in danger of going out of business.

As for his father's life style, Buñuel has observed that he 'did absolutely nothing' (Buñuel, 25). After rising, he bathed, breakfasted, read the newspaper, checked to see if his Havana cigars had arrived, went out on a few errands, and had an aperitif before lunching at home. After lunch, he took a siesta, then changed his clothes and went to his club where he played bridge or cards with his friends before dinner. The routine was that of a wealthy bourgeois who had no financial worries and who was able to move freely in the higher echelons of Zaragoza society. His wife, María, was a devoted, sincere and devout woman who imposed strict control over servants and children alike. In terms of material surroundings and the nature of daily life, the household in which Buñuel grew up could not, then, have been more bourgeois. In his own words: 'We were undoubtedly the last scions of an ancient way of life' (Buñuel, 17).

After he left home at the age of seventeen, Buñuel's life could not have been more different from the one he left behind. In going to Madrid to study for a degree, he evidently followed his parents' wishes, for his father had categorically opposed his desire to study music in Paris on the grounds that music was not a serious activity (Buñuel, 52). But it was not long before, in abandoning Agricultural Engineering for the natural sciences and then an Arts degree, he revealed that independence of spirit that would characterize the rest of his life. Furthermore, his increasing involvement at the Residencia de Estudiantes and outside it in the avant-garde movements described earlier, stemmed from a personality that was unconventional and increasingly anti-bourgeois. And it is no coincidence that his arrival in Paris in 1925 should have occurred almost immediately after the death of his father, who, as we have seen, had earlier opposed such a move. Although for a while Buñuel was able to survive only by means of financial support from his mother, he had effectively distanced himself from the bourgeois background of his childhood and adolescence.

As far as his political views were concerned, Buñuel has suggested that he and his friends had little political consciousness until 1927–28, two to three years after he left Madrid: 'Up until that moment, we paid only minimal attention to the infant Communist and anarchist publications, although they did introduce us to Lenin and Trotsky' (Buñuel, 55–6). Against this, however, is his admission, referred to earlier, that by the age of seventeen, before his arrival at the Residencia, he had already been exposed to the work of Karl Marx. And it seems clear enough that during his eight years at the Residencia, where all kinds of debate and argument took place and where the general atmosphere was very liberal, Buñuel's left-wing leanings would have been reinforced. Indeed, he recalls the irony of an occasion when the then dictator, Primo de Rivera, arrived at the Café Castilla and unwittingly bought drinks for a group of young men of left-wing sympathies, among whom Buñuel included himself (Buñuel, 57). And when the King, Alfonso XIII, visited the Residencia and asked an astonished Buñuel for directions, the young man regarded his failure to remove his hat in deference to royalty not as an act of discourtesy but as a testimony of his own integrity and honour (Buñuel, 57).

It was, though, Buñuel's arrival in Paris and his growing interest in Surrealism that consolidated his political views. Despite the fact that he and Dalí made *Un Chien andalou* before they became part of the official surrealist group, this does not mean that they were unaware of the political implications of the surrealist movement, and the film itself was certainly designed to shake bourgeois complacency. Furthermore, when he joined the surrealists in 1929 and embarked on the filming of *L'Âge d'or*, Buñuel was in no doubt at all that his and their intentions, as we have seen in Chapter 1, was to transform the social order (Buñuel, 107).

During his childhood in Calanda and Zaragoza, Buñuel had accepted the conditions of the poor as a fact of life and was therefore unmoved by them, as in the case of a ragged child seen in the course of the journey from Calanda to La Torre:

As we rolled along, our children's cart often passed a thin village child
dressed in rags who was collecting horse manure in a shapeless basket to
fertilize his family's scanty vegetable garden. When I think back, it seems
to me that these images of abject poverty made no impression on us what-
soever. (Buñuel, 17)

Twenty or so years later this indifference would be completely reversed when
he exposed in *Las Hurdes* the abject poverty and misery to which the inhabitants of that region were condemned by the negligence of the powers-that-be.
In Paris, Breton, Aragon, Éluard, Unik and others helped channel Buñuel's
political leanings towards Communism, and there were other left-wing associates too who were not members of the surrealist group. Yves Allegret, for
example, was an influential figure in the guerrilla October Group theatre and
a committed Trotskyist who had considered making a documentary about Las
Hurdes two years before Buñuel completed his. And he had been accompanied to the region by the communist Eli Lotar, who was subsequently
Buñuel's cameraman for the filming of *Las Hurdes*. It is also perfectly clear,
by his own admission, that he attended meetings of the Party, which suggests
the possibility, despite his own denials quoted earlier, that he was in fact a
paid-up member and, according to Francisco Aranda, continued to be so until
1937, when, on arrival in America, his subscription lapsed.[2] At all events,
Surrealism and Communism coincided in those areas that appealed to
Buñuel's aggressive, rebellious and uncompromising personality, and, in
particular, his hatred of the greed, vanity, and egotism that characterised the
prevailing bourgeois social order.

   This said, Buñuel was too much of an independent and anarchic spirit to
belong to any organisation, and it is no surprise that he separated from the
official surrealist group in 1932, convinced that its members had become in
their way too bourgeois:

> [. . .] it wasn't only the political dissension among the surrealists that
> cooled my ardour for the movement, but also their increasing snobbery,
> their strange attraction to the aristocracy [. . .] In addition, I wasn't too
> happy with the surrealist journal *Minotaure*, which had become increas-
> ingly slick and bourgeois. (Buñuel, 138–9)

But this is not to say that Buñuel abandoned surrealist, or for that matter,
communist principles. Indeed, for the rest of his life his films were essentially surrealist both in their emphasis on the world of dreams and in their
subversion of bourgeois values, while his communist sympathies also
remained strong for many years. Furthermore, his lifestyle, distinguished by
its austerity, largely reflected his anti-bourgeois stance. His house in Mexico

---

2   See Aranda, *Luis Buñuel: A Critical Biography*, 126.

City had nothing of the opulence or elegance of the bourgeois houses we encounter in such films as *L'Âge d'or*, *He*, *Viridiana*, *Tristana*, *Belle de jour*, *The Discreet Charm of the Bourgeoisie* or *That Obscure Object of Desire*. On the contrary, Carlos Fuentes has described its interior as being 'as impersonal as a dentist's office'.[3] On the second floor Buñuel's bedroom was as austere as a monk's cell, and the director, seventy-three at the time, slept on wooden boards, covering himself only with a rough blanket. It was a practice he had followed for many years, as his sister Conchita has described in relation to his stay in Madrid when, during the making of *Viridiana*, they stayed in the Torre de Madrid:

> [. . .] as always, Luis lived like an anchorite. Our apartment was on the seventeenth floor of the only skyscraper in the city, and he occupied the space like Simeon on his column [. . .] We had four beds, but he slept on the floor, with a sheet and a blanket and all the windows wide open.
>
> (Buñuel, 235)

The austerity of Buñuel's Mexican house had its counterpart in his dress and his habits. As Carlos Fuentes noted and photographs prove, he favoured 'short-sleeved sports shirts, grey cardigans, formless gabardine slacks'.[4] He invariably rose at 5 a.m. and went to bed at 9 p.m. He walked for two hours every day and regularly spent time in the gymnasium on the third floor of his house, his favourite pastime consisting of exercising on crutches, which he considered to be good for the spine. His taste in food was generally simple and, by his own admission, he derived more pleasure from two fried eggs with sausage than from *langoustes à la reine de Hongrie* or *timbales de caneton Chambord* (Buñuel, 228). And although alcohol was always one of Buñuel's greatest pleasures, he favoured drinking in bars that were distinguished by their silence and solitude. In addition, he hated publicity and did everything in his power to avoid it, including appearances at film festivals. Buñuel's way of life in general was therefore very different indeed both from the bourgeois environment to which he had been exposed in his father's house and from that which he portrays in many of his films. Carlos Fuentes noted that even after Buñuel's income greatly increased with the success of *Belle de jour*, the simplicity of his life was not affected.[5]

Buñuel's uncompromising attitude towards the bourgeoisie has been forcefully expressed both in his autobiography and elsewhere. In the former, as we have already seen, he has described the opposition of the surrealists to the society in which they found themselves (Buñuel, 107). As for himself, he was

---

[3] See Carlos Fuentes, 'The Discreet Charm of Luis Buñuel', in Mellen (ed.), *The World of Luis Buñuel: Essays in Criticism*, 62–4.

[4] Fuentes, 63–4.

[5] Fuentes, 64.

attracted in 1929 by what he regarded as the moral character of Surrealism, whose essence was to reject bourgeois society in favour of completely different values:

> What fascinated me most, however, in all our discussions at the Cyrano, was the moral aspect of the movement. [. . .] It was an aggressive morality based on the complete rejection of all existing values. We had other criteria: we exalted passion, mystification, black humour, the insult, and the call of the abyss. [. . .] Our morality may have been more demanding and more dangerous than the prevailing order, but it was also stronger, richer, and more coherent. (Buñuel, 107)

Later on, in response to a question put by a journalist, he explained more precisely what he meant by and what he found wrong with bourgeois morality:

> I am against conventional morality [. . .] Morality – middle-class morality, that is – is for me immoral. One must fight it. It is a morality founded on our most unjust social institutions – religion, fatherland, family culture – everything that people call the pillars of society.[6]

And again, more than four decades after turning his back on the surrealists, Buñuel observed that his view of the bourgeoisie had not changed:

> My ideas have not changed since I was 20. Basically, I agree with Engels: an artist describes real social relationships with the purpose of destroying the conventional ideas about those relationships, undermining bourgeois optimism, and forcing the public to doubt the tenets of the established order. The final sense of my films is this: to repeat, over and over again, in case anyone forgets it or believes the contrary, that we do not live in the best of all possible worlds.[7]

Most films, he noted elsewhere, embodied and, by so doing, propagated the values and institutions that he despised, ensuring their continuity:

> How is it possible to hope for an improvement in the audiences – and consequently in the producers – when consistently we are told in these films, including even the most insipid comedies, that our social institutions, our concepts of country, religion, love, etc., are, while perhaps imperfect, unique and necessary? The true 'opium of the audience' is conformity.[8]

---

6   See Donald Richie, 'The Moral Code of Luis Buñuel', in *The World of Luis Buñuel*, 111.
7   In Fuentes, 'The Discreet Charm of Luis Buñuel', 71.
8   See Luis Buñuel, 'On *Viridiana*', in *The World of Luis Buñuel*, 216.

His own films, throughout his career, set out to mock, disturb and undermine the established order of things. Indeed, he consistently places the bourgeoisie under the microscope, subjecting it to as close a scrutiny as he would have done the behaviour of insects, had he become an entomologist.

High on the list of Buñuel's favourite items for detailed examination, inside and outside, is the bourgeois home, be it country mansion or city house or apartment. The former makes its first extended appearance in *L'Âge d'or*, when, as cars bring guests to the villa of the Marquis of X, the camera picks out the huge wrought-iron gates and railings that surround the fortress-like pile immediately behind them. Thirty-two years later, a similar episode marks the beginning of *The Exterminating Angel* as the servants leave the splendid mansion of their master, Edmundo Nobile, and the camera reveals even more massive gates, which close with a huge clang, more suggestive of a castle than a house. Before this, as cars travel along Providence Street, Nobile's house is seen to have its equivalent in other houses, similarly protected by iron railings and gates. And when, in *The Diary of a Chamber-maid*, released two years later, Célestine arrives at the country mansion of her new employer, Monsieur Rabour, we observe gates and railings which, though less ornate than those in the two earlier films, are equally strong. In each case we are presented with an image that suggests the wealth and power of the bourgeois inhabitants of these houses who use that wealth to exclude unwelcome intruders and trespassers. On the other hand, the defences that they construct can also be seen as something that cuts them off from the world at large, turning them in on themselves, emphasising their self-containment and inward-looking nature. Buñuel's houses, furthermore, are not confined to one country, for the three mentioned above are located, respectively, in Italy, South America and France, the implication being that the bourgeoisie is much the same wherever it exists. Nor does the passage of time have much effect. Buñuel's bourgeois characters of 1930 are little different from those of 1962 and 1964, or indeed from those of *The Discreet Charm of the Bourgeoisie* in 1972. And the process continues today, for moneyed people build similar houses with similar defences, even if, in the case of pop stars, film stars and football players, their origin is not specifically bourgeois. And if they live in expensive city apartments rather than country mansions, they still protect and isolate themselves from the outside world by means of security locks and alarm systems. They live, in effect, in their own self-contained world.

As gates and railings suggest certain characteristics of bourgeois life, so do the gardens that lie immediately inside them. As the lovers of *L'Âge d'or* escape into the gardens of the Marquis of X, they do so along a pathway flanked by beautiful trees and, in the foreground, an elegant vase placed on a pedestal. At the end of the garden they approach a neatly cut hedge, behind which cypresses rise at regular intervals, and in front of which there are flower beds and wicker garden chairs placed on either side of a classical statue. When the focus of attention then moves from the lovers to the guests taking their seats for a concert in another part of the garden, the background is seen to consist of two neat diagonal lines of trees and, further away, a hedge cut into the form of an arch. Just afterwards, when the young man is called away to take a telephone call, we see too that the garden contains various classical busts on top of pedestals, as well as statues. In short, the gardens of the Marquis of X have a formality and elegance that reflect the importance of these characteristics in bourgeois life as a whole. All is meticulous and studied control.

Similarly, as Célestine approaches the Rabour mansion in *The Diary of a Chambermaid*, the front of the house is seen to be marked by a row of small trees in pots placed at regular intervals on either side of the front door and downstairs windows. The same kind of formality distinguishes the back of the house, for here a row of trees grow in the middle of a long flower bed. Moving away from the latter, the camera reveals a carefully maintained lawn at the centre of which is a statue on a plinth, and even if the trees which surround the lawn are tall, evidently old, and lack the symmetry of the area immediately surrounding the house, the overall impression is that the estate as a whole is carefully looked after, as other shots of the further reaches of the estate suggest. In other films, notably in *He* and *Viridiana*, Buñuel depicts neglected estates or gardens out of control in order to suggest the state of mind of their owners, but the formal garden described above is as much a part of his depiction of and comment on the nature of the bourgeoisie as the elegant interior of their houses.

The latter, to the fore in so many of Buñuel's major films, is suggested in the greatest of detail in shots of entrance halls, drawing-rooms, dining-rooms, bedrooms and corridors. In the central sequence of *L'Âge d'or*, Buñuel portrayed the kind of bourgeois drawing-room that would become familiar to audiences of his films much later on. A panoramic shot of the room in which the guests of the Marquis of X are gathered reveals at one end three floor-to-ceiling windows and, just in front of them, four substantial pillars, which support the ceiling. Heavy drapes drawn back around the windows are echoed elsewhere in the room by curtains around doorways and covering parts of the walls, upon which numerous painting, large and small, are displayed. Flower pots and classical busts are placed on pedestals, elegant tables and chairs are distributed around the room, and a few steps lead to an impressive balcony overlooking the gardens.

Thirty-four years later, a similar scenario occurs in *The Diary of a Chambermaid*, when, after her arrival at the Rabour mansion, Célestine is taken by his daughter, Madame Monteil, into a small drawing-room, which leads into its larger counterpart. As the camera follows the two women through these rooms, we are able to form a virtual inventory of their elegant and expensive contents: mirrors and paintings on the walls, classical busts, round polished tables, flower-filled vases, Persian rugs, intricately carved cabinets and

The Exterminating Angel: the bourgeoisie at home

chairs, and porcelain ornaments, which Célestine is either not allowed to touch or with which she must take great care. Indeed, the rooms and the objects they contain acquire something of the character of a temple and their sacred relics when Célestine is instructed by her mistress to remove her shoes before walking on the expensive carpet.

The bourgeois dining-room has particular pride of place in *Viridiana* and *The Exterminating Angel*. In the former, the absence of Viridiana and Jorge allows the beggars to enter the main house and make use of the dining-room in order to fill their stomachs. Their meal ends in chaos, with wine spilled, glasses and plates smashed, and food hurled around the room, but even so we are able to form a clear impression of this splendid room. The walls are faced with expensive wooden panelling and lined with elegant glass cabinets. Beautiful vases are placed on window sills, to either side of which are heavy curtains. A white lace cloth adorns the long table, the wine-glasses are of cut glass and the plates and dishes of the highest quality. At either end of the table are two candelabra, and the chairs on which the beggars are seated are beautifully carved. To one side, emphasising the good taste of the room as a whole, is a splendid leather sofa.

In *The Exterminating Angel*, the dining-room in which Nobile entertains his sophisticated guests is even more magnificent. The long table, echoing that in *Viridiana*, contains four candelabra. Plates and cutlery are perfectly arranged on the white table-cloth, a great chandelier occupies the centre of the ceiling, beautiful ornaments of various kinds adorn sideboards, and paintings and tapestries decorate the walls.

As well as revealing the wealth and elegance of bourgeois drawing and dining-rooms, Buñuel's camera also focuses on other areas and rooms in the houses in question. In *The Diary of a Chambermaid*, a shot of Célestine walking along a corridor shows it to be lined with vases and statues of great elegance, and when she takes tea to Monsieur Rabour in his library/study, it too is revealed to us in considerable detail: the leather-backed door, potted plants, more classical busts, shelves lined with books, and a large and ornate fireplace. In an almost imperceptible but very deliberate manner, Buñuel creates with his use of the camera a finely detailed picture of the material nature of these bourgeois establishments. Indeed, in all three films mentioned above the houses and their contents bear a striking similarity to a museum, which suggests in turn both lifelessness and coldness, a surface beauty and elegance that is no more than that, a glittering but otherwise superficial façade. And even if, in *Belle de jour, The Discreet Charm of the Bourgeoisie* and *That Obscure Object of Desire*, that façade is clearly more modern, its elegance is equally superficial. In *Belle de jour*, Séverine's bedroom, with its wall-lights, pictures and bedside table, is much less cluttered than the interiors of the three earlier films, but its more modern minimalism is equally an image of lives in which surface and façade are all-important.

Buñuel's portrayal of bourgeois houses, be they mansions and villas inhabited by wealthy aristocrats or smart apartments occupied by well-to-do professionals, is clearly characterised by a strong element of repetition, for similar interiors, objects and decoration are evident in many of his films. But it is important to understand that this in no way points to carelessness or laziness on Buñuel's part. On the contrary, his habit of creating bourgeois scenarios that echo each other is very deliberate, for it underlines his conviction that the bourgeoisie changes very little from one generation to another; is, indeed, rooted in a way of life of which one significant aspect is sameness and stagnation, something that is also reflected in bourgeois dress. When, for example, the guests arrive at the home of the Marquis of X in *L'Âge d'or*, the men without exception wear the customary morning-dress, as does the rebellious young man when he gatecrashes the dinner-party, for he knows full well that, in order to be accepted, he must at least appear to be indistinguishable from the other male guests.

Thirty-two years later, in *The Exterminating Angel*, nothing has changed, for the male guests at Nobile's home are in their dress identical to those in the earlier film. And later still, in *The Discreet Charm of the Bourgeoisie*, the men who arrive for dinner at the Colonel's house also wear dinner-jackets, though tails are no longer part of their formal attire. As for the female guests in these three films, fashion has changed rather more over the period of time in question, so that the women in *The Exterminating Angel* and *The Discreet Charm of the Bourgeoisie* look much more 'modern' and elegant than those in *L'Âge d'or*, although the formal evening gown is common to them all. As for more informal occasions, bourgeois attire has also remained much the same over many years. At home in his study, Monsieur Rabour wears a dressing-gown and cravat, as does Mattieu – minus cravat – thirteen years later in *That Obscure Object of Desire* when he attempts to make love to Conchita at his country house. Otherwise, the men in these films are invariably dressed in expensively tailored suits, the women in smart suits or dresses. In short, whatever the film in which the bourgeoisie plays a prominent part, dress acquires the character of a uniform, as much a mark of identity as that of a soldier or a priest. It is as much a façade as the elegance of the bourgeois house.

Closely connected with these two aspects of bourgeois life in Buñuel's microscopic analysis are bourgeois manners. When the guests in *L'Âge d'or* arrive at the Marquis of X's villa, they are greeted by their host and his wife with exemplary courtesy and formality, the former shaking hands with each male guest and kissing the hand of his wife, the guests reciprocating the gesture. Subsequently, they are engaged by their hosts and by other guests in conversation whose polite nature – this being a largely silent film – may be seen from their body language and their facial expressions. Their exchanges could almost be said to be choreographed in terms of posture, gesture and movement, and the same is true of *The Exterminating Angel* when we see Nobile's guests congregated in the drawing-room. Once again the immaculately dressed company is arranged in groups, individuals are introduced to others, and although, as we shall see, Buñuel deliberately introduces comments into their exchanges that are quite the opposite of what we would expect of people of their refinement, their dialogue is always beautifully shaped and quite as elegant in its form as those who speak it.

As well as possessing a constant formal elegance, which is in itself a kind of repetition, bourgeois conversation is also repetitive in its subject matter, for its range of topics are invariably limited and circumscribed by questions of good manners and propriety. Moving from one dinner-party and one drawing-room to another, the Marquis of X, Nobile, and others like them, repeat endlessly the same conversations. Furthermore, repetition is a constant of their activities as a whole. In *L'Âge d'or*, for example, cars draw up one after the other at the Marquis of X's villa, as they have done on many other occasions, and in *The Exterminating Angel* the process is repeated when a succession of cars deposits Nobile and his guests at the front door of his house. Their attendance at the opera, followed by dinner, is also something that they do regularly, as is the repeated dining out practised by the six characters of *The Discreet Charm of the Bourgeoisie*. The point is emphasised even more when, in *The Exterminating Angel*, Nobile and his guests enter the house and then repeat the exercise, as does Nobile himself when he proposes a toast to Silvia and, apparently forgetting that he has already done so, toasts her again a few moments later. As well as this, the characters of this film, trapped in the drawing-room for several weeks, succeed in escaping only when they find themselves in positions identical to those immediately prior to their entrapment. And some time later, their earlier situation is repeated when, having entered a church to give thanks for their deliverance, they discover that they are unable to leave. On the element of repetition in human behaviour, Buñuel has made the following observation:

> In everyday life we repeat ourselves every day. Every morning we get up, we brush our teeth with the same brush and with the same hand and movements, we sit at the same breakfast table, we go to the same office, meet the same people [. . .] And how many times has it happened in a party where we say hello to someone and an hour later we again shake hands, say hello, and then exclaim, 'Oh, what are we doing, we just said hello a minute ago.'[9]

The point is, however, that if repetition of the kind described is part and parcel of the everyday lives of ordinary human beings, Buñuel transforms it, when practised by the bourgeoisie, into pure ritual, a kind of codified form of behaviour which, practised from generation to generation, has become the very essence of their way of life. But if this is so, it is also the case that the rituals in which this class of people are so immersed – polite chit-chat, dinner-parties, visits to restaurants and the theatre – are as superficial and as empty of true meaning as the elegance of the houses in which they live and the objects that adorn them: in short, a façade which, from film to film, Buñuel constructs in the greatest detail.

His more important objective is, though, to expose in no uncertain fashion the reality that lies behind the façade when this is stripped away, a reality that manifests itself to the full in *L'Âge d'or*. As mentioned previously, three important incidents occur while the Marquis of X and his guests are engaged in polite conversation in the drawing-room. Firstly, a horse-driven cart containing two drunken peasants lumbers noisily through the room; secondly, a screaming female servant, attempting to escape a fire that has broken out in the kitchen, collapses at the feet of the assembled company; and thirdly, the Marquis's gardener shoots and kills his small son when he steals and runs off with his cigarette. Neither of the first two incidents succeeds in distracting the group. As for the third, the sound of the shot draws them to the balcony, from which they observe the bloodstained face of the dead boy, but their

---

[9]   See Juan Luis Buñuel, 'A Letter on *The Exterminating Angel*', in *The World of Luis Buñuel*, 255.

reaction to the incident is what Buñuel wishes to emphasise. The camera, moving in close-up from left to right along the line of bourgeois faces, reveals at most a mild disapproval of what has occurred, as if to suggest that such barbarity is only to be expected of individuals outside their social circle. Nor does the murder of the boy hold their attention for more than a few moments, for they soon return to the drawing-room in order to renew their sadly interrupted conversations. All three episodes, therefore, underline Buñuel's view of bourgeois self-absorption and indifference to the fate of others.

This particular point is emphasised even more strongly in *Las Hurdes*, which suggests by implication that the powers-that-be have for many years turned a blind eye to the human misery that exists in the region. Furthermore, as we have already seen, the reaction to the film of a largely bourgeois audience at its first screening in Madrid was extremely cool, and that of the influential Dr Gregorio Marañón at a subsequent private screening was decidedly hostile. These were individuals who were doubtless uncomfortably aware of their long-standing indifference to the problems of the area in question, but, even so, still resolved to interest themselves only in their own affairs, to the exclusion of all else. Indeed, the reaction to any intrusion into the activities of the bourgeoisie is vividly illustrated in *L'Âge d'or* when the young man arrives at the dinner-party, his thoughts focused entirely on the young woman. Annoyed by her mother when she engages him in conversation, thereby distracting him from his quest, and further enraged when she accidentally spills a glass of wine over his clothes, the young man slaps her face and is immediately pounced upon, manhandled and ejected from the room by the other guests. In short, the bourgeoisie, determined to protect itself and maintain the status quo, ruthlessly rejects all those who threaten its conventional values. We are at once reminded of the behaviour of the scorpion in the film's opening documentary sequence, for it too, as a title reminds us, 'rejects the intruder who arrives to disturb its solitude'. The bourgeoisie, Buñuel suggests, is just as poisonous in its reaction.

This incident is also indicative, of course, of bourgeois intolerance, of which examples occur throughout Buñuel's films, not least in response to what the bourgeoisie regards as sexual impropriety, which usually means an open display of erotic feelings. The first example occurs in *Un Chien andalou* when the androgynous female is seen in the street prodding an amputated hand with a stick and observed by a crowd of people who are held back by two policemen. Shortly afterwards, one of the policemen speaks to the young woman, clearly reprimands her for her behaviour, and places the hand in the box that she carries with her. The implication of this dream-like episode is, quite clearly, that a public display of sexual activity will not be tolerated, and it is no coincidence either that it is forbidden by the police, instrument of the bourgeoisie in many Buñuel films, or that a few moments later the young woman is killed by a car, an incident that may be seen not only as Buñuel's desire to put paid to the kind of sexually aggressive woman he feared, but also as the revenge of bourgeois society on a woman who has caused grave offence.

Other examples occur in *L'Âge d'or* and *Tristana*. In the former, the lovers, locked in a passionate embrace on the ground while the formal ceremony of laying the foundation stone is being conducted close by, are set upon and dragged apart as soon as they are spotted by the crowd. In the latter, Tristana and her lover, Horacio, are seen kissing at night in a quiet street by a middle-aged husband and his wife and daughter. The husband, described in the filmscript as a *'bourgeois of mature age who has the appearance of a bureaucrat or a businessman'*, takes them to task: 'That sort of thing should be done indoors.'[10] He puts into words in this respect the actions of the policeman towards the young woman in *Un Chien andalou*.

Bourgeois intolerance towards the sexual behaviour of others does not mean, however, that the bourgeoisie is averse to indulging itself in similar activities, especially in private, and, in the case of married couples, behind the back of the husband or wife. In *L'Âge d'or* the young woman's father is seen in his laboratory shaking a bottle half full of liquid in a manner that is strongly suggestive of masturbation and, perhaps, sexual fantasy. In *The Exterminating Angel* Eduardo and Beatriz, who have not met previously and both of whom are to be married to others in a few days' time, soon become lovers who express their passion for each other hidden in a cupboard, away from the attentions of their fellow guests. In *The Diary of a Chambermaid* Monsieur Monteil is a sexual predator who is determined to get his hands on Séverine behind his wife's back, while the latter, rather like the Marquis of X, conducts strange experiments with tubes and flasks in the privacy of her bathroom. Again, in *Belle de jour* bourgeois individuals such as the gynae-cologist, no doubt a highly respected member of his profession, indulge their fantasies behind closed doors in the privacy of the brothel, this particular individual demanding that the prostitute, Charlotte, first beat him with his own leather whip, then walk on him as he lies prostrate on the floor. In another episode, which appears to be one of Séverine's dreams or daydreams, a Duke, in the seclusion of his country house, persuades her to play the part of his dead daughter and to lie in a coffin, naked apart from a black veil, while he, after placing flowers on her, masturbates beneath it. And in *Tristana*, Don Lope is, to all appearances, the guardian of the young, orphaned girl, but, away from the public gaze, he quickly makes her yield to his sexual advances in the privacy of his bedroom. Buñuel thus presents us with an entire gallery of bourgeois characters who, for all their surface respectability and, in many cases, intolerance of the behaviour of others, show little hesitation in indulging in the very things they condemn.

---

10 See Buñuel, *Tristana*, 83.

This suggests, of course, hypocrisy, and Don Lope is certainly guilty of it, for between his public and private behaviour there is often a considerable gulf. In conversation with his friends in a café, he claims that all women are fair game for a man's sexual advances, except for the wife of a friend or an innocent girl, but this does not prevent him from making the young and naive Tristana his mistress. Again, he claims to despise material wealth, but is more than delighted when he inherits his sister's money, for this, after a period of relative deprivation, allows him once more to live in his accustomed style. And thirdly, in spite of the fact that, shortly after taking Tristana into his care, he vows to rid her of what he regards as religious superstition, he ends up by spending his winter evenings in the company of priests who are quite as hypocritical as himself, for their apparent interest in his welfare and state of health merely disguises their desire to drink his chocolate and to persuade him to remember them in his will.

Hypocrisy is also the hallmark of the Ambassador of Miranda in *The Discreet Charm of the Bourgeoisie*. Here is a diplomat who represents a poor, backward, starving, South American banana republic, but who in his private life craves money, food and women. Condemning the use of marihuana when offered it by an army colonel, he is in reality a major drug pusher. Again, holding a female terrorist at gunpoint in his apartment, he takes advantage of the need to search her for weapons in order to touch her breasts and genitals, and, shortly afterwards, his apparent generosity in letting her go is followed by his signal to the police to arrest her in the street. And finally, although the episode proves to be a nightmare in which terrorists break into the Ambassador's house and shoot everyone but him, his insatiable craving for food is revealed when, concealed beneath the table and in fear for his life, he cannot resist reaching up for a piece of roast meat, which he greedily devours. The disparity between the Ambassador's private and public life could not be greater.

While some of the bourgeois activities mentioned earlier consist of private sexual indulgence or the pursuit of fantasies that border on the perverse, other bourgeois characters are shown by Buñuel to be addicted to certain forms of fetishism. This, in relation to sexual behaviour, refers to the pleasure derived from focusing the attention on a part of the human body or on a piece of clothing belonging to a particular person, a pleasure that is vividly portrayed in *He*, *Viridiana* and *The Diary of a Chambermaid*. The first of these three films begins with its male protagonist, Francisco, observing a priest washing the feet of altar boys. His gaze, matched by the movement of the camera, travels along the line of naked male feet and eventually stops at a woman's shoe-clad feet before moving upwards from feet to legs to the face of Gloria, the woman he will soon marry. In *Viridiana*, as mentioned previously, Don Jaime keeps his dead wife's clothes in a large chest, frequently putting on her shoes and wrapping her corset around his waist. And in *The Diary of a Chambermaid*, Monsieur Rabour keeps in a cupboard a collection of women's boots and shoes which, at his request, Célestine puts on. As she reads to him, he strokes the boots, calls her Marie, and has her walk up and down in front of him. Later on he is found dead in bed, half naked and clutching a pair of boots. In the case of Don Jaime and Rabour items of clothing and footwear have become a substitute for a dead wife and, presumably, a past lover, in both instances the female substituted by an object without which sexual satisfaction cannot be achieved. With regard to Fernando, the situation is more complex. His focusing on Gloria's feet may well point to his fear of actual physical contact with a woman, the fetish being the safer option, a possibility reinforced by the fact that his subsequent marriage to her drives him into a state of total paranoia. At all events, Buñuel seems to suggest that the fetishes described above are the special if not exclusive province of the bourgeoisie, a further example of lives that are empty, sterile, and often pathetic.[11]

Bourgeois society, because it is basically patriarchal, is also shown by Buñuel to relegate women to a position of secondary importance. To a large extent, this attitude towards women may be attributed to the influence of the Church, which in the past has played a significant part in bourgeois education, as we have already seen in relation to Buñuel himself. For the fathers of Christianity, such as St Paul, woman was important only in the sense that she could bring children into the world, thereby contributing to the continuity of the Christian flock. It is an attitude that explains in part the relatively large size of the family in Catholic countries in particular, and also the domestic role of the mother. As well as this, the Church's condemnation of sexual relations as a source of pleasure had the effect of dividing women into two categories: dutiful wives on the one hand, and women of much lesser moral fibre, including prostitutes, on the other. It is a view which, deeply rooted in the psyche of Catholic countries in particular, continues today to label women either as saints or whores, and when this is combined with the traditional view of the male as head of the family, its effect in reducing the female to an inferior role, be she dutiful wife, beautiful accessory or casual plaything, is very clear.

In *L'Âge d'or*, the elegant bourgeois women who accompany their dinner-jacketed husbands to the Marquis of X's dinner-party are little more than accessories, helped out of the car on arrival, clinging to their spouse's arm as they enter the house, smiling and paying dutiful attention to the men's conversation but clearly playing little serious part in it. And much the same can be said of the women in *The Exterminating Angel* and *The Discreet Charm of the Bourgeoisie*. Séverine, in *Belle de jour*, has a flawless beauty and a beautiful wardrobe, which make her the most elegant wife in the whole of Buñuel's cinema, but, as we have already seen, her bourgeois husband fails

---

[11] On fetishism and paranoia in Buñuel's films, see Evans, *The Films of Luis Buñuel: Subjectivity and Desire*, 111–24.

to treat her as a woman of flesh and blood, seriously neglecting her deep sexual desires.

Women as the victims of male exploitation are also, of course, very frequent. Tristana is used by Don Lope for his sexual gratification and, because she is financially dependent on him, she is initially unable to escape. But he also uses her as a servant, for although at one moment he objects to her mopping up some spilt cleaning-fluid on the grounds that it is not her job to do so, he is more than happy for her to bring him his slippers and to kneel before him in order to put them on his feet. And, thirdly, he undoubtedly regards her as an attractive accessory, a young woman for whom he buys quite elegant clothes, and whom he likes to show off when they go out walking. Similarly, Viridiana, the totally innocent novice nun, becomes the object of the sexual desires of Don Jaime and his more predatory son, Jorge. Drugged by the former so that he can possess her, she is, after his death, subjected to Jorge's sexual innuendo. And when, at the end of the film, she becomes his mistress, sharing him with the servant, Ramona, it is perfectly clear that both women will be dispensed with when Jorge has tired of them, for earlier on he has done precisely that with another young woman. His predatory nature in this respect is suggested by Buñuel when Jorge's advances to Ramona in the attic of the house are immediately followed by a shot of a cat pouncing on a mouse.

Sexual motives, which reduce the significance of a woman to that of a sex-aid, also dominate the bourgeois male characters of *The Diary of a Chambermaid* and *That Obscure Object of Desire*. In the former, as we have seen, Célestine is required by Rabour to wear the boots which he keeps in a cupboard, but any woman would serve his purpose, for his thoughts as he strokes and kisses the boots are on Marie, who seems to belong to his past. And when she is not performing this service for Rabour, she is frequently pestered by his son-in-law, Monsieur Monteil, who has evidently made similar advances to Célestine's predecessors. As for *That Obscure Object of Desire*, Conchita is seen by the bourgeois Mathieu not as a woman to be loved and respected for herself, but simply as a body to be possessed sexually. He pursues her relentlessly, spending considerable amounts of money to that end, following her from Paris to Seville, and finally buying a small house where he can visit her. But there is no suggestion in his behaviour that he sees her as anything but a sexual challenge. Indeed, he belongs to a generation which saw, and which probably still sees, single women in this way, and in that particular regard he is no different from Don Lope in *Tristana*. Against this, of course, it could be argued that men who are of an altogether lower class and of lesser education also see women in the same light, but the fact remains that the wealth, power and sophistication of the bourgeoisie allows it to pursue and indulge its desires with much greater resolve and cunning.

While Buñuel pillories the bourgeoisie for all the things mentioned above, he also highlights its complacency, emotional paralysis and lack of imagination. As to the first point, there is a striking moment in *L'Âge d'or* when, shortly after the arrival of his guests and in apparently earnest conversation with two of them, the Marquis of X is seen in close-up to have a number of flies on his face. Nothing, however, can ruffle bourgeois complacency, and he continues the conversation as if the flies did not exist, a point that is reinforced by the indifference of the group as a whole to the three incidents which then follow and which have been referred to earlier: the appearance of the rustic cart, the collapse of the terrified servant, and the gardener's shooting of his son. Even the latter fails to attract the attention of the Marquis's guests for more than a few moments, after which they return to the drawing-room as if nothing unusual had occurred. Similarly, in *The Exterminating Angel* Nobile's bourgeois companions complacently accept the fact that they are unable to leave the drawing-room at the end of the evening. They merely sit around, remove their jackets when it is time to go to sleep, and, when daylight arrives, attempt to continue their normal activities. After weeks of captivity and lacking food and water, they become desperate and bourgeois sophistication is transformed into animal savagery, but release from their plight quickly restores their habitual complacency, for when we see them in church they are once again their former selves, and when they find they cannot leave the church any more than they could the drawing-room, they appear to be quite unruffled.

Complacency goes hand in hand with a lack of genuine passion, for these are people who, as the consequence of their education and upbringing, have been taught the importance of restraint, reserve and self-control to such an extent that these characteristics have become a way of life. The male protagonist of *Un Chien andalou*, identified by his dark grey suit and tie as essentially bourgeois, is, as we have seen, unable to respond to the young woman who desires him. And Pierre, Séverine's reserved and cold husband in *Belle de jour*, is unable to arouse her. Both men could not be more different from the eager, passionate young man of *L'Âge d'or*, or more like the stiff, reserved guests of the Marquis of X who, as the orchestra plays, sit in neat rows of chairs while, in another part of the garden, the young man and his beloved indulge their desperate feelings for each other. Indeed, when true, uninhibited passion manifests itself, the bourgeoisie seeks to stifle it, as do the onlookers in the case of the androgynous female prodding the dismembered hand in *Un Chien andalou*, and those disturbed by the lovers' ecstatic cries in the early part of *L'Âge d'or*. Certainly, we cannot imagine the Marquis and his guests behaving as the lovers do. And although the young woman in the latter is, for most of the time, as responsive to the feelings of the young man as he is to hers, she ultimately reverts to her more restrained and 'correct' way of life when, as if responding to a sudden attack of conscience and guilt, she abandons him and returns to the bosom of her family.

There are, though, as we have seen, various bourgeois characters in Buñuel's films who are the very opposite of the inhibited young man of *Un*

Chien andalou. Jorge in *Viridiana*, the Ambassador in *The Discreet Charm of the Bourgeoisie*, and Mathieu in *That Obscure Object of Desire*, are certainly not restrained in their pursuit of women. They play a large part in Jorge's activities, and the three we encounter in the course of the film are evidently only a small proportion of those he has pursued and will pursue during his adult life. In the case of the Ambassador, he makes advances not only to the female terrorist but also to the wife of Monsieur Thévenot. And Mathieu, as we already know, devotes a considerable amount of his time to pursuing and attempting to possess Conchita. But, this said, none of these men are driven by the kind of passion felt by the young man of *L'Âge d'or* or Alejandro in *Wuthering Heights*. On the contrary, their attempts to seduce the women in question amount to little more than a game in which there is a great deal of calculation and very little, if any, genuine feeling. They have that coldness and, in the final analysis, emptiness that Buñuel saw as being typical of bourgeois life.

The repetitious and stereotyped nature of bourgeois activity suggests, in addition, a lack of imagination. Throughout Buñuel's films, elegant houses echo each other, one dinner-party is much like another, encounters, gestures, and conversations are constantly repeated, and little happens that is unpredictable. In such circumstances there is clearly little scope for the imagination, which implies the very opposite of activities that are dull, repetitious and devoid of excitement. For Buñuel, imagination was, for obvious reasons, synonymous with freedom, for, like dreams and fantasies, it allows man to escape the shackles of reason and conventional morality:

> When I was younger, my so-called conscience forbade me to entertain certain images – like fratricide, for instance, or incest. I'd tell myself these were hideous ideas and push them out of my mind. But when I reached the age of sixty, I finally understood the perfect innocence of the imagination . . . I was free to let my imagination go wherever it chose. (Buñuel, 174–5)

In *L'Âge d'or* imagination allows the young man, in the hands of the two brutal policeman and separated from his beloved, to transform advertisements into her image and thus to transcend time and space, while she, gazing into the mirror in her bedroom and thinking of him, sees not her own image but the romantic landscape of her dreams. In this respect, imagination has a positive, creative function, for it sustains and motivates the lovers, adding to the richness of their lives. It is difficult to visualise the Marquis of X and his circle behaving in such a way.

As well as attributing to the bourgeoisie the litany of faults and deficiencies described above, Buñuel also takes great delight in shocking its complacency to the very foundations. Sometimes this takes the form of outrageous and unacceptable behaviour on the part of particular individuals, as in the case of *L'Âge d'or*, when the unrestrained ardour of the lovers disrupts the ceremony of laying the foundation stone, and when, later on, the enraged young man slaps the wife of the Marquis of X across the face. On both occasions bourgeois formality is seriously undermined. Again, in *Viridiana*, the drunken behaviour of the beggars, which almost wrecks the elegant dining-room of Don Jaime's house, is an unwelcome shock to Jorge and Viridiana when they return to the house. And in *Tristana*, the episode in which Tristana and Horacio kiss in public certainly ruffles the feathers of the bourgeois family that witnesses it.

Much more common, though, is the disruption of the normal pattern of bourgeois life by unpredictable and unexpected events, of which *The Exterminating Angel* offers a number of relevant examples. Firstly, before Nobile and his guests arrive at his house for dinner, the servants and cooks decide to leave for unexplained reasons, much to the consternation of their masters and thereby disrupting preparations for the rest of the evening. At the end of the evening, as we have seen, Nobile's guests prepare to leave for their respective homes but are inexplicably unable to leave the drawing-room. And prior to this, we see that their conversation, although distinguished by the shape and formal structure that normally characterises bourgeois dialogue, is shot through with unintended comments and observations, as if they have no control over what they are saying. Such is the exchange between Raul and the Doctor:

> RAUL: Poor Leonora! . . . How is her cancer? Is there any hope?
> DOCTOR: None. In three months she'll be completely bald.

And just afterwards, Juana is in conversation with Juan:

> JUANA: It's your fourth child?
> CHRISTIAN: I don't know. I've lost count.
> JUANA: And you're sure who the father is? (*Pause.*) I mean . . .
> CHRISTIAN: You'd better ask her . . .

Quite clearly, this loss of control over what one says, in complete contrast to the good manners and total control normally exercised by the bourgeoisie, is disturbing for them and it is also, of course, a rich source of mocking humour for Buñuel himself.

Disturbances of a rather different kind occur in *The Discreet Charm of the Bourgeoisie*. Here, the attempts of the six bourgeois characters to have dinner – symptomatic in itself of bourgeois greed and materialism – are thwarted by a series of misunderstandings and chance events. In the very first sequence, the Ambassador, Monsieur and Madame Thévenot, and the latter's sister, Florence, arrive for dinner at the elegant home of Monsieur and Madame Sénéchal, but do so on the wrong evening. In order not to miss out on dinner, they immediately take the embarrassed hosts to a nearby restaurant only to discover that no preparations have been made because the owner has just died and his corpse is laid out in the next room. These failures are followed by a third when the Ambassador, Monsieur and Madame Thévenot, and Florence visit the Sénéchal house once more, this time for lunch. As they arrive, the hosts are still getting dressed, but then, overcome by a sudden erotic impulse, they remove their clothes and begin to make love, obliging their puzzled guests to wait downstairs. Furthermore, unable to restrain their feelings for each other but also anxious not to have their guests hear Madame Sénéchal's ecstatic cries, they depart the house by climbing down from the bedroom and disappearing into the garden, leaving their visitors high and, literally, dry.

The same characters are then subjected to three further disappointments and shocks. When the three women order tea in an elegant tea-room, the waiter returns to inform them that there is only coffee, and, not long afterwards, that it has run out too. In addition, while they are waiting for the coffee, they are subjected to a harrowing tale told by a young army lieutenant who describes how, at the instigation of his dead mother, he poisoned the man he has always believed to be his father, but who in reality was his natural father's murderer. Little wonder that the three women leave the tea-room shaken and without a drink. On another occasion, as the group attend the Sénéchal house yet again for a meal, they are interrupted by the arrival of fifteen soldiers, and, after they have turned waiter in order to feed them, by the sudden commencement of military exercises, including heavy shelling. And finally, when they once more sit down to lunch at the Sénéchal's, they are unexpectedly arrested and taken away to the police station.

In all, the characters of *The Discreet Charm* fail to enjoy their meal on six occasions, but, as well as this, they are also thwarted in this respect in their dreams. Indeed, in both *The Exterminating Angel* and *The Discreet Charm* Buñuel uses dream and nightmare in a variety of ingenious ways both to shock and to undermine bourgeois complacency. In the first of these two films, Ana is asleep on a sofa but clearly very agitated. She slowly sits up, her face bathed in perspiration, while in the background the loud ticking of a clock is heard, and then a continuous creaking. As she opens her eyes, her attention is drawn to a cupboard, which opens slowly and from which a white severed hand drops to the floor and begins to slide towards her. It disappears beneath a table, but then reappears, wriggling and writhing under the scarf that she has thrown onto the surface of the table, and then falling to the floor again. As it slides away from her, she attempts to strike it with a bronze statuette. The clock strikes three, its ticking grows even louder, and then, without warning, the hand climbs up the front of her body and begins to choke her. She throws it onto the table and attempts to stab it with a long knife but it moves away, at which point the lights go on and the other guests are seen standing around her. In this immensely powerful sequence, highly Freudian in its implications, the elegant façade of bourgeois elegance is stripped away as the fears and anxieties – no doubt sexual – buried in the unconscious mind come to the surface, leaving the individual in question in no doubt, whatever his or her apparent self-assurance, that there are within them powerful and often shameful things that they cannot control.[12]

As time passes and these trapped individuals are gradually overtaken by panic and hysteria, the kind of dream that Ana experiences becomes a more general nightmare. As the camera moves slowly around the drawing-room, all the guests are seen to be asleep or drowsing, some lying on sofas, some on chairs and others on the floor. The tolling of bells is heard, followed by screams and cries, all of them suggestive of anguish and desperation. Voices then begin to sing the Te Deum and vocal effects are accompanied by a series of disturbing visual images. A close-up of Leticia's head becomes that of Raul superimposed on a cloudy sky to the accompaniment of a horrible grinding sound. More voices cry out in agony, a saw cuts through a tree trunk, a hacksaw slices through the strings of a cello, another saw cuts through the fingers of a hand, and this in turn becomes a hacksaw opening up a woman's head, the visual impact of these images reinforced by the sound of the saws. As in the earlier sequence concerning Ana, all these sounds and images are inside the heads of the characters, pointing to their deepest and, perhaps, unacknowledged fears and phobias. For all their wealth and self-importance, these people are at bottom little different from the under-privileged urban children of *The Forgotten Ones*, in which Pablo's nightmare, in which he sees himself struggling with the older and violent Jaibo for a piece of meat held out by Pablo's mother, is a projection of his fear of his rejection by her, as well as a recollection of Jaibo's murder of another boy, in which Pablo was an accomplice. In making the connection, Buñuel is, of course, pricking the bubble of bourgeois self-importance, but he also takes great delight in subjecting the bourgeoisie to such horrors in order to under-mine its habitual self-satisfaction and frighten it out of its wits.

In *The Discreet Charm of the Bourgeoisie*, as noted previously, the charac-ters' quest for a good dinner is unsuccessful in their dreams as well as in reality, as though their persistent failures become a kind of nightmare. The first dream is set up by Buñuel quite ingeniously, for what we, the cinema audience, initially consider to be a real event is revealed to be Sénéchal's dream, but this in turn is later seen to be Thévenot's dream of Sénéchal dreaming of himself and his companions arriving for dinner at the house of the Colonel, the commander of the troops who had earlier interrupted their meal. In what seems to be Sénéchal's dream, there are from the outset discon-certing elements, for the whisky proves to be coca-cola, and the chickens are made of cardboard. Without further ado, moreover, the guests discover that they are not in a dining-room but on the stage of a theatre, for the curtains to

---

[12] Buñuel's suggestion for a crawling hand was incorporated into Robert Florey's Hollywood film of 1945, *The Beast with Five Fingers*.

The Discreet Charm of the Bourgeoisie: a bourgeois nightmare

one side of the room suddenly part to reveal the audience in their seats, while a prompter whispers to those on stage the opening line of the play.

This bizarre event is seen to be a dream only when Sénéchal wakes up. Almost immediately he receives a telephone call from Thévenot, who informs him that he and his friends are already at the Colonel's house, waiting for Sénéchal and his wife to arrive. The evening at the Colonel's home is, as is to be expected, typically bourgeois in terms of its stylised conversation and polite exchanges, but an argument breaks out between the Ambassador and the Colonel in the course of which the Colonel strikes the Ambassador and, in response, the Ambassador shoots him three times. It is clearly the horrific nature of the incident that finally awakens Thévenot from his sleep, much relieved, though shaken, in the knowledge that the traumatic episode has been but a dream.

The final sequences of the film reveal the group arriving for dinner once more at the Sénéchal home. No sooner are they seated at the table, however, than the sound of breaking glass is heard and three terrorists burst into the dining-room, pointing their guns at the bourgeois group, apart from the Ambassador who has quickly concealed himself beneath the table. The terrorists quickly mow down the five individuals standing in front of them, and then their leader draws attention to the hand of the Ambassador, which reaches up from beneath the tablecloth for a piece of roast meat. As a loud burst of gunfire shatters the silence, the Ambassador wakes up in his bed, his hands in a defensive position, shouting, his jaws champing at a piece of imaginary meat. Agitated and sweating profusely, but comforted by the knowledge that his assassination was only a dream, he consoles himself further by going to the kitchen where he finds some cold meat in the refrigerator. He proceeds to consume the only completed meal in the film.

In *The Discreet Charm of the Bourgeoisie*, in particular, Buñuel also ruffles the poise of his bourgeois characters by having them listen to a number of unnerving horror tales. The story told in the tea-room by the army lieutenant describes, as we have seen, his murder of his 'father' when he discovers that he is the murderer of his real father. He tells the three women how his dead mother appeared to him one night, revealing to him that her first husband was killed in a duel by her present husband and that she wants him poisoned. Obedient to his mother, the boy introduces the poison into a glass of milk, and his 'father' dies in agony, collapsing on his bed. The story is, of course, narrated to the listening audience, and the images we see on screen – much more vivid than words – clearly correspond to those in the lieutenant's imagination. At all events, the story's Oedipal implications, dark undercurrents and its elements of 'grand guignol' are certainly sufficient to disrupt the polite chat of the three bourgeois women and the sophisticated ambience of the tea-room.

Similarly, after the sudden arrival of soldiers has disrupted the meal at the Sénéchal home, the Sergeant insists on describing to the assembled company a recent dream, which we, the cinema audience, see in flash-back. In the dream in question the Sergeant finds himself in a dark and deserted street where he meets a pale young man who smells of the earth and who tells him that, having lived in the street for six years, he will do so forever. When the Sergeant then enters a dark shop, he encounters a second young man who informs him that the individual he has just met has been dead for six years, and, shortly afterwards, a young woman whom he accuses of having rejected him but who now embraces him. The Sergeant then enters another shop, vainly searching for the first young man, and emerges only to find that the second young man and the woman are no longer in the street. As tears stream down his face, he calls out for his mother, for whom he is searching. This story, much less clearly structured than the one described earlier, but powerful in its emphasis on death and solitude, is certainly dark and suggestive enough to put the bourgeoisie off its food.

Buñuel, then, uses dreams and horror stories to disturb the elegant surface of bourgeois behaviour, but, in doing so, he also makes a complacent bourgeoisie aware that there are things buried deep in its own unconscious that it may prefer to hide or ignore, but which at any moment may rise to the surface. He delights, of course, in this method of subversion, and even if, in the end, a character like the Ambassador is able to seek temporary refuge from his nightmare of annihilation in a piece of meat, there still exists the possibility that that nightmare might return.

A rather different threat to bourgeois composure is to be found in political activity of different kinds, as the terrorist attack in *The Discreet Charm* suggests. Indeed, the bourgeoisie seems in Buñuel's films to be constantly on edge, ever aware of its vulnerability to outside forces that threaten its conservative way of life. For this reason, as we have seen, it goes to considerable lengths to protect itself by means of walls, railings and gates against all manner of intruders, be they burglars, terrorists or revolutionaries, but the threat of disruption is always present. In *Rehearsal for a Crime: The Criminal Life of Archibaldo de la Cruz*, Archibaldo is the child of rich bourgeois parents and is left one night, as often happens, in the care of his governess, while, having appeased the child with the gift of a musical box, his parents go to the theatre. During their absence, the governess tells Archibaldo the story of a king who could rid himself of his enemies simply by opening a musical box, and shortly afterwards, as the boy opens his new gift, the governess dies in front of him. Although he believes that he is responsible for her death and that thereafter he has the power of life or death over all women, the governess is in reality killed by a stray bullet from the street where a revolution has broken out. In other words, although the causes of Archibaldo's behaviour in adult life are complex and attributable to a number of factors in his childhood, revolution plays a significant and disruptive part in shaping it.

Similarly, a revolution breaks out in the streets at the end of *The Exterminating Angel* as Nobile, his friends and many other worshippers find themselves unable to leave the church. Bullets rip through the air, soldiers attempt to break up the crowds outside, and, as the film ends, church bells toll ominously. In other words, the bourgeois individuals, whose complacency has been shaken by their incarceration in Nobile's house and the realisation that, beneath the surface, they are little more than savages, are now, though apparently calm at the prospect of a further imprisonment, surrounded by forces that may well get out of control and threaten their very existence.

Central and South America are, of course, parts of the world in which, especially in the past, the threat of revolution and bourgeois apprehension of it were relatively constant, lending themselves naturally to Buñuel's subversive aims. But he does not restrict this kind of danger to his Mexican films, for, as we have seen, terrorism figures prominently in *The Discreet Charm of the Bourgeoisie*. At one point, for example, the female terrorist who later finds her way into the Ambassador's apartment is seen in the street where, in order to conceal her real purpose, she pretends to be selling toys. Spotting her from his window, the Ambassador recognises her as a member of a group of South American terrorists who have been pursuing him for some time, produces a rifle, and fires some shots from the window, forcing her to flee in a waiting car. Although he appears decisive and relatively calm here, the presence of terrorists who could kidnap or even kill him evidently preoccupies him, for, as we have seen, he dreams the later sequence of the film in which the terrorists break into his house in order to murder him and his friends.

Five years later, in *That Obscure Object of Desire*, terrorist activities are again in evidence, for, as Mathieu sits in his car in a quiet residential area of Seville in one of the film's early sequences, a terrorist bomb explodes nearby, destroying the vehicle containing a wealthy bourgeois on his way to a bank. Later on, as Mathieu arrives at his country house near Paris, bent on making love to Conchita, police cars race past in response to a terrorist attack on a power-station. And, at the end of the film, when he and Conchita are window-shopping, a loudspeaker announcement warns of the activities of left-wing extremist groups who have carried out numerous atrocities, including an assassination attempt on the Archbishop of Sienna, and who have provoked an equally violent response from right-wing extremist groups. The announcement precedes an even bigger explosion than that towards the beginning of the film. And if, in one sense, the explosions that occur at intervals suggest Mathieu's desire for Conchita and its disruptive effect on him, they also point to the unease that revolutionary or terrorist movements create in the bourgeois mind. Indeed, it is no coincidence that both *The Discreet Charm of the Bourgeoisie* and *That Obscure Object of Desire* were made after the left-wing student riots in Paris in 1968, for Buñuel, who was in Paris at the time checking locations for *The Milky Way*, saw clear parallels between the students and the surrealists of the 1920s and 1930s (Buñuel, 125). The student opposition to traditional conservative values, which undoubtedly created apprehension in French bourgeois circles, was thus a direct influence in relation to Buñuel's aim in these films to disrupt the otherwise tranquil façade of the middle and upper classes.

As the preceding argument suggests, Buñuel's scrutiny of the bourgeoisie is comprehensive and minute, engaging his attention from his first film to his last, even if in later years his attitude becomes not so much outraged as mocking and ironic. But if his films repeatedly reveal the elegance of bourgeois houses, the ritualistic nature of bourgeois life, and all the imperfections, moral or otherwise, that lie behind the bourgeois façade, they also suggest that, far from crumbling to dust, this is a social class distinguished by its resilience and capacity for survival. The point is tellingly made in *The Exterminating Angel*, for there Nobile and his companions, despite the trials of hunger, thirst and degradation they are obliged to endure, emerge relatively unscathed from their incarceration, rising Phoenix-like from the ashes to continue their former way of life. They possess, in effect, a survival instinct which, strangely, stems from their complacency and self-assurance, for this enables them to shrug off and surmount the inconveniences that come their way, a point effectively made in the persistence displayed by the characters of *The Discreet Charm of the Bourgeoisie* in their pursuit of a meal regardless of the disappointments they experience. The surrealists may have wished, as we have seen, 'to explode the social order, to transform life itself' (Buñuel, 107), but Buñuel seems to have realised from an early stage the ultimate futility of that aim, that 'we do not live in the best of possible worlds', and that the most a creative artist can do is express that view in whatever form he sees fit.

4

'THANK GOD I'M STILL AN ATHEIST'

Surrealist opposition to the conventional values embodied in western society and embraced by the bourgeoisie in particular, inevitably meant that religion, and especially the kind of morality advocated by the Catholic Church, would become a major focus of attack. As we have already seen, freedom of all kinds lay at the heart of surrealist beliefs, be it the freedom from the dictates of reason allowed by instinct and passion, the freedom associated with the imagination, or that connected with dreams and the expression of the unconscious mind. Christianity, on the other hand, based in part on the dictates of the Commandments that 'thou shall not', was seen by the surrealists to be essentially restrictive of the freedom that they worshipped, and, because religious teaching formed such a central part of the education provided by Catholic schools throughout Europe, to be a decisive and detrimental influence upon young and developing minds. Furthermore, the Catholic Church was regarded by the surrealists as walking hand in hand with the bourgeoisie, the latter contributing financially to the well-being of the former, and the Church supporting the bourgeoisie in its suppression of the lower classes and in its championing of traditional moral values. In this context, it is not difficult to understand the close links between many of the surrealists and the communists, for both sought a revolution in society that would free the individual, the latter in an economic sense, the former in a moral and spiritual sense, from the power hitherto exercised over them by others.

This said, there are evidently certain parallels between Christianity and Surrealism, for if the latter places great store on the inexplicable and the marvellous, so does the former in relation to some of its key elements: the Immaculate Conception, the Resurrection, the miracles, the transformation of bread and wine into the body and blood of Christ. And if Christianity offers man the possibility of salvation, so in a rather different way does Surrealism in offering him another and better way of life. But if these parallels exist, there is also a fundamental difference in the sense that Christianity codifies its principal values into rules of behaviour based on reason, moderation and self-discipline, while Surrealism advocates freedom from such restrictions. In effect, it would not be unfair to state that for those who were part of it, Surrealism was an alternative religion. Indeed, the arrival in Paris in 1920 of Tristan Tzara was seen by André Breton as 'the coming of the Dada Messiah'.[1]

Breton was, as noted earlier, the son of a lower middle-class family. Brought up in the provincial town of Lorient on the western coast of France, he was exposed as a child to the attempts of a narrow-minded mother to bring him up with puritanical strictness. An intelligent and independent boy, he instinctively reacted against such an upbringing, rejecting the religious values that his mother embodied. As he matured and then embraced both Surrealism and Communism, he felt that he belonged to the great intellectual rebels of the past, including the religious heretics, and, regarding himself as a subversive, he refused to accept those things with which men seek to comfort themselves in a difficult and even hostile world: hope in the future and the solace of religion. His rejection of the latter has been effectively described as follows:

> As for religion, again in line with Communism, he views it as an institution at the service of bourgeois society which it helped strengthen by giving solace to the economically exploited with the promise of a better world in the hereafter.[2]

Paul Éluard, like Breton and many other surrealists, saw religion as something that inhibited both freedom of thought and action, and his creativity as a writer, but this did not mean that he was not a religious individual in a broader sense. It has been said of him, for example, that he 'stands in the tradition of the non-believer who has abandoned God, while remaining essentially a religious person'.[3] In this particular sense, Éluard's concerns were with his own solitude but also with the solidarity of all men – which explains his Communist affiliation – in a world subjected to constant flux and change. Quite clearly, within the surrealist movement, there were writers and creative artists of very different kinds – polemicists, novelists, poets, painters and film-makers – but all of them were united in their rejection of orthodox religion.

Buñuel's birthplace of Calanda, to which he returned regularly for many years, was, as has been suggested earlier, a village dominated by religious practices.[4] When a funeral occurred, the coffin was placed in front of the church door, holy water was sprinkled over it, priests chanted – there were seven in Calanda – and ashes were scattered over the corpse. As the coffin was carried to the village cemetery, the mother of the deceased, accompanied

---

[1] See Brandon, *Surreal Lives: the Surrealists 1917–1945*, 163.

[2] See Anna Balakian, *André Breton: Magus of Surrealism* (New York: Oxford University Press, 1971), 163.

[3] See Robert Nugent, *Paul Éluard* (New York: Twayne Publishers, 1974), 133.

[4] See p. 18.

by other relatives, wailed pitifully. All this was, Buñuel has observed, 'an integral part of our lives' (Buñuel, 12). As a child, despite the family move to Zaragoza not long after his birth, he was frequently involved in the religious activities of Calanda in a personal way. One of his uncles, known as Tío Santos, was a priest for whom the young Luis acted as an acolyte. He also sang and played the violin in the Virgin of Carmen choir and, together with two fellow musicians, was sometimes invited to the Carmelite convent on the edge of the village. At home, like Lorca, his close friend when he moved to Madrid, the young Buñuel acted out the Mass in the attic, dressed in an alb – the long white garment worn by a priest over his cassock – surrounded by a collection of religious artefacts made of lead, and assisted in the ceremony by his sisters. And then, as well as this, there was the miracle of Calanda, in which he believed totally for the first thirteen years of his life.

The miracle concerned a local inhabitant, Miguel Juan Pellicer, who in 1640 had his leg amputated after it had been crushed by the wheel of a cart. Pellicer had always been an extremely religious man, regularly attending church and dipping his finger in the oil that burned in front of the statue of the Virgin. He continued to do so after his accident, rubbing the oil into the stump of his leg, and one morning, when he awoke, he discovered that his leg had been restored. Attributed to the Virgin of Pilar and acknowledged by ecclesiastical and medical authorities, the miracle seemed to Buñuel much more impressive than that associated with the Virgin of Lourdes, and he recounted it to others for years to come (Buñuel, 13).

Buñuel's childhood was, as this account suggests, extremely traditional, and his mother, a very devout woman, played no small part in it. She ensured that her seven children were brought up according to the strict moral conventions of the day, doting on Luis, her first-born, to the extent that, as Francisco Aranda has suggested, she later kept photographs of him 'on an improvised altar in a wardrobe where they were surrounded by photographs of the late Popes'.[5] His father, to judge by what we know of his involvement in the social life of Zaragoza, was probably far less devout than his wife, but both parents were clearly instrumental in the decision to send their son, firstly, at the age of six, to the College of the Brothers of the Sacred Heart of Jesus, and then, a year later, to the Jesuit Colegio del Salvador. As we have already seen, his seven-year education under the Jesuits affected him profoundly.

Quite apart from the Jesuits' insistence on the evils of sex, life at the school, where Buñuel was a day pupil, not a boarder, was distinguished by its discipline. The day began at seven-thirty with Mass and ended with evening prayer. In the winter, which is extremely cold in northern Spain, only one of the classrooms was heated, and the pupils, wrapped in heavy scarves and thick clothing, spent much of their time in freezing conditions, their fingers

5   Aranda, *Luis Buñuel: A Critical Biography*, 12.

and feet numb. Order and discipline were rigorously enforced by the teachers, misdemeanours of any kind severely punished, and every move on the part of the pupils closely watched. In the classroom, the dining-room and the chapel, absolute silence was demanded, and no one was allowed to shout or run until, having marched in two columns for recess in the courtyard of the school – a practice seen at the beginning of *Viridiana* – a bell gave them permission to break ranks.

As for the curriculum, the pupils studied, among other subjects, apologetics – that area of dogmatics that deals with the proofs of Christianity – the catechism, and the lives of the saints, and they also acquired an excellent knowledge of Latin. The teaching methods were still very much based on the kind of scholastic argumentation that had predominated in the Middle Ages, in which the challenge or *desafío* played an important part. This involved two members of the class challenging each other on a particular topic until one of them proved victorious. As well as this, of course, the Jesuits ridiculed the philosophical arguments of those philosophers and scientists who in any way attempted to undermine the truths of traditional Christian belief: Galileo, Descartes, Kant and Darwin. Jesuit teaching was therefore marked by its inflexible attitudes and its rigorous discipline. As far as the young Buñuel was concerned, it clearly affected his sexual attitudes to women, but it also gave him a deep knowledge of the Bible, of the issues that were central to the Catholic faith, and, in addition, a mental discipline that is very evident when religious matters came to the fore in his later films.

During his schooldays at the Colegio del Salvador, Buñuel proved to be an assiduous student, receiving good marks for several subjects and also for good conduct and piety – somewhat ironic in the light of his subsequent career! Nevertheless, at the age of fourteen or so, he began to have doubts about the credibility of what he was being taught. How was it possible, for example, that millions of dead in many countries and over many centuries could be resurrected, and where could their bodies be accommodated? And how could it be fair or just that a last judgement, immediately after death, should be final and irrevocable? These were the questions awakened in a young and developing mind already touched by scepticism and, no doubt, by a growing awareness of the intransigent methods and cruel punishments employed by the Jesuits to indoctrinate their young charges. At all events, Buñuel left the Colegio del Salvador at the age of fifteen and soon afterwards, while he was at the local high school, began to read Rousseau, Marx and Darwin's *The Origin of the Species* (Buñuel, 30). His earlier blind acceptance of the Catholic religion was being seriously undermined.

His subsequent eight years at the Residencia de Estudiantes, as well as exposing him to liberal ideas and avant-garde movements in the arts and deepening his political affiliations with the Left, cemented his hostility towards the Catholic Church itself. It is interesting to note, in the context of Buñuel's loss of faith, that at the Residencia he and Lorca were both heavily involved in the annual production of José Zorilla's nineteenth-century play, *Don Juan Tenorio*, in which Buñuel frequently played the role of Don Juan. Zorrilla's play, first performed in 1844 and a great favourite with Spanish audiences ever since, contains various themes that would have greatly appealed to him. Don Juan takes great pleasure, for example, in shocking and scandalising the public and in pursuing a life of unmitigated pleasure that defies all the moral principles of Christian teaching. He is, in short, a rebel against all social and religious conventions and in that sense provided a kind of role model for Buñuel himself at that period of his life. It has to be said, on the other hand, that, for all his scandalous behaviour, Don Juan is at bottom a believer who is convinced that he can repent and find salvation when the day of reckoning comes, as indeed occurs when, at the end of the play, he is redeemed through his genuine love of Doña Inés. His appeal for Buñuel lay, therefore, in that part of the play that has to do with Don Juan's rebellion rather than his redemption, though, given his schooling with the Jesuits, the latter would also have been of considerable interest to him.

Buñuel's hostility towards the Catholic Church can also be more easily understood in the context of historical and political events in Spain between 1923 and 1936. Prior to this, the Church, invariably in collusion with the Right, already exercised enormous power, and this gained further strength when in 1923 Spain became a dictatorship under General Miguel Primo de Rivera. Although he was successful in some ways during his seven-year period in power – new schools were built, new roads and railways constructed – Primo de Rivera's increasing conflict with left-wing intellectuals drove him more and more into the arms of the Church, and his plan to allow Jesuit and Agustinian colleges to grant degrees created a furore that ultimately played no small part in his downfall. In early 1930, as we have already seen, the dictatorship came to an end, and the Spring of 1931 saw the inauguration of the Second Spanish Republic under a largely left-wing government, which held power until 1933. The steps that it now took in relation to the Catholic Church illustrate perfectly the latter's power up to this point and the hostility that this inspired in those with socialist affiliations.

As Buñuel's experience has shown, the Church, through its schools, was able to shape and influence the minds of young people, depriving them to a considerable extent of true freedom of thought. When the new Parliament debated the religious question in late 1931, it was therefore resolved that the various religious Orders should be deprived of the right to teach, for if the Republic was based on the principle of freedom, it was very clear that, in indoctrinating the young, the schools run by the Church struck at the very heart of the Republic itself. Furthermore, none of the Orders were to be allowed to increase their already enormous wealth from the sale of goods, and the Jesuit Order, which professed allegiance to an authority other than the State, was abolished. Naturally enough, the Church itself was incensed by such interference in its affairs, as it was by the presence of what it saw as a communist-inspired Government. Only a few weeks after its formation, the Cardinal Primate of Spain, Mgr Pedro Segura, had described its members as 'the enemies of Jesus Christ' who were 'sold to Moscow gold'.[6]

If the Government took action against the Church on moral and political grounds, the actions of ordinary people of left-wing persuasion were inspired by long-standing resentment and hatred of the old order. In May 1931, for example, an article in the right-wing newspaper *ABC* in support of the now-exiled King, and a left-wing demonstration outside a monarchist club in the centre of Madrid, led to an attack on churches and convents in the city. This in turn motivated similar attacks in other cities, and in a short period of time 102 churches and convents were completely destroyed in Madrid, Malaga, Murcia, Granada, Valencia and Seville. Had Buñuel been in Spain at this time, there can be little doubt where his sympathies would have lain, for in his autobiography he has described his reaction to the murder of an archbishop a few years earlier, while he was still at the Residencia:

> [. . .] we heard that the anarchists, led by Ascaso and Durutti, had assassinated Soldevilla Romero, the archbishop of Saragossa, an odious character who was thoroughly detested by everyone, including my uncle, the canon. That evening, at the Residencia, we drank to the damnation of his soul.
>
> (Buñuel, 55)

We can well imagine Buñuel setting fire to a church, just as elsewhere he expresses the attraction of 'burning down a museum' (Buñuel, 107).

In the General Election of November 1933, the parties of the Left were heavily defeated by those of the Right who, with the support of the centre parties, remained in power for the next two years. This in turn meant that much of the anti-clerical legislation approved by the previous government was allowed to lapse and that church schools continued to be in charge of a good deal of the education system. In short, the close link between the Church and the representatives of the Right was re-established, and, although the Left was once more restored to power in the General Election of February 1936, the outbreak of the Civil War in July of that year, and the ensuing military dictatorship headed by General Francisco Franco, ensured that the Church would continue to rule supreme.

In the early years of the dictatorship, which lasted for forty-six years, the connexion between the regime and the Church was particularly strong. During the Civil War the priests had been persecuted by the Left, and many executed, but under Franco they came back into favour. The educational system was recatholicised, and great efforts were made, especially in the 1940s, to create the link between the rulers and the clergy that was known as

---

6 See Gerald Brenan, *The Spanish Labyrinth* (Cambridge: Cambridge University Press, 1960) (first published 1943), 236.

'National Catholicism'. As well as this, the Church became an integral part of the political system, for bishops had seats in the Spanish Parliament, and two organisations, the ACNP (the Catholic Association of Propagandists) and the Opus Dei, acquired considerable power, the latter, in some ways similar to the Freemasons, being known to its opponents as 'the Holy Mafia'.[7] There were, of course, those who disliked the close association of State and Church, not least because the political programme so often involved persecution of opposition groups such as Basque and Catalan nationalists, or those who initiated strikes against the regime. On the whole, the older priests and bishops supported Franco, while the younger members of the clergy held more liberal and, indeed, Christian views. By the 1970s, the latter were in the ascendancy as the older men retired or died and the stranglehold of the dictatorship relaxed its grip.

Although Buñuel left Spain for Paris in 1925, he was, as we have seen, often back there until the beginning of the Civil War, and, even after he departed once more in late 1936, worked for the Republican cause. Before the War and during it he therefore had ample opportunity to observe the links between the Church and the Right and the oppression that was enacted in their name. That close association remained vivid in his memory for the rest of his life:

> I've always been impressed by the famous photograph of those ecclesiastical dignitaries standing in front of the Cathedral of Santiago de Compostela in full sacerdotal garb, their arms raised in the Fascist salute toward some officers standing nearby. God and Country are an unbeatable team; they break all records for oppression and bloodshed. (Buñuel, 170)

After the Civil War, he did not return to his homeland for twenty-four years.

Buñuel's doubts regarding religious faith began, as noted previously, at the age of fourteen, and were those of a curious and intelligent schoolboy. Later on, they were consolidated by a much more mature intellectual probing of all the issues involved. Buñuel regarded the role of chance in life as all-important, for even the moment of conception is the result of the chance meeting of an egg and a sperm. Subsequently, chance also plays a crucial part in influencing the pattern of human lives, and its existence therefore denies the possibility of a logical and ordered world in which God is the organiser and supreme controller. Furthermore, Buñuel found it impossible to believe that God was watching him at every moment, for if that were the case, he would be obliged to believe, given the wrongs he had done in his life, that his eternal damnation was inevitable, which is in itself a contradiction of the Catholic belief in free will. To believe that God pays any attention to human beings was, for Buñuel, also quite absurd. On the contrary, the universe is a

---

7   See Raymond Carr, *Spain 1808–1975* (Oxford: Clarendon Press, 1982), 701–2.

complete mystery, and therefore mystery and chance, which are the negation of an all-powerful, all-seeing God, are the only meaningful things in human existence. In wrestling with arguments of this kind and reaching the conclusion that God does not exist, Buñuel was, ironically, putting into practice the kind of disciplined arguments he had learned at school with the Jesuits when one pupil was called upon to refute a proposition advanced by another. In other words, the influence of his religious education stayed with him throughout his life, even if the path he later followed proved to be very different. In this respect, his famous observation 'Thank God I'm still an atheist' neatly sums up both his fascination with religious issues and, in its juxtaposition of opposites, the contradictory aspects of his character.[8]

Nowhere is that contradiction better illustrated than in his return visits over many years to his native Calanda in order to participate in the custom known as the Drums of Good Friday. The drums of Calanda beat almost without interruption from mid-day on Good Friday until noon on Saturday, in memory of the darkness that descended upon the world at the moment of Christ's death on the cross. Just before noon on Good Friday, the drummers – during Buñuel's childhood there were about two hundred, nowadays there are over a thousand – gather in the village square opposite the church and wait there in complete silence until the church bell tolls. At once the drums thunder in unison and continue to do so for two hours until the procession leaves the square and makes its way around and through the town. The participants in the procession chant the story of Christ's agony until they return to the square around five o'clock, at which point the drums begin once more and continue through the night and up until noon the following day. Saturday morning commemorates the burial of Christ, and then, at mid-day, the drums become silent.

Despite his rejection of religion, Buñuel has described the mysterious and inexplicable effect that the drums of Calanda have always had on him:

> I don't really know what evokes this emotion, which resembles the kind of feeling often aroused when one listens to music. It seems to echo some secret rhythm in the outside world, and provokes a real physical shiver that defies the rational mind. (Buñuel, 20)

The key to understanding his reaction to this ceremony lies, of course, in his reference to the irrational, and also, slightly earlier, to the 'mysterious power' that the drums of Calanda exercised over him. For all his rationality in rejecting religion, Buñuel could not, then, deny his emotions and instincts, so beloved of the surrealists. In some ways, his response was that of the mystic, of which there are, of course, many examples in Spanish history. And in some

---

[8]   See Joan Mellen, 'An Overview of Buñuel's Career', in Mellen (ed.), *The World of Luis Buñuel: Essays in Criticism*, 6.

ways this was also reflected in the harsh and austere way of life to which he also often subjected himself, sleeping on planks of wood or eating sparsely. Even his physical appearance in later life was not unlike that of a monk.

The close liaison between the Church and those sympathetic to the Right, in particular the bourgeoisie, is almost as much a focal point in Buñuel's films as his emphasis on the bourgeoisie itself. The point is made very clearly, for example, in *L'Âge d'or*, for the group of people who arrive on the shore prior to the laying of the foundation stone is seen to consist of various bourgeois dignitaries, including three men wearing chains of office and medals, and representatives of the Church in the form of a number of priests and nuns. Furthermore, as the new arrivals wend their way across the rocky terrain, they come face to face with a number of skeletons dressed in the full regalia of archbishops, in the presence of whom they stop and remove their hats in homage before continuing their journey. Later, when two guests arrive by car for the dinner-party at the home of the Marquis of X, they are seen to be accompanied by a censer, which is removed from the back seat before the guests alight, and then replaced. Later still, as the orchestra plays in the garden, three Marist priests are seen walking across a bridge, and then, scurrying to catch up with them, a fourth who, half way across, turns and runs in the opposite direction. And finally, when the camera focuses on the musicians in the orchestra, it reveals two of the priests to be members of the orchestra, Church and bourgeoisie firmly and closely linked. In this early film, Buñuel's presentation of the representatives of the Church and its faithful followers is largely mocking. The bourgeois group displays a reverence towards the skeletons of the archbishops that is laughable in its sheer solemnity. The censer in the back of the car becomes a kind of ludicrous accessory that accompanies the bourgeois couple wherever they go. And the sequence in which the Marist priests cross the bridge could well come from one of the madcap silent Hollywood comic films that Buñuel and the Spanish surrealists so admired.[9]

The Church and the bourgeoisie are also linked, as we have seen, in *The Exterminating Angel*. The deliverance of Nobile's companions from their imprisonment in his house becomes in the very next shot the impressive dome of a cathedral topped by a cross, and then two other smaller domes, while on the soundtrack a choir sings a Te Deum. Inside the cathedral the camera picks out a priest and deacons performing their duties, and then moves along the faces of Nobile and his companions who have evidently come to thank God for their release. As the priest and his assistants cross themselves, so do the congregation, and they are then linked once more in a rather different way when clerics and bourgeoisie alike find that they are

---

[9] On the popularity of American comic films in Spain, see C.B. Morris, *This Loving Darkness: the Cinema and Spanish Writers, 1920–1936* (Oxford: Oxford University Press (published for the University of Hull), 1980).

unable to step out of the building. Prior to this, the Church, in the form of a priest, has also been involved in an attempt to secure the deliverance of the bourgeois group from their imprisonment in Nobile's house – in marked contrast to the indifference it so often displays towards the poor and the unfortunate. The Church and the wealthy clearly cannot survive without each other.

Just as in so many films Buñuel constructs a detailed and highly critical picture of the bourgeoisie, so he presents a withering series of observations on the Church, among which its oppressive weight and power stand out. *Tristana*, for example, begins with a panoramic shot of the city of Toledo dominated by its massive cathedral, while church bells toll monotonously on the sound-track. Toledo, it should be recalled, has occupied an important position in Spanish history, both in a secular and religious context, its cathedral in particular a pointer to that fact. Buñuel's purpose at the beginning of the film is, therefore, to suggest the extent to which the influence of the Catholic Church infiltrates the lives of ordinary people in this most symbolic of Spanish cities. Later in the film, the cathedral becomes the focus of attention once more when the young Tristana visits it, accompanied by two adolescent boys. As they stand on one of the terraces, their vantage point suggests very clearly the way in which the cathedral dominates the entire city. When they then climb the spiral staircase to the great bell-tower and Tristana stands inside one of the biggest bells, the moment is meaningful in a variety of ways. Above all, the bell envelops her in precisely the way in which the lives of the people as a whole are enveloped and circumscribed by the Church itself. Again, when she attempts to push the huge bell-clapper, it proves to be almost immovable, as inflexible as church ritual and dogma. And thirdly, the sheer size and weight of the bell, echoing the massive structure of the cathedral, evokes the oppressive might of the Church in this and other Spanish cities, towns and villages.

This impression of size and weight is also suggested elsewhere in the film, not least when Tristana enters a church and gazes at the statue of a religious figure supine on top of a tomb. The tomb, as tall as Tristana herself, has the massive solidity evident in others shots of churches and convents, as does the impassive figure placed on top of it. Furthermore, just as Tristana's envelopment by the cathedral's bell points to the imprisoning influence of the Church, so the high narrow streets of this city of churches and convents symbolise the suffocating and claustrophobic grip of religion upon many of its inhabitants.

As well as size, the tomb and the statue mentioned above suggest the coldness and inflexibility that Buñuel invariably associates with the Church, something that is also underlined in other films. The beginning of *Viridiana*, for example, reveals the courtyard and cloister of a convent across which two lines of boys are walking, much as Buñuel himself had done at the Jesuit school in Zaragoza. The courtyard is surrounded by stone pillars set at

Tristana: the immovable weight of the Church

regular intervals, and when we see Viridiana for the first time, she stands immediately in front of one of them. The formal architecture of the courtyard, reinforced by the line of boys who cross it, becomes a metaphor for the inflexibility of religious doctrine, while the stonework suggests both hardness and coldness. Viridiana's position in front of one of the stone pillars is also meaningful. A visual link is established between herself and the pillar in the sense that the pale colour of the stonework is echoed in the whiteness of her habit and her face. Furthermore, the coldness of the stone has its equivalent in Viridiana, for when the Mother Superior informs her that her uncle, Don Jaime, wishes to see her before she takes her vows, Viridiana's response is decidedly cool, and later on, in conversation with his housekeeper, Ramona, Don Jaime tells her that, when he suggests that Viridiana stay with him a few days more, 'she turns to stone'. Her attitude towards her uncle, whom she is unlikely to see again, should clearly contain the compassion expected of someone who is about to devote her life to Christ, but in many ways Viridiana is initially as devoid of human feeling as the austere building in which she has received her religious instruction.

Meanness of spirit of a rather different kind is embodied in the Mother Superior herself. Informed of Don Jaime's suicide, she arrives at his house, ostensibly to offer her sympathy to Viridiana, but when the latter suggests that she bears some responsibility for her uncle's death and that, instead of returning to the convent, she will perform Christian acts in the world at large, the Mother Superior's attitude changes to one of fury and outrage. Far from attempting to console and understand her former charge, she sees her as a traitor, as someone who, guilty of pride, is lost to the cause, and who must now be dismissed because she is no longer one of them. Just as the bourgeoisie casts out intruders, so the Church, professing Christian compassion, casts out those it regards as undesirables.

A similar moment occurs in *Nazarín* when, having been stripped of his ministry as a priest, Nazarín informs the older priest, Don Angel, that his intention is to leave the town and go into the countryside where he will feel nearer to God. Torn between sympathy for him and the embarrassment of having him continue to live in his house, Don Angel agrees with the decision, but is outraged when Nazarín reveals that he intends to support himself by begging for alms, which, Don Angel claims, betrays the dignity of the clergy. Not long afterwards, another priest is seen in the company of a colonel whose horse has broken its leg. The colonel, already annoyed, vents his anger on a passing peasant whom he obliges to pay proper respect both to him and the priest, and when Nazarín intervenes and objects to the colonel's bullying on the grounds that the peasant is as much a son of God as anyone else, the priest takes the colonel's part, suggesting that Nazarín must be 'a heretic [. . .] one of those mad preachers from the north'. Not only is the priest associated here with a pompous and intolerant member of the military establishment; he is also seen, in his dismissal of Nazarín's defence of the peasant, as essentially anti-Christian. For him, as for Don Angel, Nazarín is an outsider, an undesirable, but Buñuel reveals very clearly that, of the two, it is the priest who, in his self-seeking – his desire to please the colonel – and his bigotry, stands outside the spirit of Christianity.

Hypocrisy too is one of Buñuel's targets, not least in relation to the pious façade adopted by the Church and its representatives and the reality that lies behind it. In *The Discreet Charm of the Bourgeoisie*, for example, the Bishop is asked by a peasant woman to accompany her to a barn where a dying old man requires absolution. The latter confesses to his murder, many years ago, of his employers, a married couple who treated him badly and whose photograph he keeps at his bedside. The Bishop informs the old man that the couple in the photograph are his, the Bishop's, parents, but, despite this, proceeds, in the name of Jesus Christ and the authority invested in him, to absolve him of his sins. Then, having commended him to the mercy of God, thus granting the old man's dying wish, the Bishop picks up a shotgun and blows his head off. Even if we take into account the feelings of someone suddenly confronted with his parents' killer, the disparity between the Bishop's initially compassionate manner and his subsequent bloody act of revenge – more Old Testament 'an eye for an eye' than Christian forgiveness – becomes an utter condemnation of the violence and callousness that so often lies behind the Church's mask of piety.

More than forty years earlier, the same kind of incident had occurred at the end of *L'Âge d'or*. As we have seen, the robed, bearded and compassionate figure who emerges from the Chateau de Selliny after the orgy of a hundred and twenty days bears a remarkable similarity to the traditional representation of Christ. When the young woman crawls out of the chateau seeking help and he takes her back inside, our expectation that he will show her mercy suddenly becomes, as we hear her scream, the realisation that he has murdered her. The sentimentality frequently associated with images of Christ is ruthlessly stripped away. The hands extended towards the individual in need of help are seen to be those of a murderer.

Buñuel also takes delight in confronting priests with the delicate sexual problems of their parishioners in order to reveal both their prudery and their reliance on religious dogma as a cover for their embarrassment. In *The Diary of a Chambermaid* Madame Monteil takes advantage of the priest's visit to her home to seek his advice about the sexual demands placed upon her by her husband. She introduces the subject gradually, but when the priest becomes aware of the nature of her enquiry, he informs her that he cannot advise her as a priest. In response, she begs him to do so as a friend, upon which she reveals that her husband demands sexual relations twice weekly. The priest, reacting supposedly as a friend but unable to set aside his opinion as a priest, is appalled. Twice a week, he insists, is excessive for any man, no matter how strong his sexual drive, and, as for Madame, she should make sure that she derives no satisfaction from the sexual act. We are reminded here of the insistence of Buñuel's Jesuit teachers that married couples, even in the act of procreation, should feel no desire. At all events, Buñuel creates a wonderfully humorous sequence by exposing both bourgeois good manners and the hidebound mentality of the Church to the, for it, embarrassing topic of sexual intercourse.

An episode in *Tristana* is also concerned with what, in the eyes of the Church, is 'correct' behaviour. When the priest, Don Ambrosio, attempts to persuade Tristana to marry Don Lope, she reveals that she cannot stand the sight of her ageing uncle. Don Ambrosio describes her feelings as unhealthy and, given that Don Lope is now much more mellow, as irrational and even satanic. The priest is, of course, only concerned with regularising a relationship that the Church regards as sinful and takes no account whatever of the feelings of resentment and even hatred that Don Lope's sexual abuse of Tristana over many years has aroused in her. In short, the Church pays little attention to the natural feelings of human beings, and it is significant too that Don Ambrosio's advice is directed to Tristana rather than Don Lope, for in the eyes of the Church woman can never be dissociated from Eve, the ultimate temptress and source of original sin.

At the same time as they pontificate on the evils of the flesh, many of Buñuel's priests are seen to be eager to indulge in earthly pleasures. In *The Diary of a Chambermaid*, Madame Monteil offers the priest two bottles of wine and a cake, both of which he gratefully accepts, commenting that he has run out of the former, and that the latter is much to his taste. And in *Tristana*, as noted previously, the priests who visit Don Lope on winter nights – and who include Don Ambrosio – greedily dunk their biscuits in the thick chocolate drink that he offers them. Indeed, given the obvious decline in Don Lope's health, of which they are well aware but to which they pay scant attention, the sensual pleasure they take in the appearance and taste of the chocolate is almost revolting.

The dogmatic and condemnatory attitude adopted by the Church towards sexual behaviour is, as Buñuel well knew, inimical to the experience of true passion and instinct. In *Un Chien andalou* the young man's attempt to pursue and secure the young woman with two ropes is, as we saw earlier, thwarted by the almost immovable weight attached to them, part of which consists of two Christian Brothers. In other words the influence of the Church, and of its educational programme in particular, is presented as totally deadening in relation to sexual desire, and it is therefore no coincidence that this sequence should occur immediately after the young man has been aroused by the young woman to the point where he caresses her breasts and buttocks. He is, in effect, pulled up short by a sudden attack of guilt and conscience, as indeed is the young woman in *L'Âge d'or* when, in the sequence in the garden, she becomes suddenly aware of the wrongful nature of her actions, breaks away from her lover's embraces and returns to the bosom of her conventionally minded family. In *Viridiana* the situation is initially very similar, even if it is finally reversed. At first, Viridiana withdraws her hand when invited to squeeze the cow's teat as if she were suddenly conscious of its sexual implications. Subsequently, she is disconcerted by Jorge's sexual innuendos. And when, later on, one of the beggars attempts to rape her and her hand grasps the penis-like handle of the skipping-rope around his waist, she faints, overcome by sexual fear. Her sexual inhibition is attributable in part to her youth and inexperience, but it must also be due in no small measure to the religious training to which she is exposed as a novice nun. Only when she has learned what the world is really like, in contrast to the enclosed and restricted life of the convent, does she begin to become aware of her deep-seated desires and, in order to fulfil them, cast aside the inhibiting lessons of her religious education.

The absurdity of total asceticism and withdrawal from the world, which might have been Viridiana's fate, is the subject of *Simon of the Desert*. Simon, we soon learn, has been on top of a column in the desert for six years, six months, and six weeks, his days devoted entirely to praying and fasting. He makes every effort to lead what he regards as a saintly existence, eating only lettuce leaves and drinking stagnant water, and avoiding all the other temptations of the world. Buñuel, however, puts temptation in his way and makes him just as aware of the weaknesses in his nature as he does the bourgeoisie of their dark subconscious. When, for example, the

young monk, Matías, brings him food, Simon is disconcerted by his good
looks and his carefree energy, and demands that he leave. And if in this
case he is made aware of erotic leanings, his repressed desire for women is
also exposed. In the course of the film, women appear to Simon in a
variety of guises. Firstly, a female peasant walks past the foot of the
column and is eyed by Daniel, another of the monks. Simon immediately
reprimands him and reminds him of the Biblical instruction: 'Do not look
upon any woman. Neither let her take you with her eyelids.' Not long
afterwards, a young girl appears, guiding a hoop with a stick and singing
to the tune of a nursery rhyme. She wears a school uniform and has shoul-
der-length blonde hair. Sitting at the foot of the column and observed by
Simon, she crosses her legs to reveal black stockings and white flesh,
smiles at Simon, and then unbuttons her blouse to expose her breasts.
Without warning, she then appears beside him, poking her tongue into his
ear. In short, she is the typical woman dressed as a schoolgirl of erotic
films, in all probability the fantasy inside Simon's head that he desper-
ately seeks to deny. When he addresses her as Satan and calls upon Jesus
Christ to come to his assistance, the girl disappears and is then seen naked,
galloping away astride a white pig.

This episode has much to do, of course, with the traditional representation
in Christian literature of woman as Satan, as temptress, as the cause, through
Eve, of man's fall from paradise. It was the view of woman that Buñuel would
have acquired at the Colegio del Salvador and that subsequently ingrained
itself on his mind, but in *Simon of the Desert* he employs it to delightful
comic effect in order to reveal in the character of his protagonist his fanatical
resolve to remain true to his calling while, at the same time, making him
unnervingly aware of his human failings.

These are also revealed in Simon's treatment of other people. He displays
impatience towards his mother, who wishes to live at the foot of the column,
telling her to leave and reminding her that her love cannot come between
him and the Lord. He is displeased with Matías when he brings him food,
thereby distracting him from his resolve to fast. Similarly, the goatherd
complains that Simon showed no gratitude when he brought him a bowl of
curds and a piece of relatively fresh bread. In the character of Simon, therefore, Buñuel embodies the intolerance towards others that is born of religious
fanaticism and that is so evident throughout the world and in all periods of
time.

This last point is effectively made when Simon is suddenly transported to
a modern city where we see him in a discothèque, dressed in the latest
fashion, while young people dance wildly to the music of a group called 'The
Sinners'. He is joined at his table by Satan, again in the form of a young
woman. She asks him to dance with her as the group plays 'Radio-Active
Flesh', but he refuses and claims that he intends to return to his column. In
response, Satan tells him that he cannot go back, for someone else has taken

his place.[10] In short, Simon's desire to return to his former way of life and his refusal to engage in the dance represents the rejection by the religious fanatic of the reality of human beings in all their imperfection, yet to accept mankind as it is in all its imperfection is, for Buñuel, the only option.

His largely comic treatment here of extreme asceticism has its counterpart in the equally absurdist presentation, four years later, of religious dogma in *The Milky Way*. In his autobiography, Buñuel has revealed that the subject of heretics had fascinated him for many years because such people are quite as convinced as orthodox Christians that only they possess the absolute truth. When at last the opportunity arose to make a film on the subject, he and his co-scriptwriter, Jean-Claude Carrière, 'did a great deal of research' and 'spent days discussing the Holy Trinity, the dual nature of Christ, and the mysteries of the Virgin Mary' (Buñuel, 244). In other words, even though he proclaimed his atheism to the world at large, Buñuel's fascination with and curiosity about religious issues remained strong throughout his life. But this did not prevent him, as a surrealist, from pointing to the absurdity of Church dogma.

In *The Milky Way* – the title of the film refers to the star that originally guided travellers to the tomb of St James (Santiago) at Compostela in north-west Spain – two modern-day travellers, Pierre and Jean, set out en route for the shrine. During the journey, they initially encounter a diabolical-looking character whom they soon recognise as God – a typically Buñuelian joke – and afterwards observe six episodes in each of which a key element of Church dogma is debated and made by Buñuel to appear completely absurd. Because the film involves travellers and an episodic structure, some critics have considered it to be influenced by the Spanish picaresque novel of the sixteenth and seventeenth centuries, but, given its religious subject-matter, it seems more than likely that Buñuel had in mind the paintings of episodes from the Scriptures that often form a sequence in churches. The religious influence, whatever form it takes, is never far away in his creative work.

In the first of the six episodes, the Eucharist is the topic for discussion between a priest and a police officer. The latter, a highly rational man, cannot bring himself to believe that the body of Christ is in a piece of bread. The priest, putting forward the orthodox view, informs him that, far from Christ being in the bread, the bread **is** the body of Christ. The innkeeper, listening to the discussion, then tries to offer his own view, arguing that the body of Christ is contained in the host as is a hare in the pâté. The debate clearly veers towards the absurd and becomes even more ridiculous when Pierre intervenes and asks the priest what becomes of the body of Christ when it enters the digestive system. Pierre and Jean are immediately shown the door.

10 See Virginia Higginbotham, *Luis Buñuel* (Boston: Twayne Publishers, 1979), 129.

Then, however, the priest suddenly changes his point of view and agrees with the innkeeper that the body of Christ is in the bread, as is the hare in the paté, upon which two male nurses appear, informing the others that the priest has escaped from an institution for the insane. Buñuel implies that there is little difference between a priest and a lunatic, between the Church and a madhouse.

The five other episodes involve discussion of the origin of evil, the nature of Christ, the Trinity, free will and the Immaculate Conception. The debate on these topics includes such tricky questions as 'How can God be Christ, a man and God at the same time?'; or, 'If Christ were God, how could he be born or die?' And, in the fifth episode involving the Immaculate Conception and a priest's eulogy of the Virgin Mary's purity before, during, and after the birth of Jesus, a young man's question as to whether the priest thinks he should marry the young woman in his room, draws from him the traditional misogynist view of woman voiced by such authorities as St Paul. In almost every case orthodox and inflexible dogma is countered by an opinion that the Church regards as heretical but from which Buñuel derives a great deal of fun.

The arrival of the two travellers at Santiago de Compostela brings them into contact with a prostitute who informs them that, contrary to their expectations, there are no other pilgrims to the shrine, for it has been revealed that the bones in the tomb were not, after all, those of St James. They were, it is now thought, those of Priscillian, the fourth-century Bishop of Avila who was executed for his heretical ideas. The empty city and the confusion over the identity of the bones so long worshipped point, Buñuel suggests, to the emptiness and absurdity of the Christian tradition and its rites and rituals. And the ending of the film suggests too the harshness and the uncertainty associated with the Christian faith.

At the beginning of the film God had commanded Pierre and Jean to have children by a prostitute and to name them 'You are not my people' and 'No more mercy'. The fulfilment of this prophecy at the end of *The Milky Way* – Pierre and Jean have sex with the prostitute mentioned earlier, suggesting that she will bear their children – points to a God who has abandoned mankind, as well as a God who shows no mercy. Furthermore, this harshness is echoed in the proclamations of Christ who now appears and, in response to his followers' pleas for guidance, tells them: 'I am not come to this world to bring peace but the sword.' Buñuel clearly has in mind the atrocities committed in the name of Christianity over a long period of time, not least in Spain and South America. In addition, although Christ cures two men of their blindness, he fails to enlighten them in other ways, for when he leads his followers into a forest, the two men move haltingly, still using their canes. Although their sight has been restored, they have no clear vision of the way ahead.[11]

---

[11] For a more detailed account of the film, see Higginbotham, 158–67.

The Milky Way, drawing so heavily on religious tradition and Church dogma, is, especially for non-Catholics, Buñuel's least accessible film. In this respect, *Simon of the Desert* has a wider appeal, for the temptation of the religious fanatic by the devil in a variety of guises has a history with which we are all familiar, and a rich and attractive comic potential. *The Milky Way*, on the other hand, is much more intellectual, dependent to a considerable extent on the audience's knowledge of the religious beliefs behind its various arguments. But it points very clearly to the mark which Buñuel's schooling with the Jesuits left on him, and, in the nature of its arguments and counter arguments, it also has much to do with the rigorous academic debates in which he participated at the Colegio del Salvador.

Quite apart from exposing the many evils of Christianity and the Church, Buñuel also sought to undermine the sentimentality with which religious figures and events have been portrayed throughout the centuries. Reference has already been made to *L'Âge d'or*, at the end of which the traditional pious image of Christ is turned on its head. And there are similar examples in *Viridiana*, the 'Last Supper' sequence being the most notorious. In Leonardo da Vinci's famous painting, the disciples certainly have human enough faces and expressions, for they are thought to have been based on real people Leonardo encountered in and around Milan. The face of Christ, on the other hand, is quite different, far more perfect and thoughtful than the others, and the hands, extended in front of him, adopt the gesture of self-sacrifice and compassion that seems to be associated with the image of Christ throughout the history of art. In many paintings of 'The Last Supper' both before and after Leonardo's – for example, Andrea del Castagno's of 1450 and Tintoretto's of 1591–94 – the saintliness of the figures at the table is suggested by the haloes that surround their heads. Buñuel, a true surrealist in his intense dislike of all sentimentality, set out to undermine the traditional image.

The sequence in *Viridiana* is closely based on Leonardo's painting. The thirteen individuals at the table have the same position as and identical gestures to the figures in the Italian painting, but they are now the beggars who have occupied the dining-room of Don Jaime's house, six of them to either side of the central figure, who, instead of Christ, is the blind Don Amalio. The subversive suggestion is, clearly, that Christianity is a faith in which the blind leads the blind – an idea which, as we have seen, is also posited at the end of *The Milky Way*. As well as this, Don Amalio is a man of violent inclinations who, soon afterwards, smashes plates and wineglasses with his stick. As for the twelve 'disciples', they embody not Christian principles but every shade of sinfulness.

An earlier sequence in the film also undermines the traditional sentimental image of the Virgin Mary. Indeed, it is no accident that this episode should be concerned with the act of painting – the lame beggar is seen working on a picture of the Virgin – for this is largely the medium in which the image of the mother of Christ has been transmitted over a long period of time. Leonardo's *Madonna of the Rocks*, Titian's *Madonna and Child with Saint Andrew and Saint Tiziano of Oderzo*, and Bellini's *Madonna of the Trees*, all depict the Virgin in an idealised manner, both reflecting and influencing the way in which she is portrayed in paintings and statues in churches wherever the Christian faith prevails. As for the lame beggar, his painting of the Virgin healing a sick woman is much more primitive, no doubt influenced by the images he has seen in village churches, but even so it still contains a good deal of sentimentality, not least in the haloed figure of the Virgin herself and the two child-like angels on either side of her. On the other hand, all this is quickly undermined by the reality that forms the background to the picture. The model for the Virgin is, for example, a scrawny, far from attractive beggar woman who complains that sitting for so long has given her cramp, and, to be quite frank, she doesn't like 'having to be the Virgin'. In truth, there are few virgins in this disreputable company – a point made a moment later when the pregnant Refugio appears and another of the beggars, the malicious Poca, suggests that 'She never even saw the father. It was dark at the time.' The juxtaposition of the painting and the harsh reality that surrounds it is both comic and highly subversive.

Buñuel adopts a similar technique in *Tristana*. Firstly, when Saturno, Tristana's deaf mute friend, throws stones at her bedroom window to signify his presence in the garden, she goes out onto the balcony and, looking down on him, opens her dressing-gown so that he can feast his eyes on her naked body. The very next shot, which begins the sequence depicting Tristana's marriage to Don Lope, is of an image of the Virgin with child seen from below, and this is followed immediately by two more shots, from a similar angle: the first of the Virgin with child and, close by, the Virgin praying; the second, of the Virgin with hands clasped and looking upwards to heaven. The contrast between the shot of Tristana on her balcony and the various images of the Virgin could not be more clear or more suggestive. The latter, in expression and gesture, suggest spirituality, piety and pure love, and have that element of sentimentality mentioned earlier. They look down upon those present in the church in an entirely compassionate manner. Tristana similarly looks down upon someone who worships her, but his is the adoration of the flesh, and her attitude to him, reflected in her cold and hard expression, is one of exploitative and triumphant sexual power. Indeed, Tristana, one leg now amputated, is a damaged woman in more ways than one: bitter, resentful, vengeful. But this, suggests Buñuel, is how things are, and there is nothing sentimental or idealised about it. The direct juxtaposition of the two contrasting sequences, the flesh and the spirit, is certainly very effective.

Buñuel's subversion of the traditional representation of Christ, evident enough in the 'Last Supper' sequence in *Viridiana*, also occurs elsewhere, but in a rather different way. In *Nazarín*, the prostitute Andara has been wounded in a fight with another woman, La Camella, and seeks refuge in Nazarín's house. He feels obliged, as a man of God, to offer her assistance, which in this case means bathing her naked shoulder and, when she faints and falls to the ground, lifting her in his arms. Her physical presence clearly makes him feel uncomfortable and he utters a prayer, while Andara, by this stage delirious, looks at the picture of Christ on the wall of Nazarín's room and sees it 'laughing heartily', as amused by the priest's unease as the latter is by the sight and feel of Andara's flesh. Prior to Andara's arrival at Nazarín's house, the picture of Christ is, of course, serious in the traditional way. In making him laugh, Buñuel once more strips away all sentimentality and makes him much more human.

In addition, Buñuel subverts in *Nazarín* the traditional idea or image of Christ accompanied on the road by some of his disciples. After he has been stripped of his ministry, Nazarín sets out to do good works and, in the course of his journey, encounters a young woman, Beatriz, who has been seduced and abandoned by her feckless lover and rejected by her family. When, at her request, he visits her sister's fever-stricken child and the child subsequently recovers, Nazarín acquires a Christ-like significance and is joined on his journey by Beatriz and the prostitute, Andara. In short, his devoted followers are not men, as in the case of Christ, but two women, of whom one has an extremely strong sexual drive – Beatriz later returns to her lover – while the other sells her body, and both, even if they are not completely aware of it, find Nazarín physically attractive, much to his discomfort. The situation is one that is shot through with typical Buñuelian irony.

Buñuel's systematic undermining of Christianity, its traditions, values and sentimental imagery, stems, of course, from his view of the true nature of humanity, which is less than flattering. Indeed, it is this unwholesome yet ruthlessly realistic picture of human beings which, in all its complexity, dominates Buñuel's films from first to last, for they present us with a panoramic view of the whole of society, from the aristocracy downwards to beggars and criminals. His vision of the world, reminiscent in many ways of the paintings of Bruegel and Hieronymous Bosch, is one in which the seven deadly sins of wrath, greed, envy, gluttony, lust, pride and sloth, are very much to the fore, illustrating his belief that 'we do not live in the best of all possible worlds'.[12]

In *The Forgotten Ones* Buñuel presents an uncompromising picture of 'the lives of abandoned children' and 'the wretched conditions of the poor as they really are'.[13] Jaibo, a young man sent to a reformatory for his crimes, succeeds in escaping and soon returns to his former way of life, vividly illustrated in an incident in which he and his gang try to steal a blind man's money and later smash his musical instruments, the source of his income.

---

[12] See Fuentes, 'The Discreet Charm of Luis Buñuel', 71.
[13] See Gwynne Edwards, *The Discreet Art of Luis Buñuel* (London: Marion Boyars, 1982), 90.

Not long afterwards, Jaibo, accompanied by a younger boy, Pedro, brutally murders Julián, an incident that soon begins to haunt Pedro awake or asleep. Rejected by his mother, Marta, Pedro is picked up by the police, found guilty of a theft committed in reality by Jaibo, and sent for rehabilitation to a school farm. When he is sent on an errand by the director, he is accosted by Jaibo, who steals the money given him by the director. A fight ensues in which Pedro accuses Jaibo of Julián's murder and is overheard by the blind man who denounces Jaibo to the police. In the meantime, Jaibo and Pedro meet again, Jaibo kills the younger boy with an iron bar, but is then shot by the police as he attempts to escape. The film ends with the young girl, Meche, and her grandfather disposing of Pedro's body on a rubbish dump.

Many of the characters of *The Forgotten Ones* represent humanity at its worst. Jaibo, in particular, has no redeeming feature of any kind. His attempt to rob the blind man exposes his indifference to someone worse off than himself, and his murder of Julián and Pedro reveals his lack of concern for human life itself. As well as this, he eyes the young girl, Meche, and later Pedro's mother, Marta, with unconcealed lust. Pedro himself is initially potentially good, but whatever qualities he might develop are corrupted and destroyed by the circumstances in which he finds himself. His mother shows him no affection and he is repeatedly, through no fault of his own, drawn into Jaibo's criminal activities. Again, although we may sympathise with the blind man, Carmelo, when he is mugged and his musical instruments smashed, he proves in reality to be just as vicious and as callous as Jaibo. When he is set upon, for example, he lashes out with his stick in which there is a sharp nail, slashing one of the boys' legs in the process, and he delights in taking revenge by denouncing Jaibo to the police. As well as this, his fawning comments to the young girl, Meche, do not disguise his desire for physical contact when he sits her on his knee and offers her sweets. She is relatively innocent at this stage in her life, but already there are clear signs that she will lose that innocence in the kind of world in which she is growing up. The way in which, though frightened of Jaibo, she allows him to kiss her on the cheek for a peso, suggests that, like many other girls in this community, she will slowly drift into prostitution.

The only note of hope in *The Forgotten Ones* is provided by the school farm to which Pedro is sent on the instructions of the juvenile court. This represents one of 'the progressive forces of our time' that are alluded to by the superimposed voice in the film's documentary-like opening sequence, and the director of the institution is clearly presented by Buñuel as someone of good intentions who, wanting to help his charges, treats Pedro with kindness and understanding. Indeed, he reveals his trust in the boy when he gives him some money and sends him on an errand to the tobacconist's shop. But the director is also resigned to the ways of the world and aware of the futility of his own idealism, an attitude that is seen to be justified when Jaibo encounters Pedro and steals the money, thereby ensuring that the latter cannot return to the school farm without it. In effect, the low-life world of *The Forgotten Ones* is a world in which, with a few exceptions, human beings are driven by primitive basic instincts or affected by their presence in others: a world, in short, of 'dog eat dog'.

Given this fact, it is no coincidence that Buñuel establishes a close relationship in the film between human beings and animals and birds. When we see Pedro for the first time, he is stroking a hen and examining its eggs, and just afterwards the other children in the house follow their mother like open-mouthed chicks demanding to be fed. In another sequence set in a stable, Jaibo holds a black kid in his arms, he and Pedro attempt to milk a jenny, and Ojitos drinks from a nanny goat's udder, all this to the accompaniment of the cackling of hens and other animal sounds. Again, when the blind man has been attacked and left on the ground by Jaibo's gang, he finds himself eye to eye with a black cockerel.

Later, Meche is seen milking a jenny, and Marta, observing the black cockerel attempting to mate with her hens, sets about it with a broom. At the school farm Pedro, enraged at being sent there, lashes out at the chickens in the chicken run, and later, when he is murdered by Jaibo, a white hen stands on his chest as he lies in the straw. And finally, as Jaibo himself lies dying, the image of a wretched dog on an empty road is superimposed on his face. The implication of all these allusions to animals and birds is that the nature of men and women is not dissimilar, and that, just as the creatures of nature are ruled by their instincts and also exposed to the savagery of others, so are human beings ultimately helpless to control their lives in what is a world without plan or purpose.

This dispiriting but, for Buñuel, realistic vision of the world is also suggested in *Nazarín* and *Viridiana*. With regard to the former, reference has already been made to the prostitute Andara, but she has her counterpart in Camella, and both of them, like the low-life characters of *The Forgotten Ones*, are ruled entirely by necessity. There is an early squabble between them over buttons, which Andara accuses Camella of stealing from her, when in fact she has herself stolen them from someone else. Subsequently they fight in the inn, their cries described in terms of 'squawking hens'. Andara steals from Nazarín's room and, in order to cover her tracks, sets fire to it. Not long afterwards, when the foreman of a railway maintenance gang intervenes in a dispute and strikes one of the men, another hits the foreman with a shovel. At another point in the film we see a dwarf suspended by children from a tree. Later still, Nazarín, Andara and the dwarf are cruelly mocked by villagers, and when Nazarín is imprisoned he is abused and beaten up by other prisoners. If there is an occasional sign of goodness in some of the film's characters – the dwarf displays affection and tenderness towards Andara, a woman offers Nazarín the gift of a pineapple – it pales in comparison with the overall impression of men and women who are selfish, intolerant, malicious, dishonest and violent.

Viridiana, completed two years after *Nazarín*, is, in a way, the third part of this triptych of films in which man is revealed in all his flawed humanity. The beggars, provided with shelter by Viridiana, almost seem to have stepped out from a medieval painting, and, as has been suggested earlier, embody every kind of sin. When they first meet Viridiana, the malicious Poca wastes no time in telling the blind Don Amalio: 'She has the face of an angel. Such a pity you can't see her!' When they are joined by the so-called 'leper' whose sores fill them with horror, they instantly marginalise him, forcing him to sit apart from them and showing him no compassion. But it is, of course, in the 'Last Supper' sequences that, inflamed by alcohol, their existing flaws are seen at their very worst. The prospect of two roasted lambs and bottles of quality wine reveals their greed. Two of the women, Enedina and Refugio, fight over Enedina's bawling baby. Enedina lifts her skirts to take a 'photograph' of her companions at the table, the camera lens her private parts. The 'leper' puts on the wedding veil and corset that once belonged to Don Jaime's wife and performs a grotesque dance. Paco drags Enedina behind a couch and attempts to rape her, and Don Amalio, informed of it by the meddling Poca, lashes out with his stick, sending glasses and crockery flying in all directions. When Viridiana and Jorge return to the house, two of the beggars attack them, one hitting Jorge with a bottle, the other attempting to rape Viridiana. The beggars, in short, embody most of the seven deadly sins. If pride is absent, it is simply because they have none.

Buñuel's portrayal of a deeply flawed humanity is not, of course, confined to the low-life characters of the three films discussed above. In *Viridiana* the workmen employed by Jorge to renovate his father's house are economically and socially superior to the beggars, but they are no less hostile to the 'leper', for they tie a tin can to his waist so that, as he approaches, it drags on the ground and warns them of his coming. Jorge, further up the social ladder, is just one example of many individuals in Buñuel's films who exploit others, often their social inferiors, to satisfy their sexual desires. As he uses the servant Ramona, so Monsieur Rabour, in *The Diary of a Chambermaid*, uses Célestine to indulge his foot fetishism, while his son-in-law, Monteil, wastes no time at all in making advances to her. Similarly, Mathieu in *That Obscure Object of Desire* uses his wealth in a constant if frustrated pursuit of Conchita. The essential difference between the beggars and these bourgeois individuals is that, in the former, their sexual needs are expressed directly, crudely, often brutally; in the latter they acquire a veneer of polish and sophistication. But, in reality, lust is lust.

Neither is the indifference and the hostility of the rich towards the less privileged much different from the way in which the latter act towards each other. In *L'Âge d'or*, as we have seen, the bourgeois guests of the Marquis of X ignore the rustic cart and the unfortunate servant, and show little interest in the gardener's murder of his son. In *Nazarín* the bullying colonel berates the passing peasant as well as Nazarín himself, and in one of the flashbacks of

The Discreet Charm of the Bourgeoisie the Chief of Police is seen to use his position of power to torture a young prisoner he clearly dislikes. As for the clergy, staunch supporters of the rich, they are revealed to be greedy, intolerant and self-seeking. In both *The Diary of a Chambermaid* and *Tristana*, especially in the latter, the fondness of the priests for food and drink is more than evident. In *Nazarín* the priest supports the bullying colonel. And in *The Discreet Charm of the Bourgeoisie* the bishop callously murders the dying peasant. Throughout Buñuel's films, then, the masters are seen to be no better morally than those below them. They too are guilty of wrath, greed, envy, gluttony, lust, pride and sloth – a point tellingly made in the second half of *The Exterminating Angel*.

The film's opening sequences, depicting the arrival of Nobile and his friends at his house, present them, as described earlier, in all their bourgeois finery in a setting that could not be more elegant. A week or so later, after they have been incarcerated in the house and deprived of even the basic amenities, the drawing-room is a scene of devastation. A fire has been lit in the doorway. Furniture has been broken up to keep the fire going, woollen stuffing ripped from sofas and armchairs. A cello is smashed to pieces. Rubbish litters the room, and the once sophisticated individuals wander about dishevelled, coughing, and rubbing their eyes. Although there are still signs of wealth and sophistication – in the architecture of the room and the remnants of elegant clothes – the scene is not far removed from what we might expect to see in one of the poor, run-down areas of Mexico City where down-and-outs warm themselves around a fire in some open area littered with glass, stones, pieces of wood and other kinds of rubbish. For *The Exterminating Angel*, read *The Forgotten Ones*.

The parallel is sustained too in the behaviour of the characters, for their customary good manners towards each other are slowly eroded by the pressure of the circumstances in which they find themselves. When, for example, Raúl discovers the box of pills which Christian has mislaid and without which his condition will deteriorate, he deliberately throws it away so that Raúl will never find it. In the darkness Mr Roc attempts to kiss Leticia and to embrace Rita. Francisco suggests pushing Leandro into the room where a bear is prowling around, and just afterwards Leandro and Juana confront each other and end up fighting on the floor. As the hunger of the trapped individuals grows, they slaughter a sheep that Nobile's wife, Lucía, had concealed in the house in order to play a joke on her friends. Deprived of water, they smash the walls in order to reach the pipes. And eventually, as they become more and more desperate and hysterical, some of them plan to dispose of their host, Nobile, in the belief that his death will secure their own release. In short, these once elegant and sophisticated people are finally revealed to be no better than savages in terms of their basic instincts. When they are released, they quickly recover their poise, but in the meantime Buñuel has made us, and them, only too aware that bourgeois sophistication is little more than skin deep and that, ultimately, there is little difference between these people, the underprivileged of *The Forgotten Ones*, and the beggars of *Viridiana*. Buñuel's portrayal of mankind, from rich to poor, is thus unflinchingly frank in terms of its exposure of human nature.

Given the flawed nature of human beings, Buñuel believed that men and women should be accepted for what they are, and that any effort to change them must prove futile. That effort is, above all, embodied in the Christian belief that man, possessing free will, is capable of making choices and, therefore, of changing for the better. Furthermore, that change can be effected by individuals who, following Christ's example, make it their mission to help others, to lead them along the path of virtue and, by so doing, to transform their lives. Of all Buñuel's characters, Nazarín and Viridiana are the two best examples of a Christian attempt to make the world a better place.

Nazarín, set in Mexico, is based on the novel of the same name by the nineteenth-century Spanish novelist Benito Pérez Galdós, but, true to Buñuel's preoccupations, has a quite different emphasis. The film, like the novel, focuses on Nazarín's Christian goodness and on his resolve to teach the virtues of Christian love, compassion, forgiveness and resignation. But whereas Galdós's character stresses the redeeming nature of his suffering and his determination to continue his work in spite of his setbacks, Buñuel draws attention to the futility of Nazarín's pilgrimage in a hostile world and to his increasing alienation both from the Church and from his initial idealism. Viridiana is in many ways a female Nazarín. Like him she sets out to do good in a world that proves to be ungrateful and, like him, she finally accepts that her efforts are in vain.

In the film's early sequences, Nazarín is seen to display the traditional Christian virtues of compassion, charity, humility and patience. When we are first introduced to him in the room of the inn where he lodges, he has been robbed, his clothes and money taken, but, far from being too upset by what has become a common occurrence, he explains to the Assistant Engineer that he doesn't really mind: 'I'm as deeply convinced of my ideas as I am of my faith in Our Lord Jesus Christ. I believe that nothing belongs to anyone. Everything belongs to the person who needs it most.'[14] As if to prove the point, he immediately gives his cooking pot to a woman who asks him for it because her own, she claims, has been broken by the children, and he allows her too to take his wood, even though it means that he will be without a fire. In many respects Nazarín is, as Buñuel himself noted, a Don Quixote figure – someone who sets out to right wrongs and impose his idealised vision of things on an imperfect world.[15]

---

[14] The translation into English is my own.
[15] See Edwards, *The Discreet Art of Luis Buñuel*, 117.

The nature of the world that Nazarín sets out to improve is vividly presented by Buñuel in the film's opening sequence. The inn in which the priest lodges is called 'The Inn of the Heroes', its name an ironic comment on the absence of any kind of heroism in the people who frequent it or live around it. The inn is in poor condition, its sign is cracked and faded, the people who pass by are shabbily dressed, and the first individuals we see are three prostitutes, La Prieta, Andara and Tinosa, their profession reminiscent of the women observed by Don Quixote when he approaches an inn on the first day of his search for chivalresque adventures. The conversation of the women focuses on the alleged theft by another prostitute, Camella, of the buttons mentioned earlier. Furthermore, when Andara learns that Nazarín has accused her cousin, La Chona, of stealing from his room, she and the other two women confront him, mock him, blow cigarette-smoke in his face, and are only prevented from attacking him by the intervention of the Engineer who shoos them away. In short, this is a world where poverty, cheating, stealing and showing aggression to others have become a way of life. When the Engineer, who has come to install electricity in the village, points out that this is a sign of social progress, the proprietress of the inn replies: 'There's no social progress here, believe me. Just lots of poor people!' Her truthful but negative remark encapsulates the reality with which Nazarín is required to deal.

His attempts to resolve particular situations by means of Christian values are shown by Buñuel to be ineffective and futile in a world where the virtues the priest embodies are either inappropriate or are ignored. Beatriz, for example, seduced and abandoned by Pinto, attempts to hang herself but fails to do so because the wooden beam in the stable is too weak. When Chanfa, the proprietress, finds her, she offers advice that is entirely devoid of sentiment before giving her some food and offering her work: 'If you really want to kill yourself, you should choose a stronger beam. [. . .] But in any case, you shouldn't give him the pleasure – he isn't worth it.' In complete contrast, Nazarín suggests that Beatriz return to her village and her family, a course of action which may be desirable but which is impossible, given the fact that her family has already turned its back on her for reasons of honour and reputation. Chanfa's pragmatism is seen to be much more effective than Nazarín's good intentions.

Later, when a young woman, Lucía, lies dying during an epidemic that has struck her village, she is attended by Nazarín, who urges her to prepare herself for the afterlife and the joy of finding herself in the presence of God. She, however, rejecting his advocacy of the spiritual life, finds more consolation in the presence of her lover, Juan, and in his last kiss. And, as far as the village as a whole is concerned, the ineffectiveness of Nazarín's involvement is made even clearer by the arrival of practical help in the form of nurses and doctors, whose appearance transforms the monotonous tolling of the church bells, suggestive of death and mourning, into a joyful pealing synonymous with life.

In another episode a policeman arrives at a village with instructions to
arrest Nazarín and Andara. The villagers seize the opportunity to vilify the
priest, knocking him to the ground, but he offers no resistance and remon-
strates with Andara when she puts up a fight, telling her she should ask
forgiveness for her violent actions. As Nazarín lies helpless on the ground,
abused and reviled by his enemies, he may seem admirable in turning the
other cheek, but the episode is also a pointer to the ineffectiveness of Christian values among people who are not given to love, hope and charity.

In the latter part of the film, Nazarín is, in effect, born to the world,
accepting human beings for what they are, not trying to change them into
people they can never be. After his arrest, he finds himself chained to other
prisoners as they march along the road. Just before this, in his prison cell, he
has been punched and kicked by a criminal who has murdered his father and,
for the first time, finds forgiveness difficult. There then follows a conversation between Nazarín and another prisoner, the Sacrilegist, punished for
stealing from churches. Encouraged by the priest to confess his sins, the
Sacrilegist makes a pertinent point: 'Look at me, I only do bad things. [. . .]
But what use is your life really? You're on the side of good and I'm on the
side of evil. [. . .] And neither of us is any use.' They are words that bring
Nazarín no comfort, and their disconsolate message is then reinforced by
other events: on the orders of the Church authorities, he is separated from the
other prisoners and made to travel with his own un-uniformed guard; Andara
is forced to leave his side; and, as he proceeds along the road, Beatriz passes
by in the company of Pinto, her head on his shoulder and her eyes closed, in
recognition of her acceptance of the triumph of the flesh. Nazarín walks in
total despair.

Despair, however, contains a seed of hope, for from disillusionment
springs Nazarín's embracing of men and women as human beings, flawed or
otherwise. When a peasant woman takes pity on him and offers him a pineapple, he at first walks on, paying no attention to her. When she approaches
him a second time, he firmly rejects the offer, but then, seeing her disappointment, takes the pineapple, holding it 'like a precious gift'. He continues along
the road, tears streaming down his cheeks as he realises that, because he is no
longer dressed as a priest, the woman has offered him the pineapple not out of
any deference to that office, but simply because she feels for him as a human
being worse off than herself. It is the moment when Nazarín learns to accept
and cherish human beings for what they are, to love man rather than God.

Viridiana is, in a sense, an even more extreme example of the futility of
religious practices, for while Nazarín attempts to put his Christian beliefs into
effect in the world, she, in proposing to take her vows, chooses to turn her
back on it, opting for isolation in the convent in preference to contact with
ordinary men and women. But when, against her will, she visits her uncle,
Don Jaime, the world inevitably impinges on her in all its ugliness. Ironically,
the woman who intends to dedicate her life to Christ becomes, on account of

Viridiana: revered objects

her physical similarity to her dead aunt, an irresistible sexual attraction to her uncle. Her chosen path – the spiritual life – becomes, as the result of her belief that her uncle has raped her, inextricably bound up with the world of the flesh. And when, as a consequence of that and of Don Jaime's subsequent suicide, for which she feels responsible, she decides that she cannot return to the convent but must take her Christian principles into the world, she is obliged, like Nazarín, to confront it in all its imperfection.

The inappropriateness of Viridiana's beliefs in a world ruled by self-interest comes into sharp relief both in relation to the beggars she chooses to help, and in relation to Jorge, Don Jaime's son, when he inherits his father's house. Jorge is, as we have seen, a pragmatist as far as his sexual relationships with women are concerned, and he is also a highly practical man when it comes to improving and modernising his father's run-down house and estate. As to the first point, his initial encounters with Viridiana establish the fundamental contrast between them. Her room is decidedly austere, the furniture consisting of a wooden table, two chairs, a simple dressing-table with no mirror, and an iron bed. When Jorge visits her there, she is kneeling, telling her beads, he is relaxed, smoking a cigar. In the ensuing conversation, he runs his eyes over her body and blows smoke towards her, while she tries her best to be formal and correct. In short, this is the conflict of the spirit and the flesh. Furthermore, Viridiana's lifeless objects – the nails, the hammer, the crown of thorns – form a marked contrast to Jorge's practical efforts to rebuild his father's house. In one telling sequence she leads the beggars in prayer, while nearby the restoration of buildings continues, the two activities juxtaposed in a series of alternating shots: on the one hand, the beggars praying under the blossoms of the almond trees; on the other, shots of cement slapped onto a dilapidated wall; lime falling into a tub of water; sand being sifted; logs falling onto the ground; stones tipped from a wheelbarrow; planks being sawed. In effect, Buñuel portrays Jorge as a man of progress, someone who, by installing electricity in his father's house, brings light where darkness prevailed, and which Viridiana, in her naivety, merely perpetuates.

If Jorge mocks her way of life, her ineffectiveness in terms of changing the world for the better is fully exposed by the behaviour of the beggars. They, short of almost every human comfort, are inevitably self-seeking and only too eager to accept Viridiana's offer of food and shelter, but their real opinion of her is expressed early on by Enedina: 'She's very good, but a bit of a simpleton.' Knowing full well that they have to remain in her good books, they are polite and respectful in her presence, but true to their selfish instincts when they are not. So it is in the sequence in which she appears with two new guests, one of them the 'leper', for, as soon as she has turned her back, the others ignore her request that they treat him 'as though he were a sick brother', threaten him, and force him out of the room. In other words, her Christian charity is accepted with a gratitude that is entirely false and does nothing to improve those on whom it is lavished.

Strangely enough, the futility of compassion in a harsh world is illustrated by the otherwise practical Jorge in relation to a dog. When a cart passes by, Jorge takes pity on the dog, which is tied by a rope to the axle and forced to run between the wheels. He buys the dog from the owner in order to save it from further suffering, but, no sooner has he done so than another cart comes in the opposite direction, with another dog in a similar predicament. The incident is amusing in one way, but it also reveals that Jorge's compassion is a drop in the ocean that really achieves very little, and the same is true of Viridiana just afterwards, when her attention is drawn to the 'leper'. The workmen, anxious to avoid him, have tied a tin can to his waist so that, when he comes near, its sound acts as a warning. As Jorge unties the dog from the cart, so Viridiana unties the can, but this by no means prevents the workmen from repeating their action when she is out of sight. Her pity offers the 'leper' only a temporary respite.

Viridiana's actions achieve in the end the very opposite of her initial intentions, as the last third of the film effectively reveals. When Viridiana and Jorge leave the house in order to take the little girl, Rita, to visit a dentist, the beggars cannot resist the temptation to enter the house, despite their promise that they will act responsibly. Subsequently, as they fill their stomachs with food and wine, their behaviour gets completely out of hand, and finally, when

Viridiana and Jorge return, he is knocked unconscious by the 'leper' and another of the beggars attempts to rape Viridiana. The fact is that none of this would have happened had not Viridiana taken the beggars under her wing. Her motives are undoubtedly good, her Christian values unquestionable, but Buñuel's suggestion is that, in a world where selfishness, greed, anger, and lust are ever present, compassion and charity merely feed those moral flaws. Indeed, the point is made even more strongly in relation to Jorge's actions during the beggar's attempted rape of Viridiana.

As the beggar pins her to the bed, her protests prove to be in vain, and when her hand grasps the phallic-like handle of the skipping-rope that the beggar uses as a belt, she faints, overcome by that same sexual association and fear that prevented her from grasping the cow's teat in an early sequence of the film. As for Jorge, he recovers his senses sufficiently to see what is happening and, in response to it, adopts a course of action that in the circumstances is entirely pragmatic and effective. Realising that, because he has been tied up, he cannot intervene directly, he appeals to the 'leper's greed by promising him money if he kills the rapist. It is a prospect that the 'leper' cannot resist and an opportunity too to take revenge on someone who had earlier threatened him with a knife. At all events, the 'leper' picks up a small shovel and strikes the rapist a number of savage blows to the head before helping himself to the money and leaving. In short, Jorge's practical intervention, based on his knowledge and experience of human nature, rescues the situation in a way that Viridiana's approach to life could never do. It is one of the film's great ironies that, in effect, she is 'saved' not by an appeal to the 'leper's better nature but to his self-interest.

As a consequence of this traumatic incident, Viridiana changes fundamentally. A sequence in which Jorge is seen supervising the installation of electricity in the house also reveals that Viridiana is now dressed differently – in a print blouse. The juxtaposition of Jorge's practical tasks and Viridiana's much more worldly appearance indicates that she is already in the process of transformation – an impression that is confirmed when, in her room a little later, she loosens her hair and studies her appearance in a mirror. Furthermore, outside her room the crown of thorns, which had been part of her religious baggage, has been thrown onto a fire. It points to the fact that Viridiana is about to rise from the ashes of her former way of life into a life that is very different and which is signalled by her joining Jorge and Ramona in a game of cards, which effectively points to a *ménage à trois*. The religious music that has earlier been heard on the sound-track becomes, significantly, a piece of jazz music to the words 'Shake your cares away'. In Buñuel's view it signifies Viridiana's salvation, her acceptance of the world as it is, and her deliverance from the chains of her earlier narrow-minded and futile beliefs.

Buñuel's preoccupation with the Catholic Church and its teachings runs through his films from *L'Âge d'or* to *The Milky Way*, sometimes very prominently indeed, at other times more marginally but rarely altogether absent.

His education during his early teenage years at a Jesuit institution marked him as much as his upbringing in a bourgeois family, and even if, afterwards, he was to rebel against it, it was something he could never shake off. Indeed, religious issues held a constant appeal for Buñuel because they so profoundly affect the behaviour of men and women – his true interest. In his films, therefore, we encounter all manner of religious individuals: dogmatic and hypocritical priests, well-intentioned people such as Nazarín and Viridiana, fanatics such as Simon, the heretics of *The Milky Way*. As for Buñuel himself, his fascination with religion may be gauged by the fact that during his final illness he spent a good deal of time with a priest, Father Julián (Rucar de Buñuel, 130). It seems hardly likely, though, that, as in the case of Don Lope in *Tristana*, the priest came to enjoy Buñuel's chocolate.

CONCLUSION

Luis Buñuel's career as a film-maker was extremely long – from *Un Chien andalou* in 1929 to *That Obscure Object of Desire* in 1977 – very largely consistent in terms of themes and technique, and singularly brilliant. It falls roughly, as the preceding chapters suggest, into three parts, though it is important to emphasise that these are not mutually exclusve, for Buñuel's work is distinguished by recurring personal, social and religious preoccupations. The first period corresponds to the years 1929 to 1934 and the completion of his three unmistakably surrealist films: *Un Chien andalou, L'Âge d'or* and *Las Hurdes*. The second period extends from around 1946 to 1960, when Buñuel spent most of his time in Mexico, making largely commercial films on low budgets and in a limited period of time. And the third period, when he divided his time between Mexico, France and Spain, saw the completion of the films for which he is best known and for the making of which he enjoyed much greater financial resources and artistic freedom than he had in Mexico: *Belle de jour, The Discreet Charm of the Bourgeoisie* and *That Obscure Object of Desire.*

As is often the case with young and committed creative artists, Buñuel's early work is the most explosive. Seventy-five years on, the disconcerting effect on the spectator of *Un Chien andalou* is as great today as it ever was, the slicing of the young woman's eye-ball with a cut-throat razor as likely to elicit reactions of horror and panic as it did in 1929. It is a moment that has written itself indelibly into the history of cinema, while the film as a whole, a mere seventeen minutes long, remains the only example of surrealist cinema to have made a truly lasting impression. Its power stems undoubtedly from the resolve of both Buñuel and Dalí to put on the screen a series of images, which in their illogicality, their dream-like nature and their sexual implications encapsulated the principles of Surrealism and struck out at traditional cinematic values as much as Picasso's *Les Demoiselles d'Avignon* turned on their head traditional ideas in painting. In many ways *Un Chien andalou* is André Breton's *Manifesto of Surrealism* put into practice. But it is also more than this, for its haunting, dream-like sequences are also a clear anticipation of the emphasis on the unconscious that would become the hallmark of Buñuel's future work.

His second film, *L'Âge d'or*, similarly anticipates Buñuel's lifelong preoccupation with the bourgeoisie. The extended dinner-party sequence at the villa of the Marquis of X is one that Buñuel introduces again, in a somewhat different form, in *The Exterminating Angel, Viridiana* and *The Discreet Charm of the Bourgeoisie*. Furthermore, although *L'Âge d'or* has little dialogue, it contains the scathing observation of the rich and the privileged, of their self-absorption and indifference to everything outside their circle, as well as of their emotional isolation, that runs throughout Buñuel's work. If *Un Chien andalou* is a visual illustration of Breton's *Manifesto of Surrealism*, then *L'Âge d'or* can equally be regarded as the cinematic equivalent of the *Second Surrealist Manifesto* of 1929, with its greater political and social emphasis. In addition, certain elements in the early part of the film and, in particular, the closing sequence, with its identification of Christ and the cruel and lustful Duke of Blangis, look forward to the lacerating attacks on the Catholic Church that distinguish such films as *Viridiana, Nazarín, The Exterminating Angel* and *Simon of the Desert*. Above all, though, *L'Âge d'or*, in the form of the two lovers, contains Buñuel's core theme, highly relevant to his own experience, of instinctive desire and passion blighted by traditional social, moral and religious values. In terms of its form – its five sections seem initially to have little to do with each other – *L'Âge d'or* is in some respects as disconcerting as *Un Chien andalou*.

If *L'Âge d'or* proved to be a surrealist bomb, as startling in its effect on those who saw it in 1930 as the explosion in the Paris street that ends *That Obscure Object of Desire* forty-seven years later, *Las Hurdes* was an altogether quieter and more subversive device, but nonetheless lethal for that. One of the striking features of this film is that, unusually, Buñuel's attack is not on the individuals who appear in it but on those outside it, those who possess administrative and governmental power and who, over many years, have shown themselves to be indifferent to the suffering of the inhabitants of Las Hurdes. Buñuel's film is also the traditional travel documentary turned on its head, for, instead of showing the interested spectator the alluring and attractive aspects of the region in question, he exposes him or her to increasingly uncomfortable horrors. In relation to the objectives of Surrealism, *Las Hurdes* has moved well away from the emphasis on the revelation of the unconscious mind, but its political aims and its stinging attack on, in this case, the unseen bourgeoisie, are very clear. In some ways the episode in *L'Âge d'or* in which the bourgeois guests of the Marquis of X appear on the balcony, rather like royalty, observe down below the body of the child shot by his father, and express little more than mild disapproval, is extended in Buñuel's third film. The only difference, certainly at the first screenings of *Las Hurdes*, was that the bourgeoisie formed the audience for the film, but, like the individuals in *L'Âge d'or*, they reacted coldly to what they saw, and, in afterwards banning it, effectively shut their eyes to what they had no wish to see or think about.

Buñuel's first three films constitute a surrealist trilogy in which, because he enjoyed total artistic freedom, he was able to remain wholly faithful to and express his beliefs without restriction. The outbreak of the Spanish Civil War in 1936, Buñuel's departure from Spain, and the relatively nomadic life that ensued, put paid to that independence and the initial creative flowering that sprang from it. Indeed, when he finally settled in Mexico in the mid-1940s and was able to resume his career as a film-maker, he was undoubtedly compromised by the constraints of the commercial film industry in terms of subject-matter, budgets and deadlines, making some twenty films in eighteen years. The free spirit of the early surrealist period gave way to stereotypical melodramas and comedies in which narrative structure and more rounded characterisation became requisites. Nevertheless, if films like *Susana* and *Daughter of Deceit* represent lesser Buñuel, the wonder is that, within such restrictions, he succeeded in making a number of films that are quite outstanding: in particular, *The Forgotten Ones*, *He, Rehearsal for a Crime: the Criminal Life of Archibaldo de la Cruz* and *The Exterminating Angel*. In all of these, and in others too, Buñuel was able to return to those themes that he had explored in the surrealist trilogy and that would distinguish his later masterpieces. *The Forgotten Ones*, for example, portrays the slum children and the underprivileged of Mexico City, and in that sense can be seen as an extension of *Las Hurdes*, and an indictment of the powers-that-be who do nothing to remedy the lot of the poor. But the portrayal of objective reality is also accompanied in this film by the revelation, through powerful and highly suggestive dream sequences, of the inner life of some of the characters. In short, *The Forgotten Ones* combines two of the essential strands of Surrealism, and the same can be said of Buñuel's magnificent *The Exterminating Angel*, made twelve years later. The bourgeois characters of this film, reminiscent of the Marquis of X's guests in *L'Âge d'or*, are precisely those people who bear responsibility for the plight of the the poor and the suffering of *Las Hurdes* and *The Forgotten Ones*. Buñuel's exposure of their self-centredness is once more uncompromising, but the truly extraordinary aspect of *The Exterminating Angel* lies in the fact that, after several weeks of deprivation and isolation, these well-to-do individuals are shown to be just as cruel and ruthless in their efforts to survive as the deprived and homeless of Mexico City. Furthermore, they are haunted by terrible dreams, expressive of deep-rooted fears and anxieties, which are little different from those experienced by the characters of *The Forgotten Ones*. In other words, although both films depict two worlds that could not be more different from each other, we are made aware of one of Buñuel's increasingly important themes – his belief that in the last resort all men are fundamentally the same, part of a common humanity.

The Mexican films remain unknown to the majority of film enthusiasts, despite their obvious merits. In contrast, many of the films made between 1960 and 1977 have become extremely well known, especially those made in France. During this period Buñuel enjoyed much greater financial resources, particularly as a result of his friendship with the producer Serge Silberman, and films such as *The Discreet Charm of the Bourgeoisie* and *That Obscure Object of Desire* are distinguished by their excellent actors, their sophistication and their technical excellence. But there are also two films of outstanding quality that were made in Spain and that are arguably more powerful and corrosive than the French films: *Viridiana* and *Tristana*, in both of which two of Buñuel's favourite targets – the bourgeoisie and the Catholic Church – are ruthlessly exposed.

Buñuel's return to Spain in 1960 in order to make *Viridiana* undoubtedly provided him with the spur to launch an attack on the Church, which still firmly backed the Franco dictatorship, and the bourgeoisie, which inevitably championed right-wing values. The coldness and, indeed, the hypocrisy of the Church is embodied in the Mother Superior when she is informed of Viridiana's decision not to return to the convent, while Buñuel's parody of Leonardo's *The Last Supper*, in which the drunken beggars substitute for Christ and the disciples, and the final burning of Viridiana's crown of thorns, contributed greatly to the banning of the film for many years both in Spain and elsewhere. In this respect, *Viridiana* is underpinned by the calculated ferocity that distinguished Buñuel's early work, a point suggested by the fact that the reaction to it was also as furious as that which had surrounded the Paris screenings of *L'Âge d'or* thirty years earlier. As for the representation of the bourgeoisie, Don Jaime, the ageing property owner, possesses the typical indolence and passivity of a class that depends on others to do the hard work. Lacking servants, he has allowed his estate to fall into ruin. Jorge, inheriting his father's property, represents, on the other hand, the new bourgeois order, for he is ambitious, calculating and entirely materialistic – in truth, little better than the beggars who abuse Viridiana's charity towards them.

Similarly, *Tristana*, made ten years later, is one of Buñuel's truly angry films. The action is placed, significantly, in the years leading up to the beginning of the Civil War, a time in which left- and right-wing values were already polarised. Despite his frequent claims to practise liberal attitudes, including free love and the undesirability of marriage, Don Lope is, in reality, a feudal overlord who does his utmost to restrict Tristana's freedom, marries her and, despite his attacks on religion, welcomes priests into his house as his health declines. Furthermore, his sexual abuse of the young Tristana, his ward, is in part responsible for turning her into the cold, manipulative woman she becomes in later life – a withering indictment of the subservient role to which, particularly in the past, women were condemned in a society influenced by the Church and by a male-dominated society that fed off its teachings in relation to the role of women.

In both *Viridiana* and *Tristana* there is a Goyesque darkness, which owes much to the fact that Buñuel was on home ground. In contrast, the French films of the 1960s, and particularly of the 1970s, have on the whole a greater sophistication and an increasing mellowness, which are also, no doubt, attributable to the director's advancing years and the damping down of his earlier fires. This is not entirely true of either *The Diary of a Chambermaid* or *Belle de jour*, but it is certainly the case in both *The Discreet Charm of the Bourgeoisie* and *That Obscure Object of Desire*.

The Diary of a Chambermaid allowed Buñuel to expose, through the experiences of the servant, Célestine, the materialism, self-centredness and sexual aberrations of the French bourgeoisie, as well as the way in which these things affect the servants, in a detailed portrait reminiscent both of parts of *L'Âge d'or* and *The Exterminating Angel*. The latter also comes to mind in relation to *Belle de jour*, for the dreams and fantasies of Séverine are not unlike those of the bourgeois characters of the earlier film, though in her case they are motivated by sexual frustration and guilt rather than fear. Indeed, in *Belle de jour*, for all its surface gloss and glamour, Buñuel delivers some telling blows against a social class whose belief in correctness and formality deadens its ability to act in accordance with natural instincts and desires. It is a film in which, in true surrealist manner, the expression of the unconscious mind through dreams and the attack on right-wing values are powerfully interwoven.

The Discreet Charm of the Bourgeoisie and *That Obscure Object of Desire* both embody Buñuel's preoccupation with bourgeois values, but, in his seventies, the iron fist has largely given way to the velvet glove, and the nature of his attack is more ironic than cutting. There is, after all, much more of a joke in the repeated failure of six bourgeois characters to settle down to a meal than in their callous exploitation of the lower classes, though the Bishop's ruthless killing of a peasant and the Ambassador's drug-trafficking are reminders of the more serious Buñuel. The film also contains, like *Belle de jour*, a number of dream sequences, but on the whole they are now introduced not so much to reveal the subconscious desires and fears of the characters as to scare them, in the manner of grim jokes and horror stories. As for *That Obscure Object of Desire*, the entire film is in some respects an extended joke against the bourgeois Mathieu, his repeated failures to possess Conchita a source of increasing amusement. Photographs of Buñuel in his seventies reveal a marked decline, a waning of physical powers in someone who once took pride in his fitness and conditioning. In the same way, the late films, though sharp and amusing, suggest that the anger that had motivated much of his earlier work had now largely subsided.

As well as voicing the concerns that lay at the heart of the surrealist movement, Buñuel's work as a whole is also, as we have seen, an expression of his sexual inhibitions and dilemmas. In his paintings of the late 1920s and the 1930s, Dalí projected his own sexual anguish, and in his plays, even though the characters are often female, Lorca dramatised his frustrations and disappointments in love. In this respect Buñuel was not much different from his two friends, but it is an aspect of his work which, despite its importance, has received little attention. Some critics would argue that knowledge of a creative artist's life does not improve the quality of his work. On the other hand, it is perfectly possible to argue that, in channelling his personal life into his work, a novelist, poet, dramatist, painter or musician, gives that work an emotional colouring that it would not otherwise have. Would Van Gogh's late paintings be as febrile as they are, had his state of mind been more stable? Would Tchaikovsky, in *Eugene Onegin*, have had Tatyana send to Onegin a written proposal of marriage, had not the composer received a similar proposal from a young woman shortly before beginning work on the opera? Looked at in this way, Buñuel's films are, from start to finish, auto-biographical – not in their detail but in the emotional conflicts their characters embody.

In terms of their cinematic style, Buñuel's films are, in comparison with present-day movies, relatively simple and straightforward. Often constrained within tight budgets and deadlines, as in the case of the Mexican films of his middle period, he worked quickly and economically, frequently shooting a film in little more than a month. Indeed, even the completion of a film as sophisticated as *Viridiana* took little longer, for work on it commenced in February 1961 and it was premièred in May of the same year. As was the case with many Hollywood directors who were obliged to work with maximum economy, Buñuel frequently employed the so-called mid or Hollywood shot (a single or a number of characters filmed three-quarter length), or the close-up in order to emphasise the significance of an object or to capture the emotion behind the facial expression of a character. At all events, there are no tricks in his method of filming. His unpretentious style has the advantage of allowing the narrative of a film to develop, without distraction, shot by shot, in an apparently effortless manner, which is, of course, the hallmark of the artist in complete command of his material. In short, there is often an artless-ness about a Buñuel film which, as in the case of a beautifully crafted piece of music, conceals the art that has produced it – invariably the sign of a true master.

FILMOGRAPHY

Buñuel as Director

UN CHIEN ANDALOU, 1929
Producer: Luis Buñuel
Screenplay: Luis Buñuel and Salvador Dalí
Photography: Albert Duverger
Art Director: Pierre Schilzneck
Music: Extracts from Beethoven, Wagner (*Tristan and Isolde*), and tangos selected by Buñuel
Editor: Luis Buñuel
Cast: Pierre Batcheff, Simon Mareuil, Jaume Miravitlles, Salvador Dalí, and Luis Buñuel
Running time: 17 minutes

L'ÂGE D'OR, 1930
Producer: Viscount of Noailles
Screenplay: Luis Buñuel and Salvador Dalí
Photography: Albert Duverger
Art Director: Pierre Schilzneck
Music: Georges Van Parys, and extracts from Beethoven, Debussy, Mendelssohn, Mozart and Wagner
Editor: Luis Buñuel
Assistant Directors: Jacques Bernard Brunius and Claude Heymann
Sound: Peter-Paul Brauer
Cast: Gaston Modot (the young man), Lya Lys (the young woman, daughter of the Marquise), Caridad de Lamberdesque (the woman), Pierre Prévert (a bandit), Max Ernst (leader of the bandits), Paul Éluard
Running time: 63 minutes

LAS HURDES/ TIERRA SIN PAN (LAND WITHOUT BREAD), 1932
Producer: Ramón Acín
Screenplay: Luis Buñuel, Pierre Unik and Julio Acín
Photography: Eli Lotar
Music: Extracts from Brahms's Fourth Symphony
Editor: Luis Buñuel

Assistant Directors: Pierre Unik and Rafael Sánchez Ventura
Sound: Charles Goldblatt and Pierre Braunberger
Cast: Abel Jacquin (narrator)
Running time: 27 minutes

GRAN CASINO, 1946
Production Company: Películas Anahuac
Producer: Oscar Dancigers
Executive Producer: Federico Amérigo
Screenplay: Mauricio Magdaleno, from the novel by Michel Weber
Photography: Jack Draper
Art Director: Javier Torres Rorija
Music: Manuel Esperón
Editor: Gloria Schoemann
Assistant Director: Moisés M. Delgado
Chief of Production: José Luis Busto
Sound: Javier Mateos and José de Pérez
Make-up: Armando Meyer
Cast: Libertad Lamarque (Mercedes), Jorge Negrete (Gerardo), Mercedes
    Barba (Camelia), Agustín Isunza (Heriberto), Julio Villareal (Demetrio)
Running time: 85 minutes

THE GREAT CAROUSER (EL GRAN CALAVERA), 1949
Production Company: Ultramar Films
Producers: Fernando Soler and Oscar Dancigers
Executive Producer: Federico Amérigo
Associate Producer: Antonio de Salazar
Screenplay: Luis Alcoriza and Raquel Rojas, from the comedy by Adolfo
    Torrado
Photography: Ezequiel Carrasco
Art Directors: Luis Moya and Darío Cabañas
Music: Manuel Esperón
Editor: Carlos Savage
Assistant Director: Moisés M. Delgado
Chief of Production: Alberto A. Ferrer
Sound: Rafael Ruiz Esparza and Jesús González Gancy
Make-up: Ana Guerrero
Cast: Fernando Soler (Ramiro), Rosario Granados (Virginia), Andrés Soler
    (Ladislao), Rubén Rojo (Pablo), Gustavo Rojo (Eduardo)
Running time: 90 minutes

THE FORGOTTEN ONES (LOS OLVIDADOS), also known as **THE
YOUNG AND THE DAMNED**, 1950
Production Company: Ultramar Films

Producers: Oscar Dancigers and Jaime Menasce
Executive Producer: Federico Amérigo
Screenplay: Luis Buñuel and Luis Alcoriza, with the assistance of Max Aub
and Pedro de Urdimalas
Photography: Gabriel Figueroa
Art Director: Edward Fitzgerald
Music: Rodolfo Halffter, based on music by Gustavo Pittaluga
Editor: Carlos Savage
Assistant Director: Ignacio Villarreal
Chief of Production: Fidel Pizarro
Sound: José B. Carles and Jesús González Gancy
Make-up: Armando Meyer
Cast: Alfonso Mejía (Pedro), Roberto Cobo (Jaibo), Stella Inda (Pedro's
mother), Miguel Inclán (Carmelo), Alma Delia Fuentes (Meche), Mario
Ramírez (Ojitos)
Running time: 88 minutes

SUSANA, 1950
Production Company: Internacional Cinematográfica
Screenplay: Luis Buñuel, Jaime Salvador and Rodolfo Usigli
Photography: José Ortiz Ramos
Art Director: Gunther Gerszo
Music: Raúl Lavista
Editor: Jorge Bustos
Assistant Director: Ignacio Villarreal
Chief of Production: Fidel Pizarro
Sound: Nicolás de la Rosa
Make-up: Ana Guerrero
Cast: Fernando Soler (Guadalupe), Rosita Quintana (Susana), Víctor Manuel
Mendoza (Jesús), Matilde Palou (Carmen), María Gentil Arcos (Felisa),
Luis López Somoza (Alberto)
Running time: 80 minutes

**DAUGHTER OF DECEIT (LA HIJA DEL ENGAÑO / DON QUINTÍN
EL AMARGAO)**, 1951
Production Company: Ultramar Films
Producer: Oscar Dancigers
Executive Producer: Federico Amérigo
Screenplay: Luis Alcoriza and Raquel Rojas (from the play, *Don Quintín el
amargao*, by Carlos Arniches and José Estremera)
Photography: José Ortiz Ramos
Art Directors: Edward Fitzgerald and Pablo Galván
Music: Manuel Esperón
Editor: Carlos Savage

Assistant Director: Mario Llorca
Chief of Production: Fidel Pizarro
Sound: Eduardo Arjona and Jesús González Gancy
Make-up: Ana Guerrero
Cast: Fernando Soler (Quintín), Alicia Caro (Mara), Rubén Rojo (Paco), Fernando Soto 'Mantequilla' (Angelito), Nacho Contla (Jonrón)
Running time: 80 minutes

STAIRWAY TO HEAVEN (SUBIDA AL CIELO), 1951
Production Company: Producciones Isla
Producers: Manuel Altolaguirre and María Luisa Gómez Mena
Screenplay: Luis Buñuel, Manuel Altolaguirre, Juan de la Cabada and Lilia Solano Galeana
Photography: Alex Phillips
Art Director: José Rodríguez Granada
Music: Gustavo Pittaluga
Editor: Rafael Portillo
Assistant Director: Jorge López Portillo
Chief of Production: Fidel Pizarro
Sound: Eduardo Arjona and Jesús González Glancy
Costume: Georgette Somohano
Cast: Lilia Prado (Raquel), Carmen González (Albina), Esteban Márquez (Oliverio), Luis Aceves Castañeda (Silvestre), Roberto Cobo (Juan)
Running time: 85 minutes

A WOMAN WITHOUT LOVE (UNA MUJER SIN AMOR), 1951
Production Company: Internacional Cinematográfica
Producer: Sergio Kogan
Screenplay: Jaime Salvador, from *Pierre et Jean*, by Guy de Maupassant
Photography: Raúl Martínez Solares
Art Director: Gunther Gerszo
Music: Raúl Lavista
Assistant Director: Mario Llorca
Chief of Production: José Luis Busto
Sound: Rodolfo Benítez
Make-up: Ana Guerrero
Cast: Rosario Granados (Rosario), Tito Junco (Julio), Julio Villa Real (Don Carlos), Jaime Calpe (Carlitos), Joaquín Cordero (Carlos), Xavier Loyá (Miguel), Elda Peralta (Luisa), Eva Calvo, Miguel Manzano
Running time: 90 minutes

ROBINSON CRUSOE, 1952
Production Company: Ultramar Films and OLMEC, for United Artists
Producers: Oscar Dancigers and Henry F. Ehrlich

Screenplay: Luis Buñuel and Phillip Ansell Roll, from the novel by Daniel
  Defoe
Photography: Alex Phillips
Art Director: Edward Fitzgerald
Music: Luis Hernández Bretón and Anthony Collins
Editors: Carlos Savage and Alberto Valenzuela
Assistant Director: Ignacio Villarreal
Chief of Production: Federico Amérigo
Sound: Javier Mateos
Make-up: Armando Meyer
Cast: Dan O'Herlihy (Robinson Crusoe), Jaime Fernández (Friday), Felipe de
  Alba (Captain), Chel López (Bosun), José Chávez and Emilio Garibay
  (mutineers)
Running time: 89 minutes

THE BRUTE (EL BRUTO), 1952
Production Company: Internacional Cinematográfica
Producer: Sergio Kogan
Executive Producer: Gabriel Castro
Screenplay: Luis Buñuel and Luis Alcoriza
Photography: Agustín Jiménez
Art Directors: Gunther Gerszo, assisted by Roberto Silva
Music: Raúl Lavista
Editor: Jorge Bustos
Assistant Director: Ignacio Villarreal
Chief of Production: Fidel Pizarro
Sound: Javier Mateos and Galdino Samperio
Make-up: Ana Guerrero
Cast: Pedro Armendáriz (Pedro), Katy Jurado (Paloma), Rosita Arenas
  (Meche), Andrés Cabrera (Andrés Soler), Roberto Meyer (Carmelo
  González), Paco Martínez (Don Pepe)
Running time: 83 minutes

HE (EL), 1952
Production Company: Ultramar Films
Producer: Oscar Dancigers
Executive Producer: Federico Amérigo
Screenplay: Luis Buñuel and Luis Alcoriza, from the novel by Mercedes
  Pinto
Photography: Gabriel Figueroa
Art Directors: Edward Fitzgerald and Pablo Galván
Music: Luis Hernández Bretón
Editor: Carlos Savage
Assistant Director: Ignacio Villarreal

Chief of Production: Fidel Pizarro
Sound: José D. Pérez and Jesús González Gancy
Make-up: Armando Meyer
Cast: Arturo de Córdoba (Francisco), Delia Garcés (Gloria), Luis Beristaín (Raúl), Aurora Walker (Esperanza), Carlos Martínez Baena (Padre Velasco), Manuel Dondé (manservant)
Running time: 91 minutes

THE TRAM-RIDE OF DREAMS (LA ILUSIÓN VIAJA EN TRANVÍA), 1953

Production Company: Clasa Films Mundiales
Producer: Armando Orive Alba
Executive Producer: José Ramón Aguirre
Screenplay: Mauricio de la Serna, José Revueltas, Luis Alcoriza and Juan de la Cabada
Photography: Raúl Martínez Solares
Art Director: Edward Fitzgerald
Music: Luis Hernández Bretón
Editor: Jorge Bustos
Assistant Director: Ignacio Villarreal
Chief of Production: Fidel Pizarro
Sound: José D. Pérez and Rafael Ruiz Esparza
Make-up: Elda Loza
Cast: Lilia Prado (Lupita), Carlos Navarro (Juan), Fernando Soto 'Mantequilla' (Tarrajas), Agustín Isunza (Papá Pinillos), Miguel Manzano (Don Manuel)
Running time: 82 minutes

THE ABYSS OF PASSION/WUTHERING HEIGHTS (ABISMOS DE PASIÓN), 1953

Production Company: Producciones Tepeyac
Producers: Oscar Dancigers and Abelardo L. Rodríguez
Executive Producer: Federico Amérigo
Screenplay: Luis Buñuel, Julio Alejandro and Arduino Mairui, from the novel by Emily Brontë
Photography: Agustín Jiménez
Art Director: Edward Fitzgerald
Music: Raúl Lavista (based on Wagner's *Tristan and Isolde*)
Editor: Carlos Savage
Assistant Director: Ignacio Villarreal
Chief of Production: Alberto A. Ferrer
Sound: Eduardo Arjona and Caldino Samperio
Costume: Armando Valdés Peza
Make-up: Felisa Ladrón de Guevara

Cast: Irasema Dilián (Catalina), Jorge Mistral (Alejandro), Lilia Prado (Isabel), Ernesto Alonso (Eduardo), Luis Aceves Castañeda (Ricardo)
Running time: 91 minutes

THE RIVER AND DEATH (EL RÍO Y LA MUERTE), 1954
Production Company: Clasa Films Mundiales
Producer: Armando Orive Alba
Executive Producer: José Ramón Aguirre
Screenplay: Luis Buñuel and Luis Alcoriza, from the novel by Manuel Alvarez Acosta
Photography: Raúl Martínez Solares
Art Director: Gunther Gerszo
Music: Raúl Lavista
Editor: Jorge Bustos
Assistant Director: Ignacio Villarreal
Chief of Production: José Alcalde Gámiz
Sound: José D. Pérez and Rafael Ruiz Esparza
Make-up: Margarita Ortega
Cast: Columba Domínguez (Mercedes), Miguel Torruco (Felipe Anguiano), Joaquín Cordero (Gerardo), Jaime Fernández (Rómulo), Víctor Alcocer (Polo)
Running time: 93 minutes

REHEARSAL FOR A CRIME: THE CRIMINAL LIFE OF ARCHIBALDO DE LA CRUZ (ENSAYO DE UN CRIMEN: LA VIDA CRIMINAL DE ARCHIBALDO DE LA CRUZ), 1955
Production Company: Alianza Cinematográfica
Producer: Alfonso Patiño Gómez
Executive Producer: Roberto Figueroa
Screenplay: Luis Buñuel and Eduardo Ugarte, from the novel by Rodolfo Usigli
Photography: Agustín Jiménez
Art Director: Jesús Bracho
Music: Jorge Pérez Herrera
Editor: Jorge Bustos
Assistant Director: Luis Abadíe
Chief of Production: Armando Espinosa
Sound: Rodolfo Benítez, Enrique Rodríguez and Ernesto Caballero
Make-up: Sara Mateos
Cast: Ernesto Alonso (Archibaldo), Miroslava Stern (Lavinia), Rita Macedo (Patricia), Ariadna Welter (Carlota), José María Linares Rivas (Willy), Rodolfo Landa (Alejandro), Andrea Palma (Señora Cervantes), Eva Calvo and Enrique Díaz Indiano (Archibaldo's parents)
Running time: 89 minutes

THE BREAK OF DAWN (CELA S'APELLE L'AURORE), 1955

Production Company: Les Films Marceau, Laetitia Films
Screenplay: Luis Buñuel and Jean Ferry, from the novel by Emmanuel Robles
Photography: Robert Lefebvre
Art Director: Maz Douy
Music: Joseph Kosma
Editor: Marguerite Renoir
Assistant Directors: Marcel Camus and Jacques Deray
Chief of Production: André Cultet
Sound: Antoine Petijean
Cast: Georges Marchal (Doctor Valerio), Lucía Bosé (Clara), Nelly Borgeaud (Angela), Gianni Espósito (Sandro Galli), Julien Bertheau (Chief of Police)
Running time: 102 minutes

GARDEN OF DEATH (MORT EN CE JARDIN), 1956

Production Company: Producciones Tepeyac, Films Dismage
Producers: Oscar Dancigers and David Mage
Executive Producers: Léon Caré and Antonio de Salazar
Screenplay: Luis Buñuel, Luis Alcoriza, Raymond Queneau and Gabriel Arout, from the novel by José-André Lacour
Photography: Jorge Stahl Jr
Art Director: Edward Fitzgerald
Music: Paul Misraki
Editor: Marguerite Renoir
Assistant Directors: Ignacio Villarreal and Dossia Mage
Chief of Production: Alberto A. Ferrer
Sound: José D. Pérez and Galdino Samperio
Cast: Simone Signoret (Djinn), Georges Marchal (Shark), Charles Vanel (Castin), Michel Piccoli (Father Lisardi), Tito Junco (Chenko), Michèle Girardon (Maria)
Running time: 97 minutes

NAZARÍN, 1958

Production Company: Producciones Barbáchano Ponce
Producer: Manuel Barbáchano Ponce
Executive Producer: Federico Amérigo
Screenplay: Luis Buñuel and Julio Alejandro
Photography: Gabriel Figueroa
Art Director: Edward Fitzgerald
Music: Macedonio Alcalá
Editor: Carlos Savage
Assistant Director: Ignacio Villarreal
Chief of Production: Carlos Velo

Sound: José D. Pérez and Galdino Samperio
Costume: Georgette Somohano
Cast: Francisco Rabal (Nazarín), Marga López (Beatriz), Rita Macedo (Andara), Jesús Fernández (the dwarf), Ignacio López Tarso (the blasphemer), Ofelia Guilmáin (Chanfa)
Running time: 97 minutes

THE TEMPERATURE RISES IN EL PAO (LA FIÈVRE MONTE À EL PAO / LOS AMBICIOSOS), 1959

Production Company: Filmex, Films Borderie, Groupe des Quatre, Cité Films, Cormoran Films, Indus Films, Terra Films
Producers: Gregorio Walerstein and Raymond Borderie
Associate Producer: Oscar Dancigers
Executive Producer: Vicente Fernández
Screenplay: Luis Buñuel, Luis Alcoriza, Louis Sapin, Charles Dorat, Henri Castillou and José Luis González de León, from the novel by Henri Castillou
Photography: Gabriel Figueroa
Art Directors: Jorge Fernández and Pablo Galván
Music: Paul Misraki
Editor: James Cuenet (French version) and Rafael Caballos (Mexican version)
Assistant Director: Ignacio Villarreal
Chief of Production: Manuel Rodríguez
Sound: William-Robert Sivel (French version), Rodolfo Benítez and Roberto Camacho (Mexican version)
Costume: Ana María Jones and Armando Valdés Peza
Make-up: Armando Meyer
Cast: Gérard Phillipe (Vázquez), María Félix (Inés), Jean Servais (Alejandro), Víctor Junco (Indarte), Roberto Cañedo (Olivares)
Running time: 97 minutes

THE YOUNG ONE (LA JOVEN), 1960

Production Company: Producciones OLMEC, for Columbia Pictures
Producer: George P. Werker
Screenplay: Luis Buñuel and H.B. Addis, from *Travelin' Man* by Peter Mathiessen
Photography: Gabriel Figueroa
Art Director: Jesús Bracho
Music: Chucho Zarzosa
Editor: Carlos Savage
Assistant Directors: Ignacio Villarreal and Juan Luis Buñuel
Chief of Production: Manuel Rodríguez
Sound: James L. Fields, José B. Carles and Galdino Samperio

Make-up: Armando Meyer
Cast: Zachary Scott (Miller), Bernie Hamilton (Travers), Kay Meersman
(Evie), Graham
  Denton (Jackson), Claudio Brook (Reverend Fleetwood)
Running time: 96 minutes

VIRIDIANA, 1961
Production Company: Producciones Alatriste, Uninci, Films 59
Producers: Gustavo Alatristi, Pere Portabella
Executive Producer: Ricardo Muñoz Suay
Screenplay: Luis Buñuel and Julio Alejandro
Photography: José F. Aguayo
Art Director: Francisco Canet
Music: selections from Beethoven, Handel's *Messiah*, and Mozart's *Requiem*,
  arranged by Gustavo Pittaluga
Editor: Pedro del Rey
Assistant Directors: Juan Luis Buñuel and José Puyol
Chief of Production: Gustavo Quintana
Cast: Silvia Pinal (Viridiana), Francisco Rabal (Jorge), Fernando Rey
  (Jaime), Margarita Lozano (Ramona), Victoria Zinny (Lucía), Teresa
  Rabal (Rita), Lola Gaos (Enedina)
Running time: 90 minutes

THE EXTERMINATING ANGEL (EL ÁNGEL EXTERMINADOR), 1962
Production Company: Producciones Alatriste, Uninci, Films 59
Producer: Gustavo Alatriste
Executive Producer: Antonio de Salazar
Screenplay: Luis Buñuel and Luis Alcoriza
Photography: Gabriel Figueroa
Art Director: Jesús Bracho
Music: Raúl Lavista, selections from Beethoven, Chopin, and Scarlatti.
Editor: Carlos Savage
Assistant Director: Ignacio Villarreal
Chief of Production: Fidel Pizarro
Sound: José B. Carles
Costume: Georgette Somohano
Cast: Silvia Pinal (Leticia), Enrique Rambal (Edmundo Nobile), Jacqueline
  Andere (Alicia de Roc), José Baviera (Leandro Gómez), Augusto
  Benedicto (Doctor Carlos Conde), Claudio Brook (Julio)
Running time: 93 minutes

THE DIARY OF A CHAMBERMAID (JOURNAL D'UNE FEMME DE CHAMBRE), 1964

Production Company: Speva Films, Ciné Alliances Filmsonor, Dear Films
Producers: Serge Silberman and Michel Safra
Screenplay: Luis Buñuel and Jean-Claude Carrière, from the novel by Octave Mirbeau
Photography: Roger Fellous
Art Director: Georges Wakhevitch
Editor: Louisette Taverna-Hautecoeur
Assistant Directors: Juan Luis Buñuel and Pierre Lary
Chief of Production: Henri Baum
Sound: Antoine Petijean
Costume: Jacqueline Moreau
Cast: Jeanne Moreau (Célestine), Michel Piccoli (Monteil), Georges Géret (Joseph), Françoise Lugagne (Mme Monteil), Daniel Ivertiel (the Captain), Jean Ozenne (Rabour), Gilbert Geniat (Rose), Jean-Claude Carrière (the priest), Bernard Musson (the sacristan), Muni (Marianne), Dominique Sauvage (Claire)
Running time: 98 minutes

SIMON OF THE DESERT (SIMÓN DEL DESIERTO), 1965

Production Company: Producciones Alatriste
Producer: Gustavo Alatriste
Screenplay: Luis Buñuel and Julio Alejandro
Photography: Gabriel Figueroa
Music: Raúl Lavista and the *saetas* and drums for Holy Week in Calanda
Editor: Carlos Savage
Assistant Director: Ignacio Villarreal
Chief of Production: Armando Espinosa
Sound: James L. Fields and Luis Fernández
Make-up: Armando Meyer
Cast: Claudio Brook (Simón), Silvia Pinal (the Devil), Hortensia Santoveña (Simón's mother), Jesús Fernández (dwarf), Luis Acedes Castañeda (Trifón)
Running time: 42 minutes

BELLE DE JOUR, 1966

Production Company: Paris Films Production, Five Films
Producers: Robert and Raymond Hakim
Executive Producer: Robert Demollière
Screenplay: Luis Buñuel and Jean-Claude Carrière
Photography: Sacha Vierny
Art Director: Robert Clavel
Editor: Louisette Taverna-Hautcoeur

Assistant Director: Pierre Lary and Jacques Fraenkel
Chief of Production: Henri Baum
Sound: René Longuet
Costume: Hélène Nourry and Yves Saint-Laurent
Make-up: Janine Jarreau
Cast: Catherine Deneuve (Séverine), Jean Sorel (Pierre), Michel Piccoli (M. Husson), Geneviève Page (Mme Anaïs), Francisco Rabal (Hippolyte), Pierre Clementi (Marcel), Georges Marchal (the Duke), Françoise Fabian (Charlotte), Marie Latour (Mathilde), Francis Blanche (M. Adolphe), Macha Meril (Renée), Iska Khan (the Asiatic client), François Maistre (the gynaecologist), Muni (Pallas)
Running time: 100 minutes

THE MILKY WAY (LA VOIE LACTÉE), 1969
Production Company: Greenwich Film Production, Fraia Film
Producer: Serge Silberman
Associate Producer: Ully Pickard
Screenplay: Luis Buñuel and Jean-Claude Carrière
Photography: Christian Matras
Art Director: Pierre Guffroy
Music: Luis Buñuel
Editor: Louisette Taverna-Hautcoeur
Assistant Director: Pierre Lary
Chief of Production: Ully Pickard
Sound: Jacques Gallois
Costume: Jacqueline Guyot
Cast: Paul Frankeur (Pierre), Laurent Terzieff (Jean), Alain Cuny (man in cape), Edith Scob (María), Bernard Berley (Jesus), François Maistre (mad priest), Julien Bertheau (Richard), Muni (Jansenist nun), Michel Piccoli (Marquis de Sade), Pierre Clementi (the Devil), Georges Marchal (Jesuit), Claudio Brook (bishop), Jean Claude-Carrière (Priscillian), Delphine Seyrig (prostitute)
Running time: 98 minutes

TRISTANA, 1970
Production Company: Epoca Films, Talía Films, Selenia Cinematográfica and Les Films Corona
Executive Producers: Joaquín Gurruchaga and Eduardo Ducay
Screenplay: Luis Buñuel and Julio Alejandro, from the novel by Benito Pérez Galdós
Photography: José F. Aguayo
Art Director: Enrique Alarcón
Editor: Pedro del Rey
Assistant Director: José Puyol

Chief of Production: Juan Estelrich
Sound: José Nogueira and Dino Fronzetti
Make-up: Julián Ruiz
Cast: Catherine Deneuve (Tristana), Fernando Rey (Don Lope), Franco Nero
  (Horacio), Lola Gaos (Saturna), Jesús Fernández (Saturno)
Running time: 96 minutes

THE DISCREET CHARM OF THE BOURGEOISIE (LE CHARME DISCRET DE LA BOURGEOISIE), 1972
Production Company: Greenwich Film Production
Producer: Serge Silberman
Screenplay: Luis Buñuel and Jean-Claude Carrière
Photography: Edmond Richard
Art Director: Pierre Guffroy
Editor: Hélène Plemiannikov
Assistant Director: Pierre Lary
Chief of Production: Ully Pickard
Sound: Guy Villette
Cast: Fernando Rey (Rafael), Jean-Pierre Cassel (Sénéchal), Stéphane
  Audran (Alice), Paul Frankeur (Thévenot), Delphine Seyrig (Simone),
  Bulle Olger (Florence), Julien Bertheau (bishop), Muni (peasant woman),
  Michel Piccoli (minister), Bernard Musson (waiter), François Maistre
  (police inspector)
Running time: 100 minutes

THE PHANTOM OF LIBERTY (LE FANTÔME DE LA LIBERTÉ), 1974
Production Company: Greenwich Film Production
Producer: Serge Silberman
Screenplay: Luis Buñuel and Jean-Claude Carrière
Photography: Edmond Richard
Art Director: Pierre Guffroy
Music: Galaxie Musique
Editor: Hélène Plemiannikov
Assistant Directors: Pierre Lary and Jacques Fraenkel
Chief of Production: Ully Pickard
Sound: Guy Villette
Costume: Jacqueline Guyot
Make-up: Monique Archambault
Cast: Adriana Asti (woman in black), Julien Bertheau (prefect), Jean-Claude
  Brialy (Foucauld), Adolfo Celi (doctor), Paul Frankeur (innkeeper),
  François Maistre (instructor), Monica Vitti (Mme Foucauld), Muni
  (maid), Bernard Musson (monk), Hélène Perdrière (aged aunt), Pierre
  Maguelon (Gérard)

Running time: 104 minutes

THAT OBSCURE OBJECT OF DESIRE (CET OBSCUR OBJET DU DÉSIR), 1977

Production Company: Greenwich Film Production, Les Films Galazie, In Cine
Producer: Serge Silberman
Screenplay: Luis Buñuel and Jean-Claude Carrière, from the story, *La Femme et le pantin*, by Pierre Louÿs
Photography: Edmond Richard
Art Director: Pierre Guffroy and Pierre Bartlet
Music: extracts from Wagner and flamenco music
Editor: Hélène Plemiannikov
Assistant Directors: Pierre Lary and Juan Luis Buñuel
Chief of Production: Ully Pickard
Sound: Guy Villette
Costume: Sylvia de Segonzac
Make-up: Odette Berroyer
Cast: Fernando Rey (Mathieu), Angela Molina (Conchita), Carole Bouquet (Conchita), Julien Bertheau (Édouard), André Weber (Martin), Bernard Musson (police inspector), María Asquerino (Conchita's mother), Muni (concierge)
Running time: 103 minutes

Buñuel as Assistant Director

MAUPRAT, 1926, directed by Jean Epstein

TROPICAL SIREN (LA SIRÈNE DE TROPIQUES), 1927, directed by Henri Etievant and Marius Nalpas

THE FALL OF THE HOUSE OF USHER (CHUTE DE LA MAISON USHER), 1928, directed by Jean Epstein

Buñuel as Executive Producer at Filmofono

DON QUINTÍN, THE EMBITTERED ONE (DON QUINTÍN EL AMARGAO), 1935, directed by Luis Marquina

THE DAUGHTER OF JUAN SIMÓN (LA HIJA DE JUAN SIMÓN), 1935, directed by José Luis Sáenz de Heredia

SENTINEL, ON GUARD! (¡CENTINELA ALERTA!), 1936, directed by Jean Grémillon

WHO LOVES ME? (¿QUIÉN ME QUIERE A MÍ?), 1936, directed by José Luis Sáenz de Heredia

GUIDE TO FURTHER READING

La Révolution surréaliste (New York: Arno Press) reproduces numbers 1–12 (1924–29) of this important magazine and contains articles, surrealist texts and poems. No. 12 has the *Second Surrealist Manifesto* and the screenplay of *Un Chien andalou*. *André Breton, What is Surrealism?: Selected Writings*, ed. Franklin Rosemont (London: Pluto Press, 1978), presents a useful collection of articles, in translation, by the founder of Surrealism, written between the 1920s and the 1960s. Sarane Alexandrian, *Surrealist Art* (London: Thames & Hudson, 1970), focuses on Surrealism in painting and is lavishly illustrated, but due attention is also given to surrealist writings, in particular, poetry. Ado Kyrou, *Le Surréalisme au Cinéma* (Paris: Le Terrain Vague, 1963), provides expert comments on different aspects of surrealist cinema by one of the early writers on the subject. An informative account of the evolution of the surrealist movement, together with a discussion of the surrealist object and the surrealist image, is to be found in Anna Balakian, *Surrealism: the Road to the Absolute* (London: Allen & Unwin, 1972, first published 1959). The importance of the object as an extension of our subjective self, together with its significance in the writings of Breton and a consideration of Salvador Dalí's paranoia-critical method, is examined by Haim N. Finkelstein in *Surrealism and the Crisis of the Object* (Michigan: UMI Research Press, 1979). Mathew Gale writes on the roots of Dada in the Avant-Garde and considers the way in which it led to Surrealism in the lavishly illustrated *Dada and Surrealism* (London: Phaidon, 1977). And Ruth Brandon, in the very lively *Surreal Lives: the Surrealists 1917–1945* (London: Macmillan, 1999), traces the way in which the literary elements of Surrealism moved eventually to painting and provides a vivid account of the surrealists' private and public lives.

As far as Spanish Surrealism is concerned, Francisco Aranda, *El surrealismo español* (Barcelona: Editorial Lumen, 1981), makes a convincing case for a distinctive Spanish, as opposed to French, Surrealism. In contrast, C.B. Morris takes the opposite view, emphasising the effect of French Surrealism on Spain in *Surrealism and Spain* (Cambridge: Cambridge University Press, 1972). Robert Havard pursues the Aranda line, with particular emphasis on the poetry of Rafael Alberti between 1927 and 1936, in *The Crucified Mind: Rafael Alberti and the Surrealist Ethos in Spain* (London:

Tamesis, 2001). There is also substantial discussion of the work of Dalí, Buñuel, Lorca, Maruja Mallo, Giménez Caballero, and Vicente Aleixandre. Havard is also the editor of *Companion to Spanish Surrealism* (London: Tamesis, 2004), a collection of specialist essays on Surrealism in general, as well as on particular individuals such as Dalí and Buñuel.

Studies of Spanish cinema include John Hopewell's lively and informative *Out of the Past: Spanish Cinema After Franco* (London: British Film Institute, 1986), which, despite its title, looks back as well as forward, frequently referring to Buñuel. Similarly, Virginia Higginbotham's *Spanish Film Under Franco* (Austin: University of Texas Press, 1988), contains a chapter on Buñuel and his influence on younger Spanish film-makers, as well as many other references to his work. In *This Loving Darkness: The Cinema and Spanish Writers* (Oxford, London: University of Hull, 1980), C.B. Morris examines the enthusiasm for and opposition to the development of cinema in the Spain of the 1920s and 1930s, and considers the influence of the cinema on Spanish poets, playwrights and novelists. Marsha Kinder's *Blood Cinema: The Reconstruction of National Identity in Spain* (Berkeley, Los Angeles, London: University of California Press, 1993), applies contemporary critical theory to Spanish cinema and examines the work of key film-makers, including Buñuel. *Spanish Cinema: The Auteurist Tradition*, ed. Peter William Evans (Oxford: Oxford University Press, 1999), consists of twenty-one essays covering the work of film-directors from the 1950s to the present. It includes a piece by Jo Labanyi, 'Fetishism and the Problem of Sexual Difference in Buñuel's *Tristana*'.

Buñuel's autobiography, *Mon dernier soupir* (Paris: Éditions Robert Laffont, 1982), provides an essential insight into many aspects of his life and career. It has also been published in English and Spanish as, respectively, *My Last Breath* (London: Jonathan Cape, 1984, and London: Fontana, 1985), and *Mi último suspiro* (Barcelona: Plaza y Janes, 1982). Though dedicated to his wife, the book has little to say about Buñuel's relationship with her, but this omission, deliberate or otherwise, is rectified by Jeanne Rucar de Buñuel's *Memorias de una mujer sin piano* (written by Marisol Martín del Campo (Madrid: Alianza Editorial, 1990), which has much to say about Buñuel's character and attitude towards her, as well as towards women in general. Of great interest too is Max Aub's *Conversaciones con Buñuel* (Madrid: Aguilar, 1985), of which the first 166 pages are the result of tape-recorded interviews with the director. The remaining 394 pages of this massive volume consist of interviews with forty-five individuals, including Jeanne Rucar de Buñuel, Rafael Alberti, Louis Aragon, Fernando Rey and Salvador Dalí.

As for studies of Buñuel's life and work, Raymond Durgnat's *Luis Buñuel* (London: Studio Vista, 1967), offers detailed and perceptive analyses of particular films, together with chapters of a more general nature on themes and cinematic technique. Durgnat's context involves Freud, Marxism, and the cultural background that influenced Buñuel. This is, though, a highly personal approach by one of Buñuel's early interpreters. There is also a Spanish translation, *Luis Buñuel* (Madrid: Editorial Fundamentos, 1973). Francisco Aranda's *Luis Buñuel: biografía crítica* (Barcelona: Editorial Lumen, 1969), published in English translation as *Luis Buñuel: A Critical Biography* (London: Secker & Warburg, 1975), contains much valuable information on both the director's life and films, and, of particular interest, a number of surrealist texts written by Buñuel, together with critical pieces and film scenarios that were never taken further. Of considerable interest too is *The World of Luis Buñuel: Essays in Criticism*, ed. Joan Mellen (New York: Oxford University Press, 1978). Its forty-one essays of varying length and quality contain contributions from Henry Miller, Carlos Fuentes and Tony Richardson, and three pieces by Buñuel himself. In general, the essays range from pieces of a biographical nature to those on Buñuel as a film-maker and to studies of individual films. Some essays included here are otherwise extremely difficult to obtain.

Virginia Higginbotham's *Luis Buñuel* (Boston: Twayne Publishers, 1979), is a well-researched account of the whole of Buñuel's career as a film-maker, but somewhat strangely groups his post-1958 films into 'Character Studies' and 'Social Satires'. The author also regards both groups as 'masterworks', which implies that such excellent films as *The Forgotten Ones* and *He* are not. Even so, information on the Mexican and Spanish background is abundant throughout. Another detailed study, with much information on the various phases of Buñuel's life and telling observations on the major themes of his films, is provided by Michael Schwarze, *Luis Buñuel* (Barcelona: Plaza y Janes, 1988), first published in German in 1981. *La imaginación en libertad (homenaje a Luis Buñuel)*, ed. Antonio Lara (Madrid: Editorial de la Universidad Complutense, 1981), consists of an introduction and four essays by different contributors on, respectively, Buñuel's deeply held beliefs, his genuinely surrealist films, censorship and a long and detailed analysis of *Tristana*.

In *The Discreet Art of Luis Buñuel: A Reading of His Films* (London: Marion Boyars, 1982), Gwynne Edwards offers close analyses of nine major films, and in *Indecent Exposures: Buñuel, Saura, Erice & Almodóvar* (London: Marion Boyars, 1995), has chapters on *Viridiana, The Exterminating Angel* and *Tristana*. The same author writes on *The Diary of a Chambermaid* in *Luis Buñuel: A Symposium*, ed. Margaret A. Rees (Leeds: Trinity and All Saints' College, 1982), which also contains essays by Michael E. Williams on Buñuel's Catholicism, Robert Havard on the significance of objects and phantoms in the montage of *Viridiana*, and Peter William Evans on the world of Séverine's domesticity and the brothel in *Belle de jour*. Paul Sandro's *Diversions of Pleasure: Luis Buñuel and the Crises of Desire* (Columbus: Ohio State University Press, 1987), seeks to apply contemporary critical theory to Buñuel's films. An introduction dealing with the context for analysis, cinema discourse, Buñuel's working contexts, and classical narrative cinema as background, leads to close examination of *Un Chien andalou*, *L'Âge d'or*, *The Exterminating Angel*, *The Discreet Charm of the Bourgeoisie*, several of the Mexican films, and *Belle de jour*. At more than 300 pages, John Baxter's *Buñuel* (London: Fourth Estate, 1994) is the work of a professional biographer and is informative enough, without throwing much light on the films. In contrast, Peter William Evans's *The Films of Luis Buñuel: Subjectivity and Desire* (Oxford: Clarendon Press, 1995), reveals a thorough knowledge of the subject. Evans has much to say on Buñuel's Mexican period and also deals at length with issues of subjectivity and desire in the light of psychoanalysis and gender theory. Similarly, in *Los mundos de Buñuel* (Madrid: Ediciones Akal, 2000), Víctor Fuentes places Buñuel's films in a wider context, analysing them in relation to important historical moments in the twentieth century, to Buñuel's personal and professional development, and to the cinematic and cultural traditions of the countries in which he worked. Four chapters deal, respectively, with the director's surrealist period, his Mexican films, co-productions in several countries and the films made in France.

Agustín Sánchez Vidal's contribution to Buñuel studies has been immense. *Luis Buñuel: obra literaria* (Zaragoza: Ediciones del Heraldo de Aragón, 1982) is a collection of the director's literary works written between 1922 and 1929, and contains prose pieces, poems, a theatre script entitled *Hamlet*, observations on cinema and some short film scenarios. An excellent introduction and explanatory notes make a strong case for the quality of Buñuel's surrealist writing. In contrast, *Luis Buñuel: obra cinematográfica* (Madrid: Ediciones J.C., 1984) is a detailed account of his films and his working methods, facilitated by the author's personal contact with him. Considerable attention is given to the lesser-known films. In *Buñuel, Lorca, Dalí: el enigma sin fin* (Barcelona: Planeta, 1988), Sánchez Vidal deals with the lives of the three great creative artists. Particularly interesting are the sections about their time at the Residencia de Estudiantes and their greater or lesser involvement in Surrealism. *Luis Buñuel* (Madrid: Ediciones Cátedra, 1991), has chapters on Buñuel's view of the nature and purpose of cinema, on his life, on his view of himself and on Buñuel as seen by others. Apart from listing the individuals involved in his films, the Filmography provides an account of each film, together with analytical comments. Finally, *El mundo de Buñuel* (Zaragoza: Caja de Ahorros de la Inmaculada de Aragón, 1993), is, as its title suggests, an informative account of the world of Buñuel and his films through the examination of such topics as the praying mantis, and of objects and parts of the body – boxes, crucifixes, hands, legs, feet – which held a fascination for him.

In celebration of the centenary of Buñuel's birth, *It is Dangerous to Look Inside, Buñuel, 100 Years/100 Años, Es peligroso asomarse al interior* (New York: Museum of Modern Art/ Instituto Cervantes, 2000), contains sections on Buñuel's work and times, one hundred pages of interviews with actors and directors, and sixty pages of photographs illustrating Buñuel's obsessions as revealed in his films. The book is superbly illustrated and the text is in English and Spanish.

SELECT BIBLIOGRAPHY

Alexandrian, Sarane, *Surrealist Art* (London: Thames & Hudson, 1970).
Aranda, Francisco, *Luis Buñuel: A Critical Biography*, trans. David Robinson (London: Secker & Warburg, 1975).
———— *El surrealismo español* (Barcelona: Editorial Lumen, 1981).
Aub, Max, *Conversaciones con Buñuel* (Madrid: Aguilar, 1985).
Babington, Bruce, and Evans, Peter W., 'The Life of the Interior: Dreams in the Films of Luis Buñuel', *Critical Quarterly*, 27, no. 4 (1985), 5–20.
Balakian, Anna, *Surrealism: the Road to the Absolute* (London: Allen & Unwin, 1972).
Baxter, John, *Buñuel* (London: Fourth Estate, 1994).
Brandon, Ruth, *Surreal Lives: the Surrealists 1917–1945* (London: Macmillan, 1999).
Buache, Freddy, *The Cinema of Luis Buñuel*, trans. Peter Graham (London: Tantivy Press, 1973).
Buñuel, Luis, *My Last Breath*, trans. Abigail Israel (London: Jonathan Cape, 1984) [cited as Buñuel].
———— *Mi ultimo suspiro* (Barcelona: Plaza y Janes, 1982).
———— *Mon dernier soupir* (Paris: Éditions Robert Laffont, 1982).
Durgnat, Raymond, *Luis Buñuel* (London: Studio Vista, 1967).
Edwards, Gwynne, *The Discreet Art of Luis Buñuel: A Reading of his Films* (London: Marion Boyars, 1982).
———— 'On Buñuel's *Diary of a Chambermaid*', in Margaret A. Rees (ed.), *Luis Buñuel: A Symposium* (Leeds: Trinity and All Saints College, 1983), 27–58.
———— *Indecent Exposures: Buñuel, Saura, Erice & Almodóvar* (London: Marion Boyars, 1995).
———— 'Luis Buñuel: The Surrealist Triptych', in Robert Havard (ed.) *A Companion to Spanish Surrealism* (London: Tamesis, 2004), 79–95
Evans, Peter William, *The Films of Luis Buñuel: Subjectivity and Desire* (Oxford: Clarendon Press, 1995).
Evans, Peter William and Isabel Santaolalla (eds), *Luis Buñuel: New Readings* (London: BFI, 2004)
Finkelstein, Haim N., *Surrealism and the Crisis of the Object* (Michigan: UMI Research Press, 1979).
Fuentes Víctor, *Los mundos de Buñuel* (Madrid: Ediciones Akal, 2000).
Gale, Mathew, *Dada and Surrealism* (London: Phaidon, 1977).
Havard, Robert G., *From Romanticism to Surrealism: Seven Spanish Poets* (Cardiff: University of Wales Press, 1988).

The Crucified Mind: Rafael Alberti and the Surrealist Ethos in Spain (London: Tamesis, 2001).

——— (ed.), *Companion to Surrealism* (London: Tamesis, 2004).

Higginbotham, Virginia, *Luis Buñuel* (Boston: Twayne Publishers, 1979).

——— *Spanish Film Under Franco* (Austin: University of Texas Press, 1988).

Hopewell, John, *Out of the Past: Spanish Cinema After Franco* (London: British Film Institute, 1986).

It is Dangerous to Look Inside, Buñuel, 100 Years/100 Años, Es peligroso asomarse al interior (New York: Museum of Modern Art/ Instituto Cervantes, 2000).

Kinder, Marsha, *Blood Cinema: The Reconstruction of National Identity in Spain* (Berkeley: University of California Press, 1993).

Kyrou, Ado, *Le Surréalisme au Cinéma* (Paris: Le Terrain Vague, 1963).

Labanyi, Jo, 'Fetishism and the Problem of Sexual Difference in Buñuel's *Tristana*', in Peter William Evans (ed.), *Spanish Cinema: The Auteurist Tradition* (Oxford: Oxford University Press, 1999), 76–92.

Lara, Antonio (ed.), *La imaginación en libertad (homenaje a Luis Buñuel)* (Madrid: Editorial de la Universidad Complutense, 1981).

Mellen, Joan (ed.), *The World of Luis Buñuel: Essays in Criticism* (New York: Oxford University Press, 1978).

Morris, C.B., *Surrealism and Spain* (Cambridge: Cambridge University Press, 1972).

——— *This Loving Darkness: The Cinema and Spanish Writers, 1920–1936* (Oxford, London: University of Hull, 1980).

La Révolution surréaliste (numbers 1–12, 1924–29) (New York: Arno Press).

Rosemont, Franklin (ed.), *André Breton, What is Surrealism?: Selected Writings* (London: Pluto Press, 1978).

Rucar de Buñuel, Jeanne, *Memorias de una mujer sin piano* (written by Marisol Martín del Campo) (Madrid: Alianza Editorial, 1990) [cited as Rucar de Buñuel].

Sánchez Vidal, Agustín (ed.), *Luis Buñuel: obra literaria* (Zaragoza: Ediciones del Heraldo de Aragón, 1982) [cited as Sánchez Vidal].

——— *Luis Buñuel: obra cinematográfica* (Madrid: Ediciones J.C., 1984).

——— *Buñuel, Lorca, Dalí: el enigma sin fin* (Barcelona: Planeta, 1988).

——— *Luis Buñuel* (Madrid: Ediciones Cátedra, 1991).

——— *El mundo de Buñuel* (Zaragoza: Caja de Ahorros de la Inmaculada de Aragón, 1993).

Sandro, Paul, *Diversions of Pleasure: Luis Buñuel and the Crises of Desire* (Columbus: Ohio State University Press, 1987).

Schwarze, Michael, *Luis Buñuel* (Barcelona: Plaza y Janes, 1988).

INDEX

Printed and bound by CPI Group (UK) Ltd, Croydon, CR0 4YY

13/04/2025

14656523-0005